TOWARDS A MODERN IRAN

Studies in Thought, Politics and Society

Edited by

Elie Kedourie
and
Sylvia G. Haim

FRANK CASS

First published 1980 in Great Britain by
FRANK CASS AND COMPANY LIMITED
Gainsborough House, Gainsborough Road,
London, E11 1RS, England

and in the United States of America by
FRANK CASS AND COMPANY LIMITED
c/o Biblio Distribution Centre
81 Adams Drive, P.O. Box 327, Totowa, N.J. 07511

British Library Cataloguing in Publication Data

Towards a modern Iran.
1. Iran – History – Cajar dynasty, 1779–1925
2. Iran – History – Pahlavi dynasty, 1925–1979
I. Kedourie, Elie II. Haim, Sylvia G.
955'.04 DS298

ISBN 0–7146–3145–0

Typeset by Computacomp (UK) Ltd, Fort William, Scotland
Printed and bound in Great Britain by
Biddles Ltd, Guildford and King's Lynn

Contents

Notes on Contributors

Peter Avery is University Lecturer in Persian and a Fellow of King's College, Cambridge. He has published *Modern Iran* (Benn, 1965), as well as translations from the Persian classics, Hafiz in 1952 and Omar Khayyam in 1979, and numerous articles. He is one of the Editors of the *Cambridge History of Iran*.

J. B. Simmons studied at the University of Chicago, at Denver and at Dartmouth College, USA, and obtained his doctorate at King's College, Cambridge. He is now teaching in Zambia.

William J. Olson is a Post-Doctoral Research Fellow in the University of Sydney. He previously held a Leverhulme Trust Research Fellowship at the University of Aberdeen, and in 1974 a Fulbright-Hays Dissertation Research Abroad Fellowship for Iran. He is now working on a diplomatic history of Anglo-Iranian relations during World War I, and an annotated bibliography entitled *Britain's Elusive Empire in the Middle East, 1900–1921*.

Edward J. Lazzerini is Associate Professor of History at the University of New Orleans, where he has taught Russian history for seven years. A specialist in the study of Russia's Muslims, especially the Crimean and Volga Tatars, he is the author of several articles in the field and of a forthcoming biography of the Crimean Tatar reformer, Ismail Bey Gasprinskii.

Mangol Bayat-Philipp is Assistant Professor of History at Harvard University, and previously taught history at the University of Shiraz, Iran for three years. She has published numerous articles, and contributed chapters to Beck and Keddie, eds., *Women in the Muslim World*, and Bonine and Keddie, eds., *Continuity and Change in Modern Iran*. She has just completed a book, *Mysticism and Dissent: Socio-religious Thought in Qajar Iran*, forthcoming.

Ervand Abrahamian teaches Middle East History and Politics at Baruch College in the City University of New York. He is also completing a book on class and ethnicity in modern Iran.

Sorour S. Soroudi (Ph.D., University of California, Los Angeles) is Senior Lecturer in Persian Language and Literature at the Department of Indo-Iranian Studies, Hebrew University of Jerusalem. He was born in Iran. He is the author of several articles on modern Persian literature.

Asghar Fathi is Professor of Sociology at the University of Calgary in Canada. He has studied at the American University of Beirut, Tehran University (law) and the University of Washington (sociology). His major interests and publications are in the fields of media of public communication and social change in developing societies. Currently he is working on a monograph with the tentative title of *The Islamic Pulpit as a Medium of Public Communication*.

Farhad Kazemi (Ph.D., University of Michigan) is Associate Professor of Politics and member of Hagop Kevorkian Center for Near Eastern Studies at New York University. He is a former executive secretary of the Society for Iranian Studies. His recent publications include: 'The Nonrevolutionary Peasantry of Modern Iran' (with E. Abrahamian), *State and Society in Iran*, A. Banani ed., special issue of *Iranian Studies*, 1978; 'The Study of Political Unrest and Violence: The Middle East', *Middle East Studies Association Bulletin*, May 1978; and *The Migrant Poor, Urban Marginality, and Politics in Iran* (New York: New York University Press, forthcoming, 1980).

Hushang Moghtader is Associate Professor of Political Science at the Faculty of Law and Political Science, Tehran University. He was educated in Tehran and London. He was a British

Council Scholar at SOAS, University of London, in 1972–3, and in 1977 did research at the Institute for Higher International Studies in Geneva. He has published a number of books on U.N. and international relations in Pharsi, and a number of articles in English on Iran's foreign relations.

Preface

The events which have been taking place in Iran in the last couple of years have taken the world by surprise. A little reflection however will suggest that they are not inexplicable prodigies. They constitute rather a manifestation – albeit sudden and astonishing – of a social, intellectual and political crisis in the throes of which Iran has found herself from at least the beginning of the century. The eleven studies included in this book are devoted to the examination of one or other aspect of this crisis, which the Shah's departure in January 1979 and the subsequent inauguration of the Islamic republic has by no means resolved. It is a safe guess that the problems of Iran will continue to engage the attention of students for many years to come. These studies will throw some light on the origins and character of the present crisis, and perhaps offer some guidance about its future unfolding.

Eight of the eleven chapters are presented here for the first time. Chapters 1, 4 and 5 have previously appeared in *Middle Eastern Studies*.

March 1980

ELIE KEDOURIE
SYLVIA G. HAIM

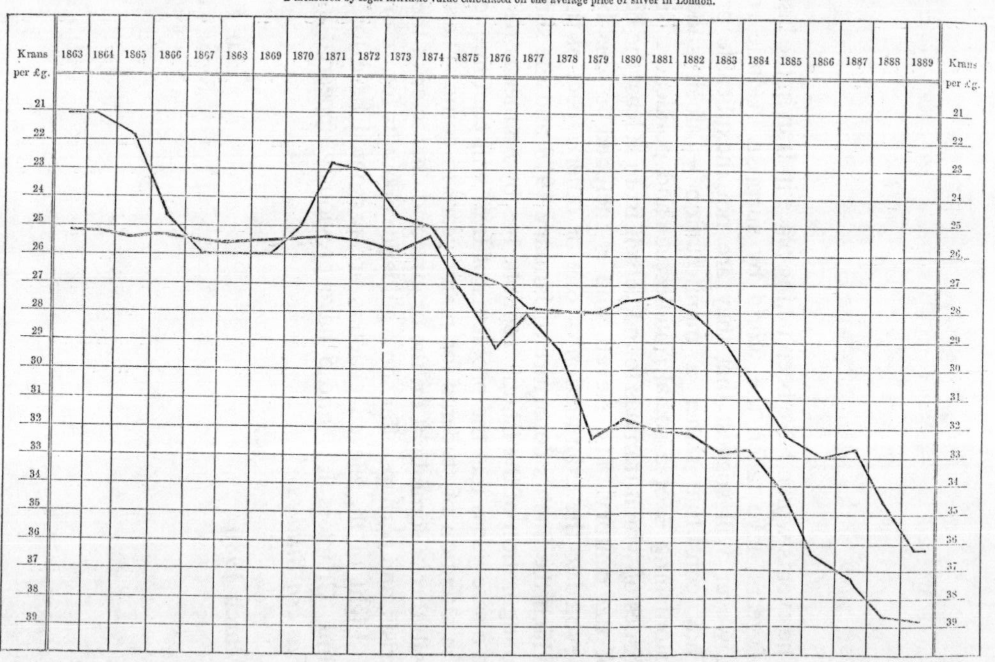
DIAGRAM
Representing the Depreciation of the Kran.
A measured by exchange on London.
B measured by legal intrinsic value calculated on the average price of silver in London.
Krans per £g.
1863 1864 1865 1866 1867 1868 1869 1870 1871 1872 1873 1874 1875 1876 1877 1878 1879 1880 1881 1882 1883 1884 1885 1886 1887 1888 1889
21 22 23 24 25 26 27 28 29 30 31 32 33 34 35 36 37 38 39
A
B
W. D. VAN LENNEP.

1

Persia on a Cross of Silver, 1880–1890

P. W. Avery and J. B. Simmons

... the nation – of London. Often ... at distances of two and three hundred miles or more from this colossal emporium of men, wealth, arts, and intellectual power, have I felt the sublime expression of her enormous magnitude in one simple form of ordinary occurrence – viz., in the vast droves of cattle ... all with their heads directed to London, and expounding the size of the attracting body, together with its force of attractive power, by the never-ending succession of these droves, and the remoteness from the capital of the lines upon which they were moving. A suction so powerful, felt along radii so vast, and a consciousness, at the same time, that upon other radii still more vast, both by land and by sea, the same suction is operating, night and day, summer and winter, and hurrying for ever into one centre the infinite means needed for her infinite purposes, and the endless tribute to the skill or to the luxury of her endless population, crowds the imagination with a pomp to which there is nothing corresponding on this planet, either amongst the things that have been, or the things that are.

De Quincey on London

Between 1880 and 1883 the Government of India was fortunate in having the services of Evelyn Baring, later the first Lord Cromer, as Financial Member of the Viceroy's Council. In 1881, in connection with expenses caused by prolonged British occupation of Qandahar after the Second Afghan War, Baring minuted that the finances of no country could be free from anxiety or capable of stability, whose 'main source of revenue is derived from payments in silver, ... whilst at the same time it owes a large sum annually in gold.' There could be no certainty 'of the sum to which the item "loss by Exchange" may not amount.'[1] By 1893 this loss induced the Government of India to cease minting silver coin, but between 1880 and 1890 the Persian Government had no Baring to diagnose the weakness of its silver-based currency.

For posterity, however, Rabino's chart traces the weakness of Persia's silver currency in that decade. In 1894 Mr Joseph Rabino was the manager in Tehran of the British Imperial Bank of Persia. He reported to the British envoy to Persia on the state of Persia's currency, and illustrated his report with the graph he had used for a Paper to the Institute of Bankers London in December 1891.[2] This graph shows the effect on the *toman* (= 10 *krans*) of the decline of the world value of silver after 1871. Due to this decline the decade 1880–1890 became critical for countries which operated solely on silver. Rabino's graph delineates Persia's currency in the grip of bimetallism's death throes.

Until about 1850 most nations, excluding Great Britain (but not British India), were bimetallic, or on a silver standard, or using some form of inconvertible paper currency internally. Although gold usually had some slight premium over silver internationally, this discrepancy was frequently altered by various nations' minting policy. Gold's premium was never sufficiently high greatly to disturb the common employment of silver bullion in the settling of international accounts.[3]

A change began in 1850. Nations started to move towards a gold standard. Gold started to leave deficit trading areas in large amounts. The first phase of this process reached its culmination in 1871, when Germany adopted a gold standard in anticipation of the income to accrue from the French war indemnity.[4] Meanwhile, Persia lacked the compensatory recuperative power to withstand the assault on its currency caused by the world's abandoning silver and the consequent depreciation in its value. Persia was nominally bimetallic, but between the 1850s and 1860s had lost most of what was left of its gold reserves. In addition to the effect of depreciation of silver, Persia throughout the nineteenth century had been subject to a bullion drain which, though for present purposes it must be kept constantly in mind, requires more particular study than it can receive in this discussion.[5] By 1871 Persia's currency was in fact silver,[6] to become increasingly isolated as the rest of the world went on to gold.

Only the United States' continued flirtation with bimetallism during the period under review postponed the day when the Persian silver *kran* was subjected to extremely serious devaluation. Throughout the nineteenth century the Persian government failed to adopt a realistic monetary policy, and, at the crucial moment, to face the problem of the collapse of bimetallism. Its international trading position, therefore, was ultimately at the mercy of fiscal decisions taken in the United States Congress.[7]

In 1873, during controversy about paper money issued in the Civil War, Congress passed a Coinage Act. The silver dollar was dropped from the list of standard coins. To supporters of silver as one of the two metals upon which to base currency, this enactment was 'the crime of '73'. Civil War paper – the 'Green Back Dollar' – was pegged to gold, redeemable after January 1, 1879. Prominent among the protesters were the Rocky Mountain mining States, injured by decreases in the demand for silver. From 1870, unusually rich new silver mines in Nevada had raised the annual world silver production from a static £8–9,000,000 to £15,000,000. The gold price of silver declined accordingly. Europe's abandonment of silver for currency accelerated this depreciation. In the end a combination of protests by the silver interests and pressure from inflationist groups swung Congress in favour of the protesters.

The U.S. dollar of 1873 contained 371.25 grains of pure silver, a little over three-quarters of an ounce, whose average bullion value for the same year was $1.00368. After the 1873 Coinage Act, this silver's value dropped in 1874 to $0.98909. The downward trend continued, but in 1878 came the Bland-Allison Act. This Congressional enactment effected a compromise among proponents of hard money, silver producers, and inflationists. Under it the U.S. Secretary of the Treasury had to purchase not less than $2,000,000 and not more than $4,000,000 worth of silver monthly at market price, for circulation either in the form of silver dollars or silver certificates. In 1878, the silver dollar was worth approximately $1.15 an ounce, to make it worth about $.89. The United States Treasury, however, continued to mint silver at the established ratio of 16 to 1 to gold.

During the next twelve years, the United States issued almost $380,000,000 in silver currency, not counting subsidiary coins of 25 and 50 cents. In spite of heavy government buying and some initial amelioration in these years, the price of silver gradually fell. The U.S. Treasury profited from this, because at the gold ratio of 16 to 1 it continued to mint coins which, regardless of what the silver cost, were legal tender.[8]

In 1890, advocates of hard money under inflationist pressure contrived a piece of legislation which appeared to call for increased use of silver. The Sherman Silver Purchase Act authorised the Secretary of the Treasury to purchase 4,500,000 *ounces* of silver a month at the current market price. This Act appeared to be a concession to the bimetallists, but its guile lay in the fact that the silver was to be held as *bullion*, and paid for by a new type of paper money (treasury notes), redeemable in *either gold or silver*.

At 1890 prices, monthly purchases of 4,500,000 ounces *weight* of silver would double the amount of silver bought; but internationally no country desired to redeem notes in silver. Therefore, a run on American gold ensued: silver's purchase price on the market plumped. By 1893 the *dollar* cost of the monthly silver acquisitions remained that of 1890.[9] Thus the price of silver was halved, and this price trend was exactly reflected in Persia.

There the diminishing value of silver rapidly became manifest because since the British Imperial Bank of Persia's establishment in 1889, Persia had a direct link with the world monetary system. Persia's bullion export price would, of course, have been just as immediately affected had the Bank existed or not. That it did exist simply ensured exceptionally careful documentation of Persian financial phenomena, both by the Bank and by British Consular officials.[10]

The Sherman Silver Purchase Act was an astute domestic compromise, designed to inveigle America's silver State senators into supporting high tariffs. People in London concerned with the Imperial Bank of Persia could not have been expected easily to foresee what its impact would mean.[11] After 1890, the United States poured out gold and silver in generous amounts. By 1893, after only three years of the Sherman Act's operation, $150,000,000 worth of silver had been paid for by treasury notes.[12] This was the year silver price fluctuations made India suspend free coinage of silver.

1893 was also the year of the Sherman Act's repeal by Congress. Neither the international monetary conference of 1881 nor that in 1892 had succeeded in establishing bimetallism. America's flirtation with bimetallism had to end, but in the meantime the Sherman Act had caused havoc in countries using silver as an exchange medium. Its repeal, and decisions like the Government of India's to cease minting silver coin made 1893 a worse year than ever for silver: the international convertibility of Persia's currency was further disastrously damaged.

In the same year Persia's situation was exacerbated when Russia, as a prelude to complete adoption of the gold standard four years later, also suspended minting silver. Russia was Persia's northern and India its southern trading partner. Both took the same step. In 1892 silver's international convertability had already been restricted by Austria-Hungary's adoption of the gold standard. In the late 1890s Japan followed suit. The productivity of South African and Australian gold mines nullified the bimetallists' threat of a 'gold famine'. The end of 1893 saw Persia's silver practically isolated. It was one of the few countries left tied to the free coinage and import and export of this metal. In its weak position, its gold having already gone, this process soon resulted in copper driving out silver as the circulating medium; but this is to anticipate the Persian economy's utter slump at the end of the nineteenth century.

Persia's peculiar vulnerability to the depreciation of silver after the 1870 Nevada silver strike, and America's inconsistencies over bimetallism, can partly be explained by its geographical position. In the nineteenth century it was placed between trading areas related to Russian and British expansion in Asia and the Indian Subcontinent. A favourable trade balance with Russia in the north and unfavourable one with British interests in the south combined with the rise to almost exclusive prominence of a north-south trading axis within Persia itself, to make it the channel for the flow of its own and Russian specie into British hands. The shift of trade on to this axis is connected with the diminution of the Persians' share of the trans-shipment of foreign goods within their country, with a resulting loss of profit. A glance at Persia's internal specie position in the first two thirds of the nineteenth century will serve to show its inability to afford any degree of specie drain.

Another factor to be considered is the change in social and especially consumer habits brought about in the nineteenth century by increased contacts with the West. The Qajar government of Persia's fiscal requirements were increased, but its lack of control over sources of production and failure to share profits with the merchant classes, whose confidence the Qajars did not enjoy, deprived the government of the means to meet its growing needs. In this context it will be necessary to look again at Nasiru'd-Din Shah's (1848–1896) 'infamous' tendency to sell concessions to foreigners. Also, the hoarding and 'cornering' so often associated with the Persian economy will have to be considered.

The change in the direction of the principal trade axis across Persia culminated a long historical process, but in the nineteenth century received its final impetus from the new proximity of the Russian and British empires. Over a long period trade's taking to the sea had gradually atrophied the Central Asian trade routes between the Far East and the West. The Persian 'middle kingdom' suffered in consequence, and efforts to find compensation through the Persian Gulf, though not entirely vain, were contemporary with Persia's unsettlement in the thirteenth century after the Mongol invasion.[13] By the time the Safavid Shahs (1502–1722) could pacify the country and attempt reconstruction of its broken economy the Europeans had reached the Gulf; the Portugese Alfonso de Albuqerque took the island of Hormuz in 1509.

Thirteenth and fourteenth century Persian efforts to gain access to the Mediterranean failed[14]. By the sixteenth century, the Ottoman Turkish Empire formed a barrier between Safavid Persia and Europe, so that for the Safavid Shahs northern and southern outlets assumed increased importance. The collapse of the Safavid Empire in 1722 resulted in a general disruption of the Persian economy, and development of trade north and south was impeded. In the late eighteenth century, however, an east-west trade axis continued to function. A deficit trade in the east with Afghanistan was balanced by a favourable trade between Persia and Turkey in the west.[15] In 1802 Scott Waring observed European gold coins in Persia which had entered by way of Constantinople.[16]

It was Malcolm's mission to Persia of 1800–1801 which began the process that was to seal the fate of this east-west axis. Captain, later Sir, John Malcolm was sent to Persia by the British Indian authorities, apprehensive of Napoleon's designs on India and the growing power of Zaman Shah, the ruler of Afghanistan. The latter's death in 1800 did not preclude the signing of the Anglo-Persian agreement of January 1801, making the Shah of Persia in effect Britain's ally against Afghanistan in the event of Afghan aggression. An annexed commercial agreement granted English and Indian traders special privileges in Persia, thus to promote the southern trading area.[17]

During the ensuing fourteen years Malcolm's preliminaries were revised and reached Treaty status.[18] Russian arms meanwhile had advanced to Persian borderlands in the southern Caucasus. The Shah was defeated in a war with Russia which resulted in the Russo-Persian Treaty of Gulistan in 1813, disadvantageous to Persia.[19] A second Russo-Persian War in 1826 ended the same way. The Treaty of Turkomanchai in 1828 confirmed the Caspian Sea's status as a 'Russian Lake' and finally excluded Persia from the Caucasus.[20]

Persia was thus confined in the north by Russia and left with no alternative in the south but to give Britain a dominant position in the Persian Gulf. The north-south polarization had come to stay, though in 1837 Muhammad Shah (1834–1848) and again in 1857 Nasiru'd-Din Shah made attempts to obtain Herat in northern Afghanistan, thus to reassert Persia's claims to an eastern outlet and important eastern entrepot city. Claims in which the Russians acquiesced, but which the British strenuously and successfully opposed.[21]

Besides the crucial position of the north-south axis in relation to the drain of specie into British hands, other factors made it bad for Persia; also for Russia. Transit and merchant services furnish a significant part of a nation's trade balance. The bulk of goods involved in Persia's deficit trade with Afghanistan in the late eighteenth and early nineteenth centuries were either of British Indian origin or replaceable by British Indian products; but so long as the bulk of these goods came overland to inland cities in eastern Persia, Persian citizens could to some extent operate to their own advantage among the merchants involved in the India trade. The same was true so long as at least some of the goods could be carried by sea in vessels of Persian ownership, before the advance of western maritime technology rendered locally managed shipping between India and the Gulf obsolete.[22]

In 1837, Persia's attack on the north Afghan city of Herat, on the route from India to Central Asian cities such as Bukhara and Khiva, elicited strong British protests, while a British officer assisted the city to withstand the Persian siege. The Russians were believed to have encouraged the Persians to undertake this campaign. The Treaty of Turkomanchai enabled the Russians to have consuls or commercial agents in the Shah's dominions, wherever commerce might require them.[23] Herat in Persian hands would have become subject to this provision to establish both Persian and Russian agents astride an Indian commercial outlet.

In 1842, when the British, after suffering ignominious reverses, evacuated Kabul, the First Afghan War's political and military objectives could not be said to have been achieved. The Amir the British had imposed on Afghanistan was killed. His rival, whom the British had opposed, was reigning. A recent historian of this war concentrates on desires to develop the Indus–Afghan–Central Asia route, to reach Central Asian markets ahead of Russia, as the chief British commercial motive for the war,[24] but the war, and the earlier Herat episode, can also be related to the development of the north-south trade axis in Persia itself. These events completed the closure of Persia's eastern outlet into Afghanistan. The southern outlet on the Persian Gulf, controlled by Britain, was substituted.

Meanwhile, Persia's south-western outlet was also threatened. In 1836 Colonel Chesney launched British steamers on the Tigris and Euphrates. Baghdad, once a centre for the onward shipment of Persian goods to the Turkish and Syrian markets, lost this trade. This loss would adversely affect Hamadan and Kirmanshah, the cities in western Persia on the route to Baghdad.

By 1875 several British commercial houses existed in Baghdad, whose trade with Europe was showing an upward trend. Goods were coming directly from London through the Suez Canal and Basrah, the port at the head of the Persian Gulf. German, French, Swiss and Greek merchants were involved, but the servicing of the goods was British. The figures are significant: for 1870–71 Baghdad's total exports, including trading in horses, was valued at about £46,000. Imports for the same year were upwards of £285,000 in value. With British steamers on the Tigris and plying up the Gulf, the former Persian trade had taken to the Tabriz–Erzeroum–Constantinople route;[25] but the northern trade outlets had also already been noticed by a British representative in Persia.

As early as 1812, Sir Gore Ouseley pointed out to the East India Company that if Gilan silk were exported from Persia through the Black Sea port of Trabzon, instead of through the Gulf, overland transport costs would go down from 21 per cent of the silk's cost to 1 per cent, and freight from Trabzon to Britain would be less than that from the Persian Gulf port of Bushire. British officials were still advocating a direct British service from Trabzon in 1823. An Armenian brought a chartered British vessel full of British goods to Trabzon in 1831. By 1847 there was a direct British steamship service from Liverpool to Trabzon, but also competition from other Europeans, Russians not excluded.[26]

Persian merchants' and animal hirers' gains from the carrying trade were clearly threatened by a maritime European nation's enterprise in embarking this trade on ships and river steamers wherever possible, to shorten goods' land passage. The threat becomes plainer when it is recalled that in the early nineteenth century a single village near Shiraz had some 2,000 mules available for hire.[27] That the Persians recognised this threat is indicated by their quick reversion, mentioned above, to the Erzeroum-Constantinople route, once Colonel Chesney had won the Tigris and trade was diverted from southwest Persia to Basrah.

Recognition that the cost of transport, added to that of exports and imports, would remain in Persian pockets so long as Persians controlled the transporting of goods within their country, seems to have been implicit in Nasiru'd-Din Shah's reluctance to grant to a British interest the Karun River Navigation Concession. In 1842 Selby and Layard experimentally took a British steamer up the Karun as far as the point where the Khuzistan Plain meets the Zagros foothills, in the vicinity of Shushtar. To extend navigation on the Tigris to the neighbouring Karun, whose estuary meets that of the Tigris at the head of the Gulf, was a natural development. It would shorten the land carriage of goods from the Gulf to Isfahan and ultimately Tehran, thus more successfully to compete with Russia.

When at last in 1888 Nasiru'd-Din Shah granted this hard-won concession, it was for all nations' shipping, not exclusively Britain's. A year later, the Persian Nasiri Company was running steamships in competition with those of the British Lynch Company. The latter, however, made an improved packroad over the Zagros to Isfahan from the riverhead, and operated its own caravans.[28]

As a counterpoise to this Concession, granted in response to British importunity, after 1888 Nasiru'd-Din Shah accepted agreements with Russia placing an embargo on all railway construction in his realms.[29] There may have been fiscal as well as political grounds for this apparently submissive policy. It is of interest that in 1881, when she was travelling in Persia, it was from her *muleteers* that Mme Dieulafoy heard complaints of the effects on old Persian institutions of the spread of Europeans' influence and technology.[30]

In the north, a similar monopoly of commercial services as that gained by the British in the south had not eluded the Russians. They were helped by the historical preponderance in the Caspian-Caucasian carrying trade of their Armenian fellow Christians. Two thousand Armenian shipmen and their families had been attracted to Astrakhan by Alexander I's 'mild government', in preference to less congenial conditions under the Shah of Persia.[31] The Treaties of Gulistan and Turkomanchai completed the process of making the Caspian Sea a 'Russian Lake'. Russian provision of roads and carriage facilities across the Caucasian isthmus to the Black Sea port of Poti set up competition with Trabzon, and increased movement in areas under Russian control.[32]

Participation, however, by Armenians, who were often Russian subjects, meant that fewer Muslim Persian villagers and caravan masters were involved in the northern trade. Also, the location of centres operating the trade meant routes to the northern frontiers shorter and less arduous than those which crossed arid and mountainous regions in central and southern Persia to reach the Gulf. Thus the Russian encroachment on the servicing of trade was less keenly felt than the British in the south, while the frontier security and mobility conferred by the Russians was of positive benefit to the Persian mercantile community. The boon was increased by the Russian pacification of Persia's transcaspian border with Turkestan after 1880, and construction of the Transcaspian Railway. By 1889, less than nine years after the railway's construction had begun, regular Russian steamship services connected its terminus on the Caspian's east coast with the ports of Baku on the west coast and Astrakhan in the north[33].

The Qajar Government participated little in the benefits Persian merchants in the north gained by these developments. The Qajars' relations with the mercantile community deteriorated throughout the nineteenth century. The Government was excluded from many of this community's secrets, and in the north the favourable Russian trade gave the merchants both power and a degree of Russian protection, so that government agents could not oppress them with the same impunity as in other provinces.

Ironically, outside those Persian mercantile circles immediately concerned, the British were the main beneficiaries of this favourable northern trade. Moreover, the favourable balance for Persia was not the only means by which Russian specie could be drawn off into British hands through the southern deficit area. Russian development of the Caucasus and Transcaspia – the Baku oilfields, road and railway construction – attracted large numbers of Persian workers.[34] Resident or migratory Persian labour's remittances home, in some instances to cities as far south as Hamadan, constituted another channel for the outflow of Russian specie through Persia.

There is evidence of the weakness of the Persian specie position as early as the end of the first fifty years of the eighteenth century. In the mid-eighteenth century, Postlethwayte's *Universal Dictionary of Trade and Commerce* stated that 'They have no gold in Persia', save ceremonial pieces struck on royal accessions or at the New Year, and 'not current among the people'. Foreign merchants imported German, Dutch and Venetian ducats. They 'must carry them to the mint as soon as they enter the kingdom', but if they could 'secretly sell them to private persons', the profit was appreciable. If they took them out, all gold coin had to be declared and 4d. duty paid 'to the king' on each ducat.[35]

Nadir Shah could have been 'the king' referred to, whose reign ended with his murder in 1747. He had struggled for some twenty years to restore Persia after the Afghan invasion and collapse of the Safavid Empire in 1722. He had endeavoured to cement friendship, which could be economically beneficial, with

Ottoman Turkey, but it was his celebrated Indian campaign in 1738–9 which most vividly demonstrated need of treasure. For treasure he looted Delhi. One estimate values his Indian spoils at from seventy millions sterling to, at lowest, 'considerably more than thirty'.[36] A later historian gives an estimate of 70 crores (70,000,000) of rupees.[37] Much of the booty was in the form of precious stones, a not always viable form of wealth.[38] On the other hand, of the 70 crores, 10 are said to have been embezzled by Nadir's officers and men.[39] Reference is made to his searching his men's baggage.[40] The house-to-house inventory in Delhi for a levy on its citizens is significant.[41] Also, the facts that Nadir gave his army gratuities in advance of pay, and the nation a three-year tax remission after the Indian campaign. At the same time, his army must one way or another have imported into Persia considerable gains in money; but for private hands, not the state, to help to capitalize private individuals in subsequent generations, but not the government. Nadir's tax remission was revoked, to be followed by taxes more onerous than before. His 'avarice' was one of the factors leading to his assassination. A 'morbid passion' for treasure was also marked in some of the Qajar rulers (1779–1925).

In 1763 Karim Khan Zand (1750–1779), who ruled southern and central Persia from Shiraz, granted privileges to the British East India Company. The agreement provided for English and Indian merchants' *purchases* of goods in Persia as well as *sales*. The foreign merchants were not to export the whole of their proceeds from sales 'in ready money as this would impoverish the kingdom and in the end prejudice trade in general'.[42]

The Khan's concern was obvious and, in not wishing monetarily to 'impoverish' Persia too much, the Company might have remembered the 1737 report of their factor at Kirman, Mr Savage. His report occasioned the Company's decision to send only one fifth of the year's woollen goods to Kirman, for which payment was to be accepted 'only in Abbasis at five Shahis, or in coined copper, or in old copper'.[43] The alternative was the unpalatable one of having to sell solely to the local governor, 'who would have obliged them to take silver at fifty per cent'.[44] Woollens had reached Kirman through the agency of Georgian merchants, who brought them from the (British) Russia Factory recently established at Astrakhan; but Mr Savage's main problem was the depreciation of Persian silver coinage, comprising Abbasis and Mahmudis.[45] In 1737 and 1763 there was as yet no profit available from a drain of Russian bullion, and further to drain Persia's specie would indeed have prejudiced 'trade in general'.

By 1793 the situation had changed. Agha Muhammad Khan Qajar had supplanted the Zands' dynasty of Karim Khan and his successors, but had inherited their specie problem. An East India Company report of January 1783 states that as a result of loss of 'gold and silver for a long Period of years', the Persians had resorted to manufacturing 'Coarse Cotton, and other Articles, for common wear'. Only a 'fifth part' of imports could be paid for in Persian produce. As no demand for Persian silks existed, the balance had to be paid for 'in the precious metals'.[46]

The change lay in the fact that, although there was no *British* demand for Persian silks, *Russia* was 'making rapid strides towards Commercial Pre-eminence' in the north, and Persian silk was being sold at Moscow 'in large quantities'.[47] The flow of Russian bullion through Persia was beginning.

Scott Waring's testimony for the continuance in the early nineteenth century of an important Perso-Turkish trade on an east-west axis was mentioned above; in 1802 he saw European gold coins in Shiraz, introduced through Constantinople. He says that European coins also reached Persia 'by way of Russia, whence large sums of money are brought to purchase various articles of merchandize, particularly silk, shawls etc'.[48] By 1802 the flow whose beginning has been noted in the preceding paragraph must have become appreciable. For though Scott Waring takes account of, besides specie from Russia, that coming 'to a large amount ... likewise' from Constantinople, he concludes that, 'notwithstanding this great importation of specie into Persia, I much doubt whether it equals the large sums which are annually exported to the different ports of India'.[49]

Scott Waring lists the foreign coins – Dutch, Venetian, Turkish, Egyptian and German – whose being 'the prevailing coin in the empire of Persia' surprised him.[50] He describes how 'monies ... current in one city, will probably not pass at the next'. Few coins can be received 'but to considerable disadvantage.'[51] In 1801, Malcolm privately reported his view that Persia's wealth and the value of its commerce had 'generally been overrated'.

Formerly, its fighting qualities had enabled rulers to bring back 'the riches of foreign conquest'. Persia, therefore, gained credit for a wealth which exceeded the reality.[52] Malcolm's comments were made some sixty years after the last great feat of Persian arms, Nadir Shah's conquest of India. His comments have at the same time to be glossed with the note that the 'credit for wealth' exaggerated was the government's, not that of private individuals unwilling to reveal to the government true statements of their accounts.[53]

Comment would not be out of place here on the Qajar government's permanent failure to collect adequate revenue for running an empire. The following table taken from returns cited by Joseph Rabino[54] demonstrates how static the government's total receipts remained in spite of the ever growing needs imposed on it during the nineteenth century.

TOTAL REVENUES OF PERSIA

1839–40 (Cash and value of payments in kind)	*krans* 34,026,150 = £1,835,994
1853–4	*krans* 33,685,580 = £1,153,163
1876–7	*krans* 54,487,630 = £1,602,580

By 1796 Agha Muhammad Khan Qajar had succeeded in conquering Persia for himself and his successors, but neither he nor they ever succeeded in bringing back 'the riches of foreign conquests'. It seems that he and his heir, Fath Ali Shah, considered minting money the best way of replenishing the lack of it in indigenous coin. Agha Muhammad Khan established mints, and Fath Ali Shah followed his example with 25 for gold and 31 for silver coin.[55] Harford Jones Brydges said that in 1811 the gold *toman* exceeded the contemporary English sovereign in quality, and the silver coinage was as sound as any.[56] The best money was that minted in Tabriz, but variation was considerable between coins of different mints and those minted specially for distribution at festivals.[57] A modern authority does not think the average output of these Persian mints could have been copious, a view borne out by what has been cited from Scott Waring.[58]

Postlethwayte, as cited above in the context of an earlier period, mentions that important foreign gold coins had to be taken to the government mint. Here is a clue to where at least some of the specie came from for the new Qajar mints, but there are ample grounds for supposing that it was not much.[59] According to the practice of the time, private specie holders could in any case present specie for conversion to legal tender at government mints for a nominal fee. The government could thus make a small profit. Of importance to the Shah was the fact that this procedure could provide him with some inkling of the qualities of concealed wealth, and who its holders were. That many of these later came forward is to be doubted.

Abdullah Mustawfi gives another clue to the origin of specie for the new mints. In his autobiography this descendant of several generations of Qajar finance officers says Fath Ali Shah minted gold and silver coins of the weight and assay of Safavid times, calling the gold by their Safavid term *ashrafis*, while the Safavid office of State Assayer, *Mu'ayyiru'l Mamalik*, was resuscitated. According to Mustawfi, the coins were minted from 'the gold and silver left in the Treasury by Agha Muhammad Khan Qajar, either in coin, ingots, plate or other made-up articles Agha Muhammad Khan's thrift had stored, thrown higgledy-piggledy into the Treasury'.[60]

It may be concluded that, though brave, this early nineteenth century venture in minting legal tender was based on extremely slender bullion resources. Fath Ali Shah's concern over the continued specie drain to India is attested by Scott Waring, who says he tried to stop 'this large exportation of gold and silver, by offering a reward to whoever should weave cloth similar to the Madras long cloths'. The observation which follows, that 'merchants cannot be supposed to interest themselves in any undertaking which would convert a portion of their profits into another channel',[61] is a further pointer to the Qajar government's lack of rapport with the mercantile community. Fath Ali Shah's offer of a reward was apparently of no avail. Nor would his minting Persian coins of such bullion as he could find to mint prevent specie leaving Persia through the southern deficit area as fast as it did in any other form. His mints were no panacea.

In 1890, when the bottom fell out of the world silver market, Persia's acute trading deficit had not changed. For the year ending September 30, 1889, Curzon estimated total Persian exports at

£2,126,000 (he calculated this figure on the basis of 31 *tomans* or 35 *krans* to the pound), and imports at £3,913,000.[62] Of these totals, he estimated that imports from British-controlled areas totalled about £2,000,000 but exports to these areas amounted to less than £1,000,000, of which some £100,000 was in specie.

These figures provide part of the background to Rabino's graph, and to understanding the critical developments in Persia after 1890, especially between this year and 1893, the period of the Sherman Act's operation. Gresham's Law and Curzon's evaluation of the *toman*'s exchange rate at T.31 or K.35 to the pound sterling must be kept in mind.

In the 1890s the growing number of private gold purchases made by wealthy Persians attracted the attention of the British Chargé d'Affaires. He said that until the 1850s both gold and silver coins were in circulation; '40 years ago gold was as common a medium of exchange in Persia as it was in England'.[63] This general conclusion is substantiated by a recent writer, who suggests that in the 1850s the prevailing exchange rate was approximately 2 *tomans* (20 *krans*) to the pound.[61] This estimate is corroborated by a British Consular despatch of 1890 from Tabriz concerning new rent demands from the British subjects who owned the Consulate building. This despatch says that a verbal agreement to pay T.200 rent for the building 'appears to have been made some 38 years ago, and at that time 200 tomans were worth nearly £100 sterling', that is, in 1852.[65]

Rabino's graph indicates how, in accordance with Gresham's Law, Persia was quickly drained of gold coins as the world abandoned monetary silver. For 1863, the exchange value of the *kran* is pegged at 21 *krans* (or 2.1 *tomans*) to the pound; but line *b* of the graph, which measures the *kran*'s value by its intrinsic silver value, puts the exchange value at only 25 *krans* to the pound sterling. Obviously a discrepancy of this order between minted currency and the real value of its metallic content arises inevitably both from minting costs, and the fact that the finished coin represents some form of legal tender.

From 1863 onwards, the *kran*'s exchange value dropped sharply. With two exceptions to be explained below, it fairly closely followed the declining world silver price. It might be inferred from this that the government and merchants of Persia could still export gold bullion as late as the early 1860s, and that this became impossible about 1863. This date is earlier than 1882–1883/1300 A.H., the date for this phenomenon suggested by Abdulla Mustawfi,[66] a suggestion which will be discussed in the context of the year 1883.

In 1873, at the time of Nasiru'd-Din Shah's first European journey, the silver *kran* briefly rallied. In July 1872, as part of the westernization and reform programme being promoted by the Shah's chief minister, Mirza Husain Khan, Baron Julius de Reuter, a British subject, received from the Shah's government an extraordinarily comprehensive concession. It granted him exclusive railway and tramway construction rights throughout Persia for seventy years, first refusal of a national bank, and of a wide range of public works including development of telegraphs. It bestowed on Reuter the right to inaugurate factories and mills: to undertake, in effect, Persia's industrialization. He could exploit the realm's entire mineral wealth, with the exception of precious metals and stones.[67] Mirza Husain Khan was eager that the Shah should visit Europe, to see at first hand the western marvels the Reuter Concession was intended to bring to Persia.

It was the first concession of such magnitude, though five years before a Prussian had lost £4,000 caution money – Reuter's was £40,000 – to the Shah through failure to implement a not dissimilar concession. Austrian and French concessionaires had also defaulted.[68] This tale of failed concessions did not deter Reuter, who was to raise £6,000,000 on the London market for his Persian enterprise. The Persian government nominally guaranteed a 5 per cent interest. However, with what Reuter's biographer calls the Shah's 'shrewdness', the guarantee's conditions were such that they 'switched the real security from the Persian Government to the profits of the enterprize itself'.[69] Reuter lent the Shah £20,000 to help defray his and the imperial suite's European expenses. The money was to be available in European capitals. It was lent to obviate 'exchange difficulties' and 'transport of bulky Persian coin'.[70] A further loan offered by Reuter was politely refused by the Shah because in return Reuter sought certain assurances about his concession.[71]

Mirza Husain Khan advocated confiding Persia's 'regeneration' to Britain, where the capital was to be found, and strict adherance to treaty obligations with Russia.[72] The Shah's and his advisers' approaches to potential European investors have been heavily criticized, often in terms which echo local protests at the time. These protests had a religious colouring. Non-Muslim foreigners' incursions into Iran's day-to-day affairs were resented as a threat to a traditional and cherished way of life, both Islamic and Persian. The incursions were an invasion of privacy, and British expansion in India, and Russian in Central Asia, portended the possibility of a more complete invasion than simply infiltration by European technicians and businessmen. One charge, repeated by subsequent historians, was that Nasiru'd-Din Shah wished to sell his country's assets to foreigners for gold. He certainly badly needed gold, and in the end Reuter got few of Persia's 'assets' in return. The concession was rescinded by the autumn of 1873, and Mirza Husain Khan sacrificed to popular protests as soon as the Shah returned from his European tour.

Anglo-Russian competition for the paramount influence in Persia during the nineteenth century is another factor frequently drawn into discussion of the cancellation of the Reuter Concession. The Imperial Russian Chancellor later confessed to Baron Reuter his misgivings over the concession, admitting that he had denounced it to the Tsar.[73] St. Petersburg was the first capital the Shah reached on his tour. His reception there was very flattering; but it can safely be assumed that he would be aware of the Russians' reaction to the concession he had granted a British subject a few months before. British India Office officials went so far as to fear that failure to find support in London might make Reuter renounce British citizenship in favour of Russian.[74] Then in 1874, the Reuter Concession's unilateral cancellation was followed by the granting of one to build railways, to General Falkenhagen, a Russian. London had in fact given Reuter little support for his schemes. Many people thought them over-ambitious. The British government, never anxious to be at odds with Russia over Persia, was careful not to afford Reuter any special backing. The British Minister in Tehran could only give him such assistance as that 'any other British subject' might expect.[75] The India Office considered Persia too 'effete' for major investment: Persia was 'even more incapable than Turkey of adopting European habits of vigorous thought or moral sense'.[76] Meanwhile, Reuter had to buy out the Shah's envoy to London, Malkum Khan, who had somehow acquired the title to a quarter of the original concession. It cost Reuter £20,000 with promises of shares in all future profits, 'to regain full ownership of his own Concession'.[77] Subsidiary deals of this kind put more British gold into Persians' hands.

Russian pressure, religious protest in Persia, the venality of Persian courtiers were certainly all involved in the cancellation of the Reuter Concession, but they should not obscure the Persian government's fundamental need to attract foreign capital. By the early 1870s, as a logical result of the bullion position, the Shah's government faced an imminent fiscal and monetary crisis. The very fact that the silver *kran* bounced upwards, for however brief a period, indicates that flirting with a scheme for attracting capital from England, where Mirza Husain Khan had apparently correctly located it, was a by no means unrealistic way of trying to cope with this crisis. The Reuter Concession promised the introduction of Western technology on an extensive scale, but it promised more. It promised unprecedented new sources of revenue; revenue, it must be noted, in hard currency.

The desire to grant a concession such as Reuter's to British interests was both logical and to Persia's advantage. Britain and British India were sapping Persia's resources: scope for the infusion of British capital in any form, especially in a way that held out the hope of developing new export markets for Persian products, was very appealing. The foreign concessionaire could reasonably be expected to waste no time in finding markets for the products he had gained the right to exploit. One historian asserts that the Shah sold Reuter a huge concession cheaply.[78] This is not quite true, but even if it were, the Imperial Treasury could have legitimately assumed that an aggressive export policy on the concessionaire's part would help to stabilize the *kran* internationally, as well as offering the Persian government a fresh source of revenue.

Russia's reaction was entirely predictable, but not solely based on political or strategic reasoning. By 1873, Russian bullion had been flowing down the Persian 'funnel' into British hands for several decades. Now a vigorous British commercial element seemed likely to step in, to quicken the whole pace of Persian commercial operations. Reuter and his group would obviously want to make profits, and the pattern of Russo-Persian trade throughout the nineteenth century showed clearly where these profits could best be made. Naturally St. Petersburg reacted swiftly to the prospect of a further development of Persia's already substantial flow of exports to Russia, and the Shah's advisers had insisted that Reuter's railway building under the concession should begin in the north. The first line was to link Rasht, close to the Caspian shore, with Tehran and central Persia.[79] Persian exports to Russia satisfied Russian requirements, but Russia had to keep the trade in line with its needs, not allow its expansion in the interest of a foreign enterprise's drive for profits.

British caution over Persian overtures between 1871 and 1873 is typical of the general British reluctance to become involved in any major investment in Persia, at least until the beginning of large-scale oil exploitation in the twentieth century. It will already have become evident that Reuter in various ways lost an appreciable amount of money in his Persian transactions. One writer has related London's scepticism over the Reuter venture, reflected in verses published in *Punch*,[80] to doubts about Reuter's character,[81] but contacts made in London by the Shah's advisers were not confined to Reuter. The fact that reputable London investment circles showed no particular interest in Persian prospects at the time of the granting of the Reuter Concession, a lack of interest reflected by Mr Gladstone's government, whose Chancellor told the House of Commons the government had 'no interest in the matter',[82] points to one conclusion. It must have been generally considered that Britain's trading position with Persia was satisfactory as it was; and certainly that there was no need 'to throw good money after bad'. Lord Granville told Reuter from the Foreign Office that it 'would be contrary to established rule for Her Majesty's Government to guarantee interest on the cost of a work undertaken in a foreign country.'[83]

The British attitude is quite understandable. Appreciable profits were, and had been, reaching British areas from Persia with only small risk to British capital. No British corporate entity would rush to put its own capital into the Persian 'funnel'. Persia's trade deficit by itself would give any potential investor less confident than Reuter cause to doubt Persia's ability to develop markets on a scale capable of yielding profits in hard currency. Many in the City must have realized that an infusion into Persia of British capital would in the long run have had to be used to cover an increasingly uncoverable balance of payments deficit. Evidence points to the Shah, in his transactions with Reuter, having been more concerned about a very 'short run' indeed, than about the full implementation of the concession. As for London, wide scope still remained in 1873 for more enticing investment prospects abroad than any Persia could offer. By 1889, however, Persia appeared as one of few relatively untouched areas left open to speculators, and more, but only slightly more, interest was then shown in it.

Not having obtained any substantial investments from Europe, in 1877 the Persian government resorted to a time-honoured method of tackling a fiscal and monetary crisis. The nineteen existing provincial mints were closed. The country's slender silver reserves were collected. Centralized production of new coins (of 900 fineness of silver) began in an automated mint in Tehran. The new *kran*'s denominations ranged in value from one quarter *kran* to five *krans*. Coins were struck from both re-smelted provincial coins and from freshly imported silver bullion. A new standard *kran*'s introduction partly restored confidence in the currency and consolidated Persia's specie supply. In spite of the continuing decline in world silver prices, the *kran* was thus temporarily stabilized. This conversion also netted the government a sizeable profit.

By farming the mint to a wealthy notable, the Shah could gain an appreciable income. On the eve of the acute currency crisis and mint scandal of the early 1890s (which is discussed below), the mint farmer paid 120,000 *tomans* (1,200,000 *krans*) a year for the exclusive right of producing coins.[84] Furthermore, both the government and the merchants could take advantage of the fact that the new standard *kran* was invariably worth more than its intrinsic silver value. As has been seen, this differentiation in value is generally applicable to legal tender. Establishment of one standard Tehran coin removed the complexities involved in pegging exchange rates between the coins of different mints. It also reduced the scope for counterfeiting. An additional benefit which could accrue to the government arose from the fact that old coins were discounted when their silver content was under par. Since none of them was accepted at more than face value, and many of the provincial coins had a greater intrinsic silver content than the new standard *kran*, the government could retain the extra silver as a bonus.[85]

Further, two outside events enabled Persia to reap greater monetary stability from the 1877 currency reform than such a measure could alone have achieved. Firstly, as has been observed, bimetallism was given a new but brief viability by the Bland-Allison Silver Purchase Act of the United State Congress; though when it was realized that the U.S. Treasury would only purchase the minimum amount of silver the Act required, after 1877 silver's world price sharply declined. Thus a wide disparity, as a glance at the graph will show, appeared between the *kran*'s intrinsic silver value and its international exchange value; then in 1879 world silver prices levelled out and held firm for about five years.

It was a second outside event which prevented the *kran*'s exchange value immediately registering the post-1877 decline in the world price of silver. In 1877 the Russians began their final and most extensive campaign against the Transcaspian Turcomans. The Russian troops across Persia's Khurasan border needed victualling. This campaign and the subsequent construction of the Transcaspian railway created an export market for Persia and, as the Baku oilfields were also to do, offered on a large scale external employment for Persian workers.

Curzon indicates that the labour force employed on the Transcaspian railway's construction, at one time over 20,000 strong, included Persians and was paid at rates ranging from 4d. to 7d. or 8d. a day. Stone for the new railway buildings was quarried in the mountains on the Persian side of the Khurasan border.[86] The Russian opening up of Transcaspia, hitherto a wild tribal waste, could begin in earnest after the Turcoman's defeat at Georg Teppe in 1881. Significantly, the *kran* rallied between 1877 and 1882. Another factor was the Caspian Fisheries Concession, granted in 1879 to a Russian subject. This concession gave the Shah's government 60,000 *tomans* (11 million *krans*) a year.[87]

From mid-1877 to 1882 the *kran* held firm at between 27 and 28 to the pound. Throughout this time its international exchange value was much greater than its intrinsic silver value. The 1887 currency reform must have seemed to the Persian authorities singularly ameliorative, and State revenues secure,[88] but this felicitous situation could not for long withstand the steady drop in world silver prices. As has been shown, the decline continued in spite of America's dabbling in bimetallism giving some support to the world silver price up to 1890. The graph shows how this decline was fairly closely reflected between 1882 and 1889 in the *kran*'s loss of value.

It is the year 1300 A.H. (November 12, 1882–November 2, 1883) which, as already mentioned, Abdullah Mustawfi cites as the year in which Persia's currency went bad. Most particularly this shrewd chronicler of his own times attributes this catastrophe to the exploitation of new silver mines in America, and to the damage to Persia's money as 'Iranian gold began to flee to Europe, to be sealed in foreign banks, and Persia changed its money from gold to silver'.[89]

This last statement has already been criticized. Gold's flight from Persia antedated 1300 A.H./1882–3 by a number of years, but Mustawfi's choice of dates shows awareness that by 1883 a crisis was unavoidable, and he also perceived a correlation between Persian monetary phenomena and events in America. It might be supposed that Mustawfi was in fact one phase of Gresham's Law behind the actual progress of events in Persia, and that he is really dating the first appearance of what was soon to become the infamous 'black money', *pul-i-siyah*, copper coins. He speaks of the 1877 currency as involving both gold and silver coins, but other sources mention only the silver *kran*.

After the 1877–1882 boost, at the outset of the decline between 1882 and 1889 there was an advantage of about 10 per cent to the minted coin over its intrinsic metallic value. This was a gap of great importance to the government, especially as by that time Persia had been largely stripped of any sort of specie reserve. However, new coins, the requisite of day-to-day business, were in such short supply that the situation in some commercial towns was becoming difficult. Mintage depended on fresh bullion imports and, because of Persia's chronic trade deficit, silver left the country as rapidly as it entered it. From 1882 to 1889 the *kran* declined in value from 28 to a little less than 36 to the pound sterling, an inflation (or devaluation) of almost 36 per cent in six years. More important, the gap between the *kran*'s intrinsic metallic value and its exchange value dropped from 5 *krans* for every pound sterling to only 2½ *krans* in the same period.[90]

In 1889, Nasiru'd-Din Shah and his chief counsellor, the

youthful Aminu's-Sultan, again had recourse to a serious quest for European investments in Persia, and large-scale concession deals. In the course of what was the Shah's third visit to Europe, he paid a second one to England. He and his entourage submitted with every sign of willingness to somewhat blatant cossetting by those political and financial circles in London who were showing a marked interest in Persia at that time, an interest Aminu's-Sultan doubtless hoped successfully to cultivate. These circles' hospitable solicitude for the Persians reflected to no small degree Lord Salisbury's preoccupations over India's defence and the Anglo-Russian 'rivalry' in Persia.[91]

Aminu's-Sultan's acquiescence in British proposals can be ascribed to his belief that they would yield tangible results. Ironically, however, any success he might have congratulated himself upon had the effect, as will be demonstrated below, of making Persia's monetary system even more vulnerable than it would otherwise have been when, in 1890, the United States by the Sherman Silver Purchase Act abruptly knocked the bottom out of world silver prices. As already mentioned, this Act's deflationary intent was disguised to seem like redoubled American support for silver's use as an integral part of the international monetary system. The Persian silver *kran* would have received substantial support from a firm United States commitment, backed by the United States' ample gold reserves, to international bimetallism. The Sherman Act's real purpose soon produced an unprecedented drop in world silver prices. The *kran* fell under tremendous inflationary pressures. Within a very short time, silver's use as an international exchange medium was inevitably terminated.[92]

The change from England's response to Persian schemes in 1873 to that which marked the period of the Shah's visit to England in 1889 was manifested in the autumn. Reuter had at last succeeded in salvaging from the wreckage of his 1872 concession the right to establish a bank in Persia, with the additional right to operate mines as an adjunct to the bank's other business. In October 1889, on issuing the prospectus and inviting subscriptions, the Bank's capital of £1,000,000 was subscribed in London over fifteen times in a matter of hours.[93] In August the Imperial Bank of Persia had received a Royal Charter of Incorporation from the British government. It thus came into existence buoyed up on the confidence of both investing circles and the British government.

In 1888 the granting of the Karun Navigation Concession had likewise been a tribute to British persistence. Though this concession was not exclusive, a fresh opening was afforded a British concern, the Lynch Company. It meant more British investment in a Persian undertaking, likely in the changed mood of the time to be applauded by parties in London now showing such eagerness to test Persian opportunities.

In 1890, however, this new British confidence in Persian ventures was severely shaken by the shock to Persian credit on the London market which followed the Lottery Concession scandal. The Shah had sold a concession for a state lottery. The desperate need for money is once more clearly implied by this sale, of a concession with which no grandiose schemes for 'regeneration', 'industrialization', 'progress' and so forth were explicitly associated. The concession, however, was rescinded, but the Persian agent in London, Malkum Khan, became involved in fraudulent speculations connected with the resale of it when it no longer existed. On the fraud's exposure investors were for a while frightened off Persia.[94]

The scare affected Major Talbot of the Imperial Persian Tobacco Corporation. Talbot had had talks with Aminu's-Sultan during the Shah's 1889 English tour. In March 1890 he obtained a 'regie' for the exploitation of all Persia's tobacco products. Although in Curzon's words, the new Corporation was 'warmly commended by high authorities and possessing many features of probable advantage', it was at first slow t obtain investors' support.[95] Nevertheless, the Regie's director, M. Ornstein, began its implementation in April, and by September 1891 the operation employed 266 people in Persia.[96]

Widespread riots in 1891–2 have made the Tobacco Concession peculiarly notorious, because it gave mass discontent a focus for opposition. Historians have seen in this opposition the first example of unified national protest against the Qajar government. They have also deplored the saddling of Persia with the obligation to pay a large indemnity in hard currency, after the concession's abolition in January 1892. The groups active in the agitation against the monopoly have been identified as the same basic combination of social forces which formed the nucleus of the Constitutional Revolution fifteen years later, with the merchant classes playing a prominent role. The Regie's minimum premium payments of £15,000 per annum to the Persians have been cited as representing a gross undervaluation of Persia's tobacco production, while the Regie deprived Persian merchants of lucrative business.[97]

However justifiable such conclusions might be, to state them regardless of the needs imposed on Persia by its adverse trading position is not. Emphasis, moreover, on the political and social aspects of opposition to trading concessions, in particular the Regie, tends to conceal how the coincidence of such concessions round the year 1890 set the scene for a sudden and extremely traumatic disruption of what remained of the Persian monetary system during the succeeding four years.

Curzon's reference to the 'probable advantage' of the Tobacco Concession[98] could with some justice be applied to all the three concessions dealt with here as associated with the period 1888–1890. The new Karun navigation, open to ships of all nations and resulting in a Persian steamship venture in the Nasiri Company, was not without advantage to Persia. The Imperial Bank could become a vehicle for increased foreign investment, and its contingent Mining Rights Corporation might have produced sorely needed exports. Successful operation of the Tobacco Monopoly would certainly have done so. Any increase in exports would have protected the *kran*'s international position. It would be an oversimplification to measure the concessions' importance to the Persian government and monetary system solely on the criteria of the concessionaire's direct payments to the government or to the Shah.

In fact, acts by the United States Congress and the failure of the Tobacco and Mining Rights concessions to realize any profit coincided, so that a cruel and unprecedented inflation was exacerbated. Expectations of development of Persia's resources under European auspices had immediately, but only briefly, attracted hard money. The Regie, the Mining Rights Corporation, the Lynch Company, the Bank, all as a natural consequence of beginning operations, in a very short time introduced new capital into Persia. The Bank, though, to its own detriment and that of Persia's future financial stability, it converted the money into silver bullion,[99] pumped in a quantity of new money. It also invested in a project such as a Tehran to Muhammara carriage way, an example of the kind of new investment being made in Persia.

Not that, even before the Lottery Concession scandal of 1890, this new British investment exceeded the bounds set by easily discernible practical considerations. The concessionaires who risked capital in the Persian 'funnel' were out for quick, safe profits, and their capital outlays were concentrated on potentially exportable raw materials, and the services required to facilitate their movement. In other words, a European bank, a road to the sea, a steamer or two on the River Karun.

Nonetheless, any degree of infusion of capital had an appreciable effect on Persia. The Shah's final sortie into the European investment world at first furnished a gratifying result. Between mid-1889 and mid-1890, the silver *kran* rose in exchange value from 36 to 30 to the pound sterling, the first such appreciation in value for almost twenty years.[100] The new gap between the value of minted *krans* and of bullion silver stood at the unprecedented figure of almost 10 *krans* to the pound sterling. The Aminu's-Sultan might well have been pleased with the bounties which dalliance with the English apparently brought. The courtier journalist and diarist Itimadu's-Saltaneh alludes to royal extravagances on the Continent of Europe on the way back to Persia. These expenses do not redound to the Shah's credit, but he probably believed that a better financial future for his country and himself had been secured.[101] An indirect British reference indicates that by the end of 1890, the *kran* might have reached an international exchange value equal to the 1882 exchange rate, the one Mustawfi cites as obtainable before the money went 'bad'.[102]

Persian merchants' reaction to this favourable turn in the terms of trade was quick. Local and international conditions made it certain that 1890 would be a year of continuing heavy imports at all Persia's major ports of entry. The danger lay, of course, in these imports' excess over any possible coverage by exports. They even surpassed the country's actual consumption capacity. In the middle of 1890, the British Consul at Bushire reported that 'much attention has been directed to Persia as an outlet for European manufacturers by the opening of the river Karun to international traffic, the visit by the Shah to Europe, and the formation of the Imperial Bank of Persia', but, the Consul added, 'possibly the attention attracted may have led to the shipment to this country of goods on a scale somewhat disproportionate to the present actual consumption'. He prophesied that 'some check may be anticipated'.[103] In September 1890, the British Consul at Tabriz also noticed a heavy increase in imports. He observed that Russia's imports had lost more ground to European, paper roubles having risen and the pound sterling fallen in value.[104]

Thus when the U.S. Congress issued silver's death warrant in the Sherman Silver Purchase Act, the silver *kran* began heavily to fall not merely from a normal exchange position, but from the peak of a speculative mountain. Persian merchants lost any advantage they might have gained from the sudden devaluation, because many of the goods imported during the boom had been bought on credit often linked to values expressed in sterling.[105] Unrestrained inflation and a sharp contraction of trade set in, to the injury of Persian and foreign merchants, but the real tragedy was the government's complete inability to cope with rising prices. Large sections of the economy were affected by uncontrollable shock waves of concurrent inflation and depression. That all classes were not immediately hit in ways characteristic of depressions or 'panics' in the West, was due to the fact that Persia was still in a stage of development where not all of the population was yet wedded to a cash economy, or market orientated.

Those who had a stake in the economy, merchants, courtiers, notables, divines, fought by all means, fair and foul, to protect their economic interests. In 1895, Sir T. E. Gordon visiting Persia noticed various 'corners' or 'rings'. Wheat rings, using local government authorities' powers, cornered a city's bread supply and raised this basic commodity's price to famine levels. After 1890, 'bread riots' had become more frequent. Gordon points out that they changed from simple attacks on local bakers to violent confrontations with 'wheat cornerers'.[106]

Mention must be made of the Tehran 'copper ring', a descendant of the old Tehran 'silver ring'. It centred round Nasru's-Saltaneh, the mint farmer and a protégé of the Shah's son Na'ibu's-Saltaneh, the Commander of the Army. In May 1894, Nasru's-Saltaneh's *krans* were given a random test at a public assay before a concourse of notables. Nasru's-Saltaneh's dismissal for fraud followed. A former Mint Master, Hajji Muhammad

Hasan, took over, supported by the court faction opposed to the Na'ibu's-Saltaneh's clique. Both British and Persian sources, while granting Muhammad Hasan a respectable degree of probity, emphasize the bribery and intrigue this change of Mint Master involved. The usually astute I'timadu's-Saltaneh chronicles a ministerial Council convened in January 1894 to discuss the problem of the serious falls in silver prices, but states that the meeting's real purpose was to open the battle for control of the mint farm.[107]

The various sources only obliquely indicate that Nasru's-Saltaneh's clearly fraudulent debasement of the silver *kran* was but the least part of Persia's problem. While world silver prices and the *kran* descended into worse periods of uncertainty, the Mint 'ring', eschewing the risks foreseeable in importing and holding bullion silver, resorted to the expedient of grinding out great quantities of copper coin, 'black money'. Nasru's-Saltaneh's 'ring' could make large profits, for copper bullion was exceedingly cheap and could be palmed off by the Mint as nominally related to the silver *kran*. The government, however, lost its former profit from minting legal tender from imported bullion silver. Gresham's Law soon operated: silver *krans* were either hoarded or exported, as 'black money' spread. Labourers' wages were soon entirely in copper; but for the purchase of commodities the copper *shahi* (20 = 1 *kran*) was only accepted at a heavy discount. Aggravated inflation thus became more widespread among the urban population.

Measures to meet the subsequent 'copper problem' lie outside the scope of discussion of the silver crisis, except in so far as they throw light on the monetary problem in general. In 1893, the Governor of Shiraz had to buy 30,000 *tomans* worth of copper coins at par, at his own expense, in order to restore some confidence in the currency. Belatedly, shortly before his assassination in 1896, Nasiru'd-Din Shah promulgated a decree which halted the mintage of copper for five years. Some government departments, including the Customs, were urged to accept copper coins as legal tender, at a fixed rate. Arrangements with the Imperial Bank enabled copper to be bought up on the government's account in small quantities from *bona fide* holders, i.e. non-speculators.[108]

The destruction of Persia's monetary system occurred on three levels. The decline of the silver *kran*'s international exchange value can easily be traced. The departure of Persia's trading partners, Russia and India, from minting silver in 1893, to leave the declining *kran* isolated, has already been noted. Parallel with these external events, at home the 'copper ring' was flooding the country with 'black money', which traded at a heavy discount and drove much of Persia's silver into the hands of hoarders.[109] On a third level, other 'rings' made 'corners' in basic necessities. An artificial inflation was added to the very acute real one. Riots were inevitable, and preoccupation with the 'Tobacco Riots' obscures the fact that, though smaller in scale, their frequency hardly diminished after the Tobacco Monopoly's cancellation. After 1890, the era of 'Bread Riots' began;[110] really, it might be said 'Copper Riots'.

In 1896 William Jennings Bryan denounced the mono-metallists on behalf of the American silver mining states, American debtor classes, and especially the heavily mortgaged farmers. He said that the world was being crucified 'upon a cross of gold'.[111] Bryan's theme, in a United States Presidential Election which he lost, was the evil consequences of the Sherman Act. He fought his campaign in the year of the assassination of Nasiru'd-Din Shah, the ruler of a country whose 'crucifixion' as a result of the Sherman Silver Purchase Act had been the cruellest of all, and on a 'cross' composed only of silver.

NOTES

1. Command 2852, 1881, *Further Papers Relating to the Occupation of Kandahar*, p. 12, para. 12.
2. Joseph Rabino's graph first appeared in the *Journal* of the Institute of Bankers 1892, Vol. XIII, Pt. 1, to illustrate a Paper he read before the Institute in December 1891, before Rabino was fully aware of the world silver crisis's impact on Persia and the recently inaugurated Imperial Bank of Persia. He was a senior official in this bank. His 1891 Paper is on the whole optimistic. Not so his 1894 report on Persia's currency, to the British Legation in Tehran, which was forwarded to London, with the graph, on June 22, 1894 under F.O. 248/566, Secret, No. 146. His use at this date of the graph used in 1891 is significant; he must have perceived that he had been thinking on the right lines in 1891–92, and that the picture the graph presented, of the silver *toman*'s downward fluctuations, was the truest indication of what Persia's currency was undergoing.

3. See R. G. Hawtrey: *The Gold Standard in Theory and Practice*: London, New York and Toronto, 1947 (5th Edition), *Bimetallism*, pp. 70–79.
4. *Ibid.*
5. Persia's bullion position in the nineteenth century is the subject of research being undertaken by one of the authors, J. B. Simmons.
6. Rabino, *Journal of the Institute of Bankers op. cit.* p. 31. Also, F.O. 248/506, No. 146. *NB* to Appendix II.
7. See *Encyclopaedia Britannica*, XI ed. Articles, *Bimetallism*, *Money*, *Silver*. Also, Ross M. Robertson, *History of the American Economy*, New York and Burlingame, 1955 (2nd Edition), pp. 311–313. Interestingly, Rabino, *op. cit.* p. 30, had taken the trouble to obtain citations from the Washington Mint, of gold and silver ratios between 1687 and 1871, 1871 and 1889, the last period registering a 'fall in silver' which had been 'unceasing'.
8. See Robertson, *op. cit.* and chart on p. 314.
9. *Ibid.*
10. E.g. Rabino's reasoning in his Paper, p. 35 and pp. 39–41 (on moving bullion without the Bank); and F.O. 248/586 No. 125, May 23, 1894, which includes Mr Crow's report on Shiraz, with a chart on exchange rates there for July 1, 1893 to June 30, 1894 inclusive. The Bank was incorporated in London for thirty years by Royal Charter in August 1889 and issued its prospectus in October.
11. That this impact was not foreseen is shown by the Bank's subsequent request for permission to devaluate its paid-up capital, (to an amount remarkably consonant with the 50% drop in world silver evaluation), F.O. 248/580 No. 189, 30th March, 1894, cf. note 92 below.
12. Robertson, *op. cit.* p. 313.
13. For the history and trade of the Persian Gulf at this time see Jean Aubin, 'Les Princes d'Ormuz du XIIIe au XVe Siècle', *Journal Asiatique*, Tome CCXLI (1953), pp. 77–138, and his 'La Survie de Shilau et la Route du Khunj-o-Fal', *Iran* Vol. VII, 1969, pp. 21–37.
14. The Il-Khanid Mongol rulers of Persia (1256–1335) attempted to reach the Mediterranean in repeated campaigns, until Abu Sa'id (d. 1335) finally made peace with the Mamluk rulers of Egypt, who had blocked the Il-Khan's advances towards the Levant. Egypt meanwhile reaped the benefit of the Indian trade diverted to the Red Sea.
15. See G. Hambly, 'An Introduction to the Economic Organization of Early Qajar Iran,' *Iran* Vol. II, 1964, especially pp. 75, 77 and 78, and A. K. S. Lambton, 'Persian Trade under the Early Qajars', in *Islam and the Trade of Asia*, Cassirer Oxford and University of Pennsylvania, 1970, especially pp. 235–236.
16. Edward Scott Waring, *A Tour to Sheeraz* (London 1807), p. 129.
17. C. U. Aitchison (compiler), *A Collection of Treaties, Engagements and Sanads*, Calcutta, 1933, Vol. XIII, pp. 49–53.
18. In 1809, Harford Jones concluded a 'Preliminary Treaty' (Aitchison, *op. cit.* p. 53), revised by Gore Ouseley in 1812 (*ibid.*, p. 56) and again revised in 1814 (*ibid.* p. 60). Malcolm's arrangements of 1801 were in effect annulled when Napoleon and the Persians signed the treaty of Finkenstein

in 1807, which in its turn became a dead letter after Napoleon's treaty of Tilsit with the Tsar two months later in the same year.

19. Aitchison, *op. cit.*, Appendix No. V.
20. *Ibid.*, Appendix No. VII.
21. Anglo-Persian engagements, designed to prevent Persia occupying Herat, were concluded in January 1853 (Aitchison, p. 77) and in March 1857, when the Anglo-Persian Treaty of Paris was signed (see especially Article 57), (Aitchison, p. 81). Muhammad Shah's Herat campaign of 1837 led to a rupture of Anglo-Persian diplomatic relations, when the British envoy left the Shah's camp in June. In June 1838, the Government of India occupied the Persian island of Kharg in the Persian Gulf, and threatened the Shah with further hostilities unless he raised the siege of Herat, which he did in the following September.
22. Waring, *op. cit.*, p. 76, describes the inland city of Yazd as an 'emporium', due to its 'situation'. While he asserts the paucity of inland trade, he ascribes to Yazd trade with Turkestan, Khurasan and Kashmir. On p. 77 he mentions that many Persian merchants visited India and Kashmir, and often undertook 'long journies' (*sic*). He made his observations in 1802–4; his 'final' visit to Basrah is dated as having been in 1804.
23. Article X and the Treaty's Annexure.
24. J. A. Norris, *The First Afghan War 1838–1842*, Cambridge, 1967, in particular the section entitled 'British Aims in Central Asia 1830–1838'. Lord Ellenborough is interestingly cited as saying that he could not see what 'Bokharians' might give in return for British imports, 'except turquoises, lapis lazuli, and *the ducats they receive from Russia*'. p. 38 (italics ours).
25. *Encyclopaedia Britannica*, IX Edition (1875–1889), Article, *Baghdad*.
26. Charles Issawi, 'The Tabriz-Trabzon Trade 1830–1900: Rise and Decline of a Route', in *International Journal of Middle Eastern Studies*, Vol. 1 No. 1, (January 1970).
27. Cited by Gavin Hambly, *op. cit.* (note 15), p. 74, Cf. William Ouseley, *Travels in Various Countries of the East, More Particularly Persia*, London 1823, Vol. II. p. 227.
28. See G. N. Curzon, *Persia and the Persian Question*, London, 1892 and 1966, Vol. II, pp. 383–387. He states that the Karun Navigation Concession was objected to because 'local traders resented competition with the hallowed monopoly of their caravans' (p. 383).
29. *Ibid.*, Vol. I, pp. 622–625.
30. In her *La Perse, la Chaldée et la Susiane* (Paris 1887), Mme Jean Dieulafoy (cited by Hamid Algar, *Religion and State in Iran* 1785–1906, California 1969, p. 176) significantly repeats *muleteers'* complaints against the spread of Europeans' influence, in the context of opposition to railway construction.
31. William Ouseley, *op. cit.*, Vol. III, p. 318. All the mariners Ouseley saw on the Caspian in 1812 were Armenians.
32. See Issawi, *op. cit.* for a fuller discussion, though L. Oliphant, *The Russian Shores of the Black Sea* (London 1852) describes Russia's self-defeating restrictions of trade.

33. Curzon, *op. cit.*, Vol. I, p. 71 and Vol. II, p. 556.
34. See T. E. Gordon, *Persia Revisited (1895)*, London and New York, 1896, pp. 8–13.
35. M. Postlethwayte, *The Universal Dictionary of Trade and Commerce*, London, 1751–1755, Vol. II, p. 445.
36. Sir John Malcolm, *History of Persia*, London 1815, Vol. II pp. 86–87.
37. L. Lockhart, *Nadir Shah*, London 1938, pp. 511, sqq.
38. Malcolm, *op. cit.*
39. Lockhart, *op. cit.* fn. 1, p. 152.
40. Malcolm, *op. cit.*
41. Lockhart, *op. cit.*
42. Aitchison, *op. cit.*, pp. 42–44. Italics are the authors', who thank Dr John Perry for drawing their attention to Karim Khan's stipulation.
43. J. G. Lorimer, *Gazetteer of the Persian Gulf, Oman, and Central Arabia*, (Calcutta, 1915), Vol. I, p. 117.
44. *Idem.*
45. *Idem.*
46. Reports on Indian Affairs (PYRME b 40, Marshall Library, Cambridge), 3rd Report of the Select Committee, *Trade with Japan and Persia* 1793; pp. 42–46 relate to Persia and the Report is dated January 1793. We are indebted to Dr Ronald Ferrier for this reference, but cf. Lambton, *op. cit.*, pp. 216, fn. and 222.
47. *Idem.*
48. Waring, *op. cit.*, p. 129.
49. *Ibid.*
50. *Ibid.*, p. 128.
51. *Ibid.*
52. Malcolm in the privacy of interdepartmental communication with H. Dundas on April 10, 1801, cited by Hambly, *op. cit.*, p. 77.
53. Hambly's estimate of the comparative prosperity of Persian cities and of Herat in Afghanistan at the beginning of the nineteenth century (*op. cit.*, p. 78) cannot be overlooked, nor the fact that Nadir Shah's army must, one way or another, have brought back money into Persia, to be retained in private hands and help to capitalize private mercantile venturers in subsequent generations. Early authorities, e.g. Waring, *op. cit.*, p. 77, attest to Persian merchants' 'shrewdness', while the same class's concealment of their assets from the government's prying eyes was also a marked feature of Qajar Persia. Rabino in his Paper, p. 33 and footnotes, speaks of the 'dearth of silver' due to 'the universal custom of hoarding'. 'Abdullah Mustawfi's *Sharh-i-Zindagani-ye-Man*, 2nd edition, Tehran, n.d. Vol. I, p. 397, refers to gold in private hands. A later development is implicit in his reference on p. 400 to gold's flight 'to Europe to be sealed in foreign banks', when money could, due to the introduction of European banking into Persia, be hoarded outside the country. (Abdullah Mustawfi had ancestors who had successfully served the Qajars as Ministers of State Revenues).
54. Rabino, *op. cit.*, p. 35.
55. Hambly, *op. cit.*, p. 76.

56. Harford Jones Brydges: *An Account of the Transactions of His Majesty's Mission to the Court of Persia in the Years 1807–1811* (London, 1834), pp. 432–433. Brydges desired to promote British export trade with Persia (p. 434), especially since 'the East India Company's Charter of exclusive trade to the East is at an end'. He stated that Persia had seldom debased its coinage.
57. William Ouseley, *op. cit.* p. 409 describes fine gold coins seen at Tabriz. In Appendix 9, Vol. II of his work, the same observer suggests that it was at Tabriz that the best money was minted, but variation, he says, was appreciable, both among the coins of different mints, and between these and coins minted for distribution at festivals as ceremonial pieces. Also, Vol. III p. 409, Ouseley described two men in Tabriz bazaar, in June 1812 (already) busy knocking out copper coin (*felus*).
58. Hambly, *op. cit.* p. 76.
59. *Ibid.*, and Postlethwayte, *op. cit.*, points out that if importers of foreign specie sold their coin 'secretly ... to private persons', they profited.
60. Mustawfi, *op. cit.* (note 53), pp. 27–28.
61. Waring, *op. cit.*, p. 8.
62. Curzon, *op. cit.*, Vol. 6II, pp. 559 and 561.
63. F.O. papers, *op. cit.*, Note 2 above.
64. Lambton, *op. cit.*, p. 238.
65. F.O. 248/505 No. 66 2nd December, 1890.
66. Mustawfi, *op. cit.*, pp. 395–400.
67. Curzon, *op. cit.*, pp. 614–615.
68. Graham Storey, *Reuter's Century 1851–1951*, London 1951, p. 73, and Firuz Kazemzadeh, *Russia and Britain in Persia 1864–1914*, Newhaven and London, 1968, Chapter 2.
69. Storey, *op. cit.*, p. 74.
70, 71. *Ibid.*, p. 77.
72. Sir Percy Sykes, *History of Persia*, London 1915 and 1951, Vol. II, p. 370.
73. Storey, *op. cit.*, pp. 80 and 81.
74. *Ibid.*
75. *Ibid.*
76. Cited by Storey, *op. cit.*, p. 75.
77. *Ibid.*, p. 77.
78. Firuz Kazemzadeh, *op. cit.*, p. 108, says that Nasiru'd-Din Shah unhesitatingly sold 'the future of generations of his subjects' for 'paltry sums'. In harmony with the tenor of E. G. Browne's *The Persian Revolution 1905–1909* (Cambridge 1910, reprinted Frank Cass, 1966), many writers on Persia, including Avery (*Modern Iran*, London 1965), have tended to criticize Nasiru'd-Din Shah and his 'venal' courtiers for corruptly selling their country's assets to foreign concession-seekers. Here it is hoped to introduce an aspect of the history of Persian concession dealings which seems hitherto to have been little regarded.
79. Storey, *op. cit.*, p. 74 and Curzon, *op. cit.*
80. Storey, p. 78. The doggerel refers perceptively to 'gold' though, as we have suggested, not as much of this commodity 'ran' for Nadir Shah as the versifier seems to have thought.

There's Reuter – let's hope 'twill be Reuter *Khan*
Instead of Reuter cannot –
Has set himself calmly the gulf to scan,
Which in Persia, since Kadjar rule began,
Hath yawned with wider and wider span,
'Twixt dried-up nature and dwindled man
Where the gold stream – for Nadir Shah that ran –
Again to Nadir has got.

81. Kazemzadeh, *op. cit.*
82. Storey, *op. cit.*, p. 78, Cf. Kazemzadeh, p. 110, citing Lord Enfield to Reuter, October 15, 1872, F.O. 60/405, and p. 131, Lord Derby to the same, March 27, 1874.
83. Storey, *op. cit.*, p. 82.
84. I'timadu's-Saltaneh, *Ruznameh-ye-I'timadu's-Saltaneh*, Tehran 1345/1966–67, p. 972. An outright gift of 50,000 tomans was included in the offer, which was in due course accepted, so that the Mint Mastership changed hands. (I'timadu's-Saltaneh was Nasiru'd-Din Shah's Minister of Press till his death in 1896, the year of this Shah's death also).
85. Rabino's report on the monetary situation, p. 7, Appendix 1(D), enclosed under F.O. 248/566 No. 146 (See note 2 above).
86. G. N. Curzon, *Russia in Central Asia in 1889*, London 1889, New Impression, Frank Cass, 1967, p. 49; Kazemzadeh, *op. cit.*, p. 162.
87. Kazemzadeh, *Ibid.*, p. 207.
88. *Vide* Rabino's graph (p. 260) for the levelling out of the *kran*'s exchange value 1877–1882 (line A).
89. Abdullah Mustawfi, *op. cit.*, pp. 395–400.
90. *Vide* Rabino's graph (p. 260).
91. See R. L. Greaves, *Persia and the Defence of India 1884–1892*, (London, 1959), especially Chapter X and Appendix IV. Also, Kazemzadeh, *op. cit.*, p. 186. Lord Salisbury, having had experience at the India Office, became Britain's Prime Minister and Foreign Secretary in June, 1885. He was interested in strengthening Persia as a 'buffer state' between Russia's Central Asian Empire and British India. This policy was reflected in the choice of the energetic Sir Henry Drummond Wolff as British envoy to Persia, where he arrived in spring 1888, one of Salisbury's instructions to him being to encourage development of Persia's resources (Wolff's *Rambling Recollections*, London 1908, p. 337). Salisbury entertained the Shah at Hatfield House, as did the Rothschilds and others at their country houses. At Lord Brownlow's according to the Shah's diary, one of his entourage, Mahdi Khan, was asked to speak into a novel recording device an American was demonstrating. On the spur of the moment he uttered two verses by the Persian poet Hafiz, beginning *agarcheh badeh farah bakhsh o bad gulbiz ast*, and meaning

    Though the wine is joy-granting and the breeze rose-scattering,
    Do not drink wine to the sound of the harp because the police are alert.
    If a cup and a comrade fall into your grasp,
    Drink with care, because the times are dangerous.

It seems that Mahdi Khan knew that something was afoot amidst all this English junketing.

92. See note 11 above: the Imperial Bank's Board of Directors in London asked the Treasury (F.O. 248/580 No. 189, March 30, 1884) for permission to depreciate the Bank's paid-up sterling capitalization from £1,000,000 to £650,000. This request opens with a reference to 'difficulties which have arisen chiefly from the depreciation of silver in the East'. In this context, it is interesting to note two somewhat fugitive comments by Andrew D. Kalmykow in his *Memoirs of a Russian Diplomat, Outposts of the Empire 1883–1897*, Yale Russian and East European Stories 10 (New Haven and London, 1971), pp. 52, 53 and 53 fn. Persia is described as 'a famed but poorly developed country with limited natural resources which had been off the gold standard since the time when Alexander the Great took all her bullion and carried it away with Macedonian efficiency'. And p. 53 fn. 'The Persians remained by sheer necessity involuntary supporters of a silver currency, whatever the opinions of learned European economists, and a hasty move in the nineties by the practical financiers of the English-run Imperial Bank of Persia brought a speedy reward in the form of a net loss of one third the original capital'. Kalmykow reached Persia in 1895, after spending a year and a half in the Persian Bureau of the Asian Department at the Imperial Russian Foreign Office in St. Petersburg.
93. G. N. Curzon, *Persia, op. cit.*, p. 475.
94, 95. *Idem* and p. 484.
96. A. K. S. Lambton, 'The Tobacco Regie: Prelude to Revolution', in *Studia Islamica* XXII and XXIII, 1965, p. 126.
97. Kazemzadeh, *op. cit.*, pp. 243–250. He cites E. G. Browne, *The Persian Revolution*, *op. cit.*, p. 33. See *Ibid.*, pp. 34–35 for specific references to the merchants' operations the Regie was to obviate, to the cultivators' advantage. I'timadu's-Saltaneh (Muhammad Hasan Khan; see note 85 above) in his *Khwab Nameh* (Mashhad 1945), pp. 104, 105, describes how the operations of the Concession benefited the cultivators because they prevented a few ('fifty or sixty') merchants, in collaboration with tribal leaders and religious dignitaries, dealing in tobacco 'futures', to the cultivators' detriment.
98. See note 96 above, and the *Khwab Nameh* cited in note 97. (Curzon is not explicit about who would benefit; I'timadu's-Saltaneh is: the tobacco-growing peasant).
99. See note 92 above.
100. See Rabino's graph (p. viii) and Report F.O. Annual Series 1890, where the British Consul General in Tabriz, writing on September 16, 1890, describes the exchange position.
101. I'timadu's-Saltaneh's *Ruznameh, op. cit.*, (note 85) p. 751, under 14th Dhu'l-Hijja 1306 A.H./August 10, 1889.
102. F.O. 248/505 No. 66 December 2, 1890, Col. Stewart, Tabriz, to Foreign Office.
103. Report 760 under British Consul Bushire's letter of May 20, 1890. Cf. Rabino's Paper, *op. cit.*, p. 32.

104. British Consul General Tabriz, reporting on September 16, 1890. Report 780, F.O. Annual Series, 1890.
105. Rabino's Paper, *op. cit.*, p. 40, and *Ibid.* for reference to long term credits.
106. T. E. Gordon, *op. cit.* (note 34), pp. 73–76.
107. I'timadu's-Saltaneh's *Ruznameh*, *op. cit.*, p. 972. Also Mirza Ali Khan Aminu'd-Dawleh, *Khatirat-i-Siyasi*, (Tehran 1963) (ed. Hafez Farma Famayan), pp. 135 sqq. Cf. F.O. 248/585, No. 108, May 4, 1894, Cunningham Greene to Lord Kimberley.
108. T. E. Gordon, *op. cit.*, pp. 74–76. See Rabino's report on the monetary situation, p. 2, for information on the rate of copper's discount, and F.O. 248/586 No. 125, May 23, 1894, Mr Crow's Report on Shiraz for 1892–93, for discount on copper and the Governor's having to purchase copper at par.
109. F.O. 248/594, No. 59, February 24, 1894, Cunningham Greene to Lord Kimberley on the Zillu's-Sultan's (see below) purchases of gold through the Imperial Bank, to hoard in Europe. F.O. 248/564, No. 162, October 15, 1893, reports the Prime Minister's complaints about silver being hoarded; a gold standard is said to be infeasible, partly because of the Shah's greed, but mainly because any gold put into circulation would promptly be hoarded. Cf. citation in note 53 above, of Rabino's Paper, p. 33.
110. F.O. 248/564, No. 167, November 7, 1893, reports rise of bread prices in Isfahan, where the Zillu's-Sultan was governor. He is described as a notorious hoarder, but this son of Nasiru'd-Din Shah was described in F.O. 248/568, No. 22 of January 22, 1891, as popular with English merchants in Isfahan, and an investor in Indian stocks. In the document of 1893, riots at Isfahan were designated 'bread riots' and other Foreign Office Papers describe bread riots in Mashhad (F.O. 248/541, No. 96 of April 16, 1892), in Fars and Shiraz (Crow's Report for 1892–93), at Yazd and Kirman (F.O. 248/541, No. 166 of November 9, 1892), and bread and 'cholera' riots in Tehran (No. 139 of October, 1892), while T. E. Gordon (*op. cit.*, p. 74), mentions the heir to the throne, who was governor in Tabriz, gaining popularity there by bringing in bread to avert riots. Thus in the period 1892–94 *after* the Tobacco Concession's cancellation, practically every major urban centre in Persia was witnessing disturbances, the 'bread riots'.
111. The relevant portions of Mr Bryan's famous speech are given in P. W. Glad, *McKinley, Bryan and the People*, (Philadelphia and New York, 1966), pp. 138–139.

2

The Mazanderan Development Project and Haji Mohammad Hasan: A Study in Persian Entrepreneurship, 1884–1898[1]

William J. Olson

In Sha'ban, 1307 (March–April, 1890), a wealthy Tehran merchant, Haji Mohammad Hasan, Amin al-Zarb, issued notices in Tehran and elsewhere proclaiming the opening of the Port of Nasiri and of a railway line in the Caspian province of Mazanderan. The circular declared that the port facilities, which included a landing pier, would help promote trade; and the railway, running from Mahmudabad on the Caspian Sea some fifteen miles inland to the small city of Amol at the base of the Elborz Mountains, would cut transportation costs. The port offered a large caravanserai, warehouses, and assorted workshops; and the railway was to make one round trip a day, more if there were a demand, carrying passengers and merchandise. Thus, after seven years of intense struggle, the Mazanderan Development Project was born; within four years it was dead. The brief life of the project, however, sheds interesting light on the problems that confronted development schemes in nineteenth-century Iran. The following discussion will first deal with the history of the railway and then examine the types of problems it encountered.

Development schemes, especially those contemplating railways, were not unusual in Iran. The late nineteenth century was replete with projects; at one time or another, British, Russian, French, German, American and Belgian interests contemplated either building or investing in railways. The Iranian government actually granted several concessions, the most famous being the Reuter Concession of 1872, although most of these projects never passed beyond reverie. Geographical obstacles, lack of funds, scarcity or absence of materials, external and internal political obstacles, separately or in combination, conspired to abrade all the schemes. Of all the projects considered only two succeeded in getting any track laid.

The better known project, the only tangible result of a larger plan, began service in 1888, from Tehran to the Shrine of Shah Abdul Azim, some six miles away. The second scheme, the Mazanderan line, began operation sometime in 1890. This project, unlike many of the others, was a Persian enterprise from inception to execution, and unique in many ways. It is, however, largely overlooked in material on railway development.[2]

Unfortunately, the available documents do not allow a precise delineation of the motives behind this project; but the climate for it developed from the relationship of three men: Nasir ad-Din Shah (1848–1896); one of his chief ministers, Ali Asqhar Khan, Amin as-Sultan; and Haji Mohammad Hasan, Amin al-Zarb, a rich, influential merchant and protégé of Amin as-Sultan. The exact role each man played is not clear but Haji Mohammad Hasan provided the main impetus.

Little is know about Haji Mohammad Hasan's early life other than that he came to Tehran from Isfahan some time in the 1850s with little more than the clothes on his back and managed, by the 1880s, to translate this meagre capital into one of the largest fortunes in Iran.[3] By the end of his career he had built an extensive commercial enterprise with agents or offices in every major, and in many minor, Persian cities, as well as cities in the Ottoman Empire, and in Batum, Baku, Moscow, and Marseilles. He traded in a wide variety of goods, acted as buyer for military equipment, and supplied such items as mirrors for room decoration and such luxuries as fresh asparagus and fine wines for the Shah's table. He was patronized by Amin as-Sultan and he in turn patronized and protected less fortunate merchants – providing monetary support or interceding in legal or political disputes.

Haji Mohammad Hasan used his political connections to enhance his standing with other merchants and to secure for himself lucrative discounts and official positions. One such position was as Master of the Mint (Amin al-Zarb), which apparently enabled him to make some of his fortune by debasing the currency and pocketing the difference. As a traditional merchant he was highly successful, and at his instigation the Mazanderan project was brought before the Shah.

Haji Mohammad Hasan wrote the Shah on several occasions expressing his views on internal development, foreign interference, and the importance of the merchant class. These letters, although very formal, are often patronizing and sometimes highly critical of government officials and important notables, including the Shah himself. In one letter Haji Mohammad Hasan sharply reproached Mas'ud Mirza, Zill as-Sultan, the Governor-General of Isfahan and one of the Shah's most powerful and influential sons, for extortion and malfeasance. In other letters Haji Mohammad Hasan bitterly criticized local officials who used their official positions to squeeze money out of merchants; and later, when the Mazanderan project was in trouble, Haji Mohammad Hasan admonished the Shah for failing to live up to his promises of energetic support.

Haji Mohammad Hasan was a vigorous defender of the position of merchants, and thus of himself, but the tone of his correspondence suggests more than just opportunistic self-interest. Haji Mohammad Hasan often used his letters to express his views on commercial and industrial development. In one of these, written some time after the Shah's second visit to Europe (1878), he wrote, 'The mines of Iran are its agriculture, commerce, and industry and the leaders of the country ought to develop these.' On another occasion, some time in 1883–84, he wrote to the Shah that the country's welfare depended upon trade that was controlled by natives and when that was the case the country could prosper, factories be built and mines dug; but when economic benefits accrued to foreign interests wealth was exported and all internal classes suffered. Haji Mohammad Hasan's letters are often forthright in urging the Shah to promote development and protect trade as a vital sector of the economy.

It is not clear what influence such ideas had on the Shah but, like many Iranians of his time, he was impressed by contemporary western technology. As a result of his support his reign saw the proliferation, and demise, of a wide variety of industrial and development schemes, including the Mazanderan development project.[4]

The exact date for the beginning of the project is not known but some time in 1303 h.g. (1885–86) the Shah granted Haji Mohammad Hasan a concession for a mining enterprise in Mazanderan. Haji Mohammad Hasan had written to the Shah about the existence of mines in Mazanderan and the Shah, perhaps with a view to his pocketbook, responded favourably. One of the mines mentioned by Haji Mohammad Hasan was an iron mine located in Mahan, a village in the Nayej area of Amol in Mazanderan. The local inhabitants used the product of this mine – in the form of cannonballs – to pay their taxes. The quality of the ore impressed Haji Mohammad Hasan and, initially overlooking the difficult location, he envisioned exploiting the mine on a commercial basis. Haji Mohammad Hasan asked for and received a concession from the Shah, which granted him control of the Nayej area and extensive rights to exploit mineral resources.[5]

Haji Mohammad Hasan began implementing his concession almost immediately by employing a foreign mining engineer to undertake initial surveys. In 1304 (1886–1887), he purchased furnaces for smelting ore, hired several French engineers to supervise work and began assembling equipment. At this stage, the planners had not envisaged the railway, which only came into being later as an attempt to rescue the entire project from collapse.

At first, the project appeared to prosper. In Rajab, 1304 (March–April, 1887), Haji Mohammad Hasan wrote that three foreign engineers and their families had gone to Mazanderan to carry on the work. But two months later, when he went to Mazanderan to inspect the operations, he suddenly changed his mind. He wrote his son in Tehran that the project was not feasible and that he was cancelling the materials ordered from Europe. Amin as-Sultan learned of this decision and he informed Haji Hosein Agha, Amin al-Zarb's son, that the Shah had heard, was displeased, and wanted to know what had happened. Then Amin as-Sultan telegraphed Haji Mohammad Hasan for particulars and offered assistance, adding darkly that if he did not follow through with the project his reputation would be damaged. This argument must have persuaded Haji Mohammad Hasan, for several days later he replied that he had reconsidered and, despite formidable obstacles – such as transportation and location – he would continue his efforts. At the same time he asked for the privilege of collecting taxes in the Mahmudabad area so that he could repair the roads, build a port and construct a factory. He also requested sanction for the purchase of rice-producing farm land around Mahmudabad and an order prohibiting the exportation of rice because of a local famine.

In Sha'ban, 1304 (May, 1887), Amin as-Sultan informed Haji Mohammad Hasan that the Shah was pleased with his resoluteness, appreciated the obstacles, and would grant all his requests while promising continued support. There was no mention of a railway at this point, although this incident played an important role in its development.

Haji Mohammad Hasan never fully explained why he suddenly gave up the idea to carry out the Mazanderan project, but in a petition written to the Shah several years later he elaborated on the occasion. He explained that after his visit to Mazanderan in 1304 he observed that transportation difficulties in the Mazanderan would have increased the cost of the iron beyond any market value; he, therefore, had decided to terminate the effort. But after hearing about the Shah's concern, he decided to reconsider means of implementing the project. This led him to the realization that he needed a place on the coast to handle and export the iron. The only way of making the whole project feasible, he concluded, was to build a railway that would facilitate transport and cut costs.

Haji Mohammad Hasan began ordering rail equipment, and then, with the Shah's somewhat reluctant approval, left Mazanderan, sometime in Sha'ban 1304 (late April or early May, 1887), and went to Baku en route to Europe. In June he left Baku for Moscow. In Moscow, Haji Mohammad Hasan received word from Amin as-Sultan that the Shah approved of the ideas both for a railway between Mahmudabad and Amol and for a horse-drawn railway between Amol and Nayej to carry ore. The Shah granted Haji Mohammad Hasan the necessary land for the right of way and also, some time in this period, perhaps in conjunction with the revived project, Haji Mohammad Hasan received a concession to build a road from Amol to Tehran.

While in Moscow Haji Mohammad Hasan made the first of several attempts to involve foreign interests in the project, entering into discussions with certain unspecified Belgian interests, with whom he concluded a draft contract for a railway from Mahmudabad to Tehran. This draft agreement apparently did not receive support from the Shah, who may have disapproved of foreign participation or feared a possible hostile Russian reaction to foreign involvement.[6]

Haji Mohammad Hasan stayed only briefly in Moscow, and, in July, he made his way to Belgium where he began contracting for railway equipment from a large Belgian firm, Cockerill & Co.

Haji Mohammad Hasan bought considerable quantities of material, including a 1.435 meter gauge vertical boiler locomotive, three passenger cars, rails, fishplates, bolts and other railway equipment. He also purchased ten miles of telegraph wire, 60 boxes of mining equipment, quantities of tin, a furnace and five cranes (a large, mobile one) for unloading ships. He engaged the services of two Cockerill engineers to supervise the initial route survey and trestle construction; and he also purchased various types of military equipment for the army as well as speciality items – such as asparagus, wine and mirrors – for the tables and homes of the Shah and prominent nobles. When he completed these arrangements he returned to Mazanderan some time in Moharram, 1305 (late September or early October, 1887), to await the arrival of the goods.

Upon his return, Amin as-Sultan sent him a warm, congratulatory telegram and informed him that he had secured transit authority from the Russians for the material. Several days later, however, Amin as-Sultan urgently telegraphed Haji Mohammad Hasan to send all available information concerning: 1) the quantity of rail purchases; 2) the route the line would follow; and 3) how many foreigners would be employed. Amin as-Sultan informed Haji Mohammad Hasan that transit authority depended upon this information. Haji Mohammad Hasan replied in detail, stating that the line would begin some 200 meters from the coast in Mahmudabad and run inland to Amol, a distance of 17,000 zar (about 10 miles). In addition, Haji Mohammad Hasan wrote that he had purchased 20,000 zar of track, to be sure of having enough, plus 14,000 zar of small gauge track for a horse-drawn cart system to bring ore from the mine to Amol. Concerning the engineers, Haji Mohammad Hasan wrote that he had engaged two engineers in Belgium plus a consulting engineer in Baku to supervise construction of the furnace, the pier, and other related projects. Evidently this information satisfied the Russians, who wanted to be sure that foreigners would not be involved and that the rails would not be transferred to any foreign concerns. On the 27 Safar (November, 1887), Haji Mohammad Hasan wrote to Amin as-Sultan that he was returning to Tehran and that all seemed well. But problems were to develop very soon.

On 7 January 1888, Haji Mohammad Hasan received a letter from one of the foreign engineers in Mazanderan indicating that everything was not well. He wrote that some local villagers had attacked and beaten his workers and that this, plus delays in the transit of the necessary materials through Russian customs, had brought all work to a standstill. He continued that the contract between Haji Mohammad Hasan and Cockerill for their services was due to expire in March, and that unless the company agreed to review it they would have to leave. This problem was just the first of many which plagued the railway throughout its life and haunted it after its death.

In this particular instance, Amin al-Zarb wrote the Shah asking for his support and explaining that the railway pursued the line of the old road from Mahmudabad to Amol and along its path were two villages. Evidently the inhabitants of these villages, at the instigation of a certain Mohammad Khan Sartip, who wanted to buy the land, attacked the foreman, the engineers and the workers in order to stop the railway's progress. Haji Mohammad Hasan complained, and wanted a clear sign from the Shah that he would put an end to such interference in the future. There is no extant copy of a reply to this petition,[7] but shortly after this, in Jamad al-Avval, 1305 (January–February, 1888), the Shah issued a *farman* accepting Haji Mohammad Hasan's petition of Ramazan, 1304 (May–June, 1887), for authorization to build a railway (and a horse-railway to the mine of Nayej). The *farman* specified that the line of the railway and the lands (which followed the old road through the forest of Galeshpol) on both sides of it, which were not already privately owned, be transferred to Haji Mohammad Hasan for 99 years.

Although the original grants seemed to confirm Haji Mohammad Hasan's position, official declarations did not always produce the desired results. In May, for example, Amin as-Sultan had to write the Governor of Mazanderan ordering him to stop certain local inhabitants from carrying on obstructive activities against the project. Even so, problems continued.

In another instance, Haji Mohammad Hasan had to settle a dispute between his local agent and one of his foreign experts, named Brandt. Haji Mohammad Hasan received a letter from two of his local employees (Seyyed Asadollah and Seyyed Mahmud) complaining that the foreign consulting engineer had confiscated the engine's throttle in lieu of a claim for back wages for one of his assistants. The Seyyeds claimed that his action kept the train from running. At the same time, Brandt, the consulting engineer, wrote a long letter complaining of endless difficulties caused by Haji Mohammad Hasan's local employees – these same Seyyeds. Brandt claimed that these men and Haji Mohammad Hasan's local agents had, against his recommendations, bought sub-standard wood for over 50,000 ties, and that because of this only 1,500 metres of track had been laid. Brandt also said that some of the local agents were trying to pick quarrels to force the foreigners to go home and that the agents were lying and cheating. Brandt accused them of allowing rails and other goods unloaded from boats to remain in the open on the beach, and consequently much valuable material had been lost or damaged. Furthermore, Brandt complained that Haji Mohammad Hasan's agents quarrelled with the transport company in Baku and that he doubted if they would send any more ships with goods. These same agents, he charged, also had interfered with work and had tried to entrust the engine to someone who did not know how to operate it. Brandt reported that one day, while he was having tea, these men took the engine and, in an hour and a half, succeeded in damaging it so seriously that it would be useless for a month until the damaged parts were repaired in Baku. Finally, Brandt said that one man, Seyyed Mahmoud, had done everything to force the Europeans to go home so that he could run affairs, and that if such conditions continued the Europeans, 'habituated to order and loyalty,' would leave.

The outcome of this confrontation is not recorded, but aggravations of this type continued. In October, 1888, another foreign engineer employed by Haji Mohammad Hasan wrote that Seyyed Mahmoud was still obstructing efforts, but the railway would still probably be finished by December, 1888, or January,

1889, thanks to the efforts of local supporters from more honest quarters. As it turned out his was an optimistic view, and problems continued to plague the effort at every turn.

The exact date of the completion of the railway is uncertain. It is likely, however, that railway operations began sometime in Sha'ban, 1307 (March, 1890), because Haji Mohammad Hasan announced the opening of the Port of Nasiri, named in honour of Nasir ad-Din Shah, by issuing a circular which described the port and its facilities. The opening of the port and the railway was a notable accomplishment; unfortunately it did not endure, as problems continued to hamper the project.

The problems encountered in the following years were varied and frustrating. Petty rivalries continued, and the operation of the railway created more difficulties. In Shavval, 1311 (April, 1894), Haji Mohammad Hasan's agent in Mazanderan, Mashadi Hasan, wrote that the port facilities needed repair, that the train had derailed, and that workers had to drag the engine to Mahmudabad for repairs. In May, the agent complained that every time the train, in operation again, passed over the tracks, the ties, which had rotted, crumbled more, and that the local inhabitants then stole the exposed or loosened spikes. In Jamadi al-akhar, 1312 (December, 1894), Mashadi Hasan wrote that the train had operated only twice in 5 months; that sections of the track were in a fairly ruinous state; and that people continued to steal spikes. Despite the difficulties, Haji Mohammad Hasan continued his efforts to make the project a success.

Finally, in late 1312 (1894–94), Haji Mohammad Hasan ordered his agent to stop paying for road guards, who were employed to protect the tracks, and other workers. He also ordered him to collect all the goods and stores for the mine and factory and to send them to Tehran. Though these orders should have marked the closing chapter of the railway's operation, letters dated from 1314 (1896–97) add a further depressing footnote.

An agent for Haji Mohammad Hasan, sent to Mazanderan to check on the state of things, wrote that people were stealing the collected stores vigorously and that if the local people – who had stolen ties, bolts, spikes, etc. – could figure a way to carry off the rails, nothing would remain. In one pitiful letter he wrote that he had considered collecting the rails but that this could only be done if he repaired the tracks so that workers could reach more isolated parts. If he repaired the track, however, there was no need to take up the rails; but if he left the rails and did not repair the tracks the people would eventually figure a way of stealing them. The agent said he was at a complete loss for what to do and asked for advice. There is no extant reply and one is left to surmise the fate of the abandoned rails. H. L. Rabino, however, reported in 1908 that:

> ... the old railway track, which formed the only means of communication between Mazanderan and Amol, was reduced to a very narrow, seldom used, path, where thorns assaulted one from either side.[8]

There was evidently one final attempt in 1316 (1898–1899) to rescue the project, for Haji Mohammad Hasan concluded a draft contract with two Russians, Nicolai Nicolaiavich Kornakof and Fiodor Yokorovich Niakief. The contract proposed to establish a company to exploit Haji Mohammad Hasan's concession for iron works, mining rights and the railway. Haji Mohammad Hasan would receive payments for the concession, half in cash and half in shares, based on a property evaluation to be made by two independent assessors plus a third assessor, to be appointed by Amin as-Sultan, to act as arbitrator, if no agreement could be reached. The Russians were to have eight months after the decision to undertake a venture to form a company and draw up articles of incorporation. Haji Mohammad Hasan would get the concession renewed, try to extend it to 70 years, and obtain permission for foreigners to join. If he failed, the Russians would be allowed to try, and if this too proved unsuccessful, the contract would be considered void. The exact reasons for the failure of this renewed effort, which may have been an attempt by Haji Mohammad Hasan to salvage some of the enormous financial losses, are not known. The Shah may have decided against it or Russian opposition may have killed it. Haji Mohammad Hasan's death in Sha'ban, 1316 (December, 1898), however, ended any chance of success, and the railway and the Mazanderan Development Project disappeared into the jungle with little visible trace.

* * * * *

The failure of this developmental project was not an isolated event. As mentioned earlier, many foreigners and Persians alike conceived various schemes only to see them wither away. The Mazanderan Project presents a unique opportunity to study more closely the possible causes of such failures.

The external and internal conditions of late nineteenth century Iran presented many obstacles to development. A demanding environment presented an array of difficulties inimical to success. These problems can be divided into at least three major categories: international political complications, local environmental difficulties, and internal political rivalries.

The consequences of international political rivalries were a major theme of nineteenth-century Iran. The clash, largely of Russian-British commercial and political interests, played an important role in determining the success or failure of developmental projects in Iran. In particular, Anglo-Russian rivalry accounts, at least in part, for Iran's entering the second decade of the twentieth century with virtually no operating railways.[9] But the failure of the Mazanderan project cannot be attributed directly to the opposition or interference of either of these two powers. Neither country actually opposed the scheme, though it may have failed because no such project was feasible in nineteenth-century Iran without their financial backing and approval. In fact, the Russians, when assured the railway would not involve foreigners, sanctioned its progress and permitted necessary equipment through Russia at the same time they were demanding from Persia a moratorium on foreign railway construction. The Russians seemed to fear foreign participation but were not opposed, overtly, to a Persian project.

The British, on the other hand, were curiously unconcerned or misinformed about the project. Sir Arthur Nicolson, British Chargé d'Affaires in Tehran, wrote to Lord Salisbury in October, 1887, that Haji Mohammad Hasan had left Tehran without permission, and that he had fallen into disfavour with the Shah because he had 'attempted to make people believe that he had powers to form a company for diverse objects. ...' Nicolson also reported that a mining project had fallen through.[10] This report came some five months after Haji Mohammad Hasan had reconsidered his decision to give up, and had gone to Europe with the Shah's permission.

For the most part British diplomatic despatches and reports are silent on the railway project. The best account of it occurs in a confidential report written by E. F. Law, the Commercial Attaché in the British Embassy in Tehran, entitled, 'Report on Railway under Construction between Mahmudabad and Amol.' This report, presented in November, 1888,[11] provides a fairly accurate summary of the project and the difficulties facing it, but the British do not seem to have taken an active interest in the plan. Neither the Russians nor the British presented any major objections to the railway, perhaps believing the line would fail anyway.

The causes for the failure of the Mazanderan Project lie largely in Persian sources. Local environmental problems and internal political rivalries presented imposing obstacles, and the enterprise was not equal to the challenge.

Almost any development project in Iran had to confront a demanding environment and the Mazanderan Project was no exception. First, there were difficulties with the terrain – steep mountains, dense forests, and mosquito-ridden marshes. Second, there were climatic problems: heavy seasonal rains and high humidity impeded work or caused necessary items to rot; large amounts of standing water provided excellent breeding ground for malarial mosquitoes. Furthermore, communications were poor and the population scattered. Added to these difficulties was Iran's basic lack of technical expertise, experience or equipment. Haji Mohammad Hasan had to import foreign engineers, as well as mining and railway equipment. He also had to import all types of necessary supplies, such as knives, spoons, axes, shovels, food – almost everything but wood. At one point Haji Mohammad Hasan had to suspend work because of a lack of hammers and shovels. He even had to import labour, largely from Tehran and Kashan,[12] because of the small population of Mazanderan. Most of these workers then came down with malaria, causing further delays. Even when healthy, however, the unskilled workers created problems, leading one frustrated agent to complain that they 'are busy at work everyday and everyday the road becomes a greater shambles.' On top of this, the humidity caused the wooden railway ties to rot, and on several occasions the train derailed – once falling into a fifteen foot culvert filled with water.

These problems alone might have proved sufficient to finish a project backed by lesser determination; but the environmental problems were not the only obstacles. Petty local rivalries and the permutations of political interests created further difficulties.

As mentioned earlier, various types of local rivalries impeded progress. Haji Mohammad Hasan's agents were not always reliable, and some local workers apparently decided to manage various aspects of the project themselves. Some caused trouble in order to drive other workers away so that Haji Mohammad Hasan would be forced to hire friends. Some of these men, like Seyyed Mahmud, interfered with the efforts of the foreign engineers in order to push their own interests. But these were not the only aggravations. Haji Mohammad Hasan also became involved in conflicts and disputes with local government officials.

On several occasions Haji Mohammad Hasan wrote to Nasir ad-Din Shah or Amin as-Sultan complaining about the interference and opposition of local officials. One such official, Mirza Abdollah Khan Mirpanjeh, the Governor of Mazanderan, caused much of the trouble.[13] Mirpanjeh vilified Haji Mohammad Hasan locally, calling him nothing but a 'cloth merchant,' and intimidating some of Haji Mohammad Hasan's agents. The governor spoke abusively of the project and even encouraged people to take steps to hinder Haji Mohammad Hasan's efforts. As a result, some local people got into the act by bullying local agents or merchants under Haji Mohammad Hasan's protection. And, although Haji Mohammad Hasan reminded the Shah of his promises of support, the constant frustration of these actions began to undermine the King's resolve.

The first evidence of the Shah's sense of frustration comes in a marginal note on one of Haji Mohammad Hasan's letters. The Shah wrote:

> One is shamed. Several thousand times orders concerning this [Mirpanjeh's activities] have been issued. When Mirpanjeh was here last I told him what to do and he agreed and the affair was at peace. Now what has happened? What are these events? I cannot read the detailed accounts. You [Amin as-Sultan] see them and give necessary orders and in the future do not disturb me with these things. Do yourself what is necessary. It is not necessary to speak to me.

After this, the Shah was disinclined to deal with the project; and Amin as-Sultan's orders do not seem to have changed the situation, for appointees protected by the Governor of

Mazanderan and his agents continued to attack Haji Mohammad Hasan's agents and victimize villagers under his protection. In addition to these problems, Haji Mohammad Hasan's enemies at court also conspired to undermine his efforts.[14] His relationship with Amin as-Sultan created enemies and his power aroused jealousies. The lack of central authority, an overlapping system of protection, and the patronage made possible by a system of office-purchasing helped create a situation in which the most insignificant men in local areas could delay or frustrate the policies of the leaders of the country. This aspect made any project difficult and precarious.

The accumulation of these problems and the declining support of the Shah, who seemed to lose enthusiasm as the difficulties increased, placed intolerable strains on the railway's chances for success; but Haji Mohammad Hasan continued to try to make the project work, perhaps as a means to salvage his investment.[15]

In Moharram, 1310 (August, 1892), Haji Mohammad Hasan negotiated a contract with a Russian concern – the Commerce and Transport Bank of Russia. The company was interested in participating in some aspects of the Mazanderan project – the port at Mahmudabad and a proposed road from Mazanderan to Tehran that had been planned earlier and dropped because of opposition. Haji Mohammad Hasan wrote to the Shah encouraging his approval for this new project, reminding him of the expenses incurred, and pointing out that he had continued with the Mazanderan project only because the King had ordered it and had guaranteed support. The Russian company, Haji Mohammad Hasan wrote, would supply the funds and engineers and take over existing assets if the Shah would grant permission. Haji Mohammad Hasan added that he did not think the Russian government would oppose this plan since the railway did not connect any important towns. Haji Mohammad Hasan forwarded a copy of the proposed contract and asked the Shah to approve it so that he could lessen the financial losses and improve the country. There is no extant reply, but nothing came of the effort. Lack of interest or Russian opposition to the participation of non-Persians helped secure the demise of the project.

Much more could be added to the list of indigenous problems. There were disputes with foreign experts over salaries, confrontations with other concessionaires over property rights, arguments, countless petty rivalries and endless instances of simple theft. Haji Mohammad Hasan wrote several bitter letters to the Shah clearly revealing his sense of frustration and defeat. Yet, despite all these aggravations, Haji Mohammad Hasan continued until his death to try to find some means of implementing the project. His personality and capacity were extremely important in the life of the Mazanderan project.

Haji Mohammad Hasan's concern for development and protection of internal trade, however, was not enough to carry out a scheme of the scope of the Mazanderan project. He was a highly successful, traditional merchant, but entrepreneurial skill alone was not sufficient to overcome the many obstacles. A development scheme, such as that conceived by Haji Mohammad Hasan, needed more than entrepreneurial talent. It needed careful planning and the necessary infrastructure – communications, skilled labour, markets, and political protection. The Mazanderan Development Project, like many of its contemporaries, suffered from a certain naiveté – a belief that intentions could compensate for knowledge. The original mining project revealed an ingenuous comprehension of the economic realities of an industrial society. Its planners saw a chance to develop a mine and make money but they failed to realize that traditional expertise or royal *farmans* would not overcome inherent deficiencies in transportation, expertise, marketing structures, and governmental authority. Haji Mohammad Hasan tried to generate the necessary systems, almost overnight, but he still lacked a clear conception of the problems and he did not possess the necessary resources to force change.

NOTES

1. The majority of the documentation for this article was obtained from materials in the private, family papers of Asghar Mehdevi in Tehran, Iran. Haji Mohammad Hasan was Dr. Mehdevi's paternal grandfather and Dr. Mehdevi has preserved an enormous quantity of his grandfather's letters, account books, and records. The correspondence mentioned in the text comes from these files and will not be individually cited in the notes. I am indebted to Dr. Mehdevi for allowing me access to these materials and his invaluable assistance in reading the often indecipherable script.
2. The definitive history of rail development in Iran remains to be done. The account in George Curzon's *Persia and the Persian Question*, Vol. I, Barnes

& Noble, N.Y., 1966 (first ed., 1892), pp. 619–20, is still one of the best. Firuz Kazemzadeh in his book, *Russia and Britain in Persia, 1864–1914: A Study in Imperialism*, and in his article, 'Russian Imperialism and Persian Railways,' *Harvard Slavic Studies* (1957), pp. 355–73, gives a somewhat partisan account of railway development and international rivalry. In neither work, however, does he mention the Mazanderan railway. Charles Issawi's book, *The Economic History of Persia, 1800–1914*, University of Chicago Press, Chicago, 1971, an annotated collection of useful primary material, contains information on railway projects but it also does not mention the Mazanderan project. Several Persian works known to the author mention the project, but not in any detail. These include: Mohammad Hasan Khan Itemad as-Sultaneh, *Ruzname-ye Khaterat Itemad as-Sultaneh*, prepared by Iraj Afshar, Amir-e Kabir Press, Tehran, 2nd edition, 1350 shamsi; Abdallah Mostofi, *Shari-i Zendegani-ye Man ya Tarikh-i va Edari-ye Doure-ye Qajariyeh*, 3 vols., Zavar Press, Tehran, 2nd edition (n.d.). Other works that deal with various aspects of investment and development problems in Iran include the following: Bradford G. Martin, *German-Persian Diplomatic Relations, 1872–1912*, Mouton & Co., 's-Gravenhage, 1959; Marvin Entner, *Russo-Persian Commercial Relations, 1828–1914*, University of Florida Monographs, 1965; A. P. Thornton, 'British Policy in Persia, 1858–1890,' *The English Historical Review*, Vol. LXX, No. 274 (1955), part II, pp. 55–71; Rose Louise Greaves, *Persia and the Defense of India, 1884–1892*; Thomas P. Brockway, 'Britain and the Persian Bubble: 1888–1892,' *The Journal of Modern History*, Vol. XIII, No. 1 (March, 1941), pp. 36–47; Graham Storey, *Reuters' Century, 1851–1951*, Max Parrish, London, 1951, pp. 72–86; and L. E. Frechtling, 'The Reuter Concession in Persia,' *The Asiatic Review* (July, 1938), Vol. 34, No. 19, pp. 519–33.

3. This information was drawn in part from C. P. Churchill, *Biographical Notices of Persian Statesmen and Notables*, September, 1909, pp. 7–8; Mehdi Bamdad, *Tarikh-i Rejal-i Iran*, Zavar Press, Tehran, 1345, Vol. III, pp. 348–62; Mehdi Qoli Hedayat, *Khaterat va Khaterat*, Zavar Press, Tehran, 1344 shamsi, pp. 100 and 488.
4. For a list of some of these projects see Mohammad Hasan Khan Itemad as-Sultaneh, *al-Masir va al-Asar*, Sanai Press, Tehran (n.d.), pp. 53–91.
5. The concession granted some time in 1303 (1885–86) consisted of seven sections. The *farman* granted Haji Mohammad Hasan a monopoly for thirty years with the right to exploit iron, copper, charcoal and land within ten *farsakhs* (about thirty-five miles) of the mine. The production from the project was exempted from customs and road fees for five years and the only metal that was exempted from the company's control was gold. The company had the right to utilize any unoccupied or derelict land and use the land adjacent to the mine for agriculture. Foreigners were excluded from owning any shares and the Shah promised to give his special attention to the company so that no one would be able to undermine its efforts.
6. The Russian government remained ambivalent to the idea of railway construction through the period and actively sought to keep foreign

investment out of northern Iran. Persian officials knew of Russia's concern and therefore acted with diffidence. When Haji Mohammad Hasan went to Europe he carried instructions from Amin as-Sultan to reassure the Russians that he was Russia's friend and would do nothing to harm their interest. The knowledge that the Russians worried about such things may have suppressed any ideas about concessions including foreigners.

7. On the back of the rough draft of this letter Haji Mohammad Hasan wrote a note to the Shah, that may have been included in the final copy, illustrating the nature of some of the problems. In reply to constant inquiries from the Shah about the slowness of progress, Haji Mohammad Hasan wrote that he had encountered obstacles that would block the efforts of two million people: 'Everytime any person tries to do anything everyone around him squelches the fire of his life.' 'Everytime anyone tries to do something for the country the functionaries of the state become upset and inconvenienced for themselves and when others see this reaction they do not want to become involved in affairs. ...' Thus there was no progress. At this point in the letter Haji Mohammad Hasan launched into his complaint against Mohamad Khan Sartip.
8. H. L. Rabino, *Mazanderan and Astarabad*, Luzac & Co., London, 1928, p. 32.
9. The conflict of political and strategic interests tended to cancel out the commercial or developmental schemes of one or another. The Russians worried about their position in northern Iran and British diplomats were concerned for the security of India. Both sides watched carefully to see that the other party did not secure some special advantage. This rivalry produced tension and some strange machinations. For an interesting and amusing story of one such affair see Arthur Hardinge, *A Diplomatist in the East*, Jonathan Cape Ltd., 1928, pp. 278–9. The rivalry, though, had serious consequences for Iran and was one of the main reasons Iran did not build any railways of significance until the late 1920s. See Kazemzadeh, *Russia and Britain in Persia* for Russian activities; and *Further Correspondence Respecting the Affairs of Persia*, part XXXIII, FO 416/55, 'Memorandum on the Trans-Persian Railway,' pp. 22–32, for the British attitude.
10. Nicolson-Salisbury, FO 60/487, 17 October 1887.
11. FO 881, item 5728.
12. The workers for the Mazanderan Project may have been available because of Iran's economic difficulties. The 1880s and 1890s were economically lean years for Iran, whose currency was tied to silver and a depression in silver prices at this time caused economic difficulties throughout the country. For an account of these difficulties see chapter 1 of this volume. See also Robert McDaniel, 'Economic Change and Economic Resiliency in 19th Century Iran,' *Iranian Studies*, Vol. IX, No. 1, Winter, 1971, pp. 36–49.
13. Mirza Abdallah Khan, Intezam ad-Dowleh, was the Shah's brother-in-law – twice. The Shah married Mirza Abdallah Khan's two sisters, in violation of Islamic law. This connection to the Royal house may have encouraged Intezam ad-Dowleh's intransigence. Furthermore, the system of

overlapping authority and office-purchase may have furthered the difficulty of the situation.

Originally the Shah granted the Governorship of Mazanderan to his third son, Kamran Mirza, Nayeb as-Sultaneh, who later sold the right to Intezam ad-Dowleh. Mirza Abdallah Khan was thus attached to Kamran Mirza, while Amin al-Zarb was a protégé of Amin as-Sultan. Amin as-Sultan and Kamran Mirza were rivals at court and their hostility and the competition and machinations of the various factions may have been one reason for the asperity between Haji Mohammad Hasan and Mirza Abdallah Khan, who may have caused trouble as an extension of this rivalry; or who may have felt that he could pursue his own personal interests and rely on support from his connections to avoid adverse consequences.

There are many stories of the problems generated by similar rivalries at court. One entertaining account is contained in E. G. Browne's *A Year Amongst the Persians*, pp. 176–79. Curzon also mentions the same story in *Persia and the Persian Question*, Vol. II, pp. 2–6. A more serious example of the effects of court rivalry is contained in A. K. S. Lambton's article, 'The Tobacco Regie: Prelude to Revolution,' in *Studia Islamica*, Vol. XXII, pp. 119–157 and Vol. XXIII, pp. 71–90.

14. Ismael Mahjuri, *Tarikh-e Mazanderan*, Vol. II, p. 212.
15. There are no exact estimates available. Mehdi Qoli Hedayat, in *Khaterat va Khaterat*, p. 100, says the investment totalled 750,000 *tomans*. Haji Mohammad Hasan said at one point he had invested 80,000 *tomans* and at another 40,000 *tomans*. The total, based on available receipts was about 100,000 *tomans*. But these are probably incomplete and hence much more may have been spent.

3

Sayyid Jamal ad-Din al-Afghani from the Perspective of a Russian Muslim

Edward J. Lazzerini

In her most recent study of Sayyid Jamal ad-Din al-Afghani, Professor Nikki Keddie remarked that 'Afghani's activities in India, Istanbul, and Russia are still rather obscure, and it is hoped that research by others into archives and papers relating to these countries can establish a picture fuller than is now possible.'[1] During the summer of 1974, while conducting research in the Soviet Union on various aspects of the *cedidi*, or Muslim modernist, movement in Russia, I took the opportunity to seek out archival references to Afghani's Russian contacts and activities during his two sojourns between May, 1887 and November, 1889. Since the study of other matters engaged most of my time, my efforts with regard to Afghani were limited and, as far as unearthing archival material, fruitless. This is not to imply in the least that significant sources do not exist in the Soviet archives. I am convinced that they do.[2] Nevertheless, I was unable to turn up any direct reference to Afghani 'papers' either through extensive examination of printed and unpublished archival guides and descriptions or through direct questioning of a number of Soviet scholars.

While our knowledge of and access to pertinent Russian archives is minimal at best, there is a set of untapped sources that is somewhat more readily available and can provide some understanding of Afghani's impact on Russia's Islamic community and the opinions of his Russian co-religionists as to his biography, personality, projects, and religiosity. The sources which I have in mind are articles and books written by Russian Muslims and published primarily though not exclusively within the Tsarist Empire. Some of these appeared in the Russian language, others in Arabic, and still others in one of the many forms of Turkic employed by Muslim publicists of the late nineteenth and early twentieth centuries.

Students of Afghani have known of two of these for some time: a short anecdotal article in Arabic by Abdürreşid Ibrahim[3] and a Russian-language article by Ahmed Bey Agaev.[4] Besides these, however, I have discovered several others, the list of which, I suspect, would not exhaust the number actually written. Three of them, composed in Turkic, were unsigned articles appearing in the Muslim periodicals *Şura* (Orenburg) and *Al-Din v'al-Adab* (Kazan').[5] A fourth, also in Turkic, was a substantial study of Muhammad Abduh and Afghani by Musa Carulla Bigi, a major figure in Russian Islamic affairs in the first third of the twentieth century.[6] A fifth, in Russian and Turkic, was little more than a brief comment on Afghani in connection with the Tobacco Protest in Persia in 1891–1892, written by the Crimean Tatar reformer, Ismail Bey Gasprinskii, in his newspaper *Tercüman/ Perevodchik*.[7] The final item, and the principal subject of this note, was a contribution to the Russian-language newspaper *Kaspii* (Tiflis) from the pen of Mehmed Ağa Shakhtakhtinskii.[8]

Of modest length and containing no great revelations, this last piece is useful, nevertheless, for its attempt to clarify (though not always successfully) certain aspects of Afghani's biography – notably his expulsion from Persia and the questions of his nationality and religiosity – and for its treatment of Jamal ad-Din's politics and panislamic orientation. In addition, Shakhtakhtinskii's article provides some relief from the generally positive response to Afghani and his ideas by Russian Muslims. While finding much of interest in Jamal ad-Din, the author also found much to dislike, criticize, and even ridicule.

What do we know of Mehmed Ağa Shakhtakhtinskii? An Azeri Turk, he was born in Erivan in 1846.[9] After completing a basic Muslim education, he attended several European universities during the early 1870s, first in Leipzig, then in Berlin, and finally in Paris, where he enrolled in courses at the École des Langues Orientales. Around 1875 his father's death forced him to return to Russia.[10] Knowledge of his activities from then until the early 1890s is minimal, although we do know that he was writing articles for a number of newspapers, including *Moskovskie Viedomosti* (Moscow), *Novoe Vremia* (St. Petersburg), and *Kavkaz* (Tiflis) on subjects ranging from linguistics and educational reform to life in Persia and the Ottoman Empire. In the early 1890s he also wrote for the newspaper *Kaspii* and served as its interim editor for three months during the summer of 1891.[11] At the end of the decade, he was again in Paris, where he attended classes at the Collège de France and the École Pratique des Hautes Études, studied Arabic, Persian, Turkish, and other languages, and often visited the experimental phonetics laboratory at the Collège. His interest in oriental languages led to his being admitted into the prestigious Société Asiatique.[12]

Upon his return to the Caucasus in 1901 or 1902, he took up residence in Tiflis. There, at the end of 1903, he founded the newspaper *Şark-i Rus*, which he dedicated to improving the quality of life of the Muslims living in the region and to reforming the Arabic alphabet. Although there is no evidence of his having participated in any of the major Muslim gatherings that took place between 1904 and 1906, his election as a deputy to the short-lived Second State Duma and his appointment to its agrarian commission[13] give credence to L. Bouvat's contention that he had become politically active during the tumultuous years around 1905.[14] After 1907, however, Mehmed Ağa completely dropped from view. About all that we know of his activities during the last twenty years or so of his life is that he participated in the work of the All-Union Central Committee For a New Turkic Alphabet during the early 1920s and was favourably inclined toward the new Soviet régime. He died in 1931.[15]

Throughout his life, Shakhtakhtinskii combined an orientalist's love for linguistics with a social reformer's concern for the problems of his native society. In a number of articles and pamphlets published over a period of more than forty years,[16] he proposed modifying the Arabic alphabet along several lines in order to overcome what he felt was a major obstacle to the spread of literacy among the Azeri Turks. On the question of literacy, of course, hinged the future development and 'modernization' of their culture. But beyond the issue of alphabet reform, Mehmed Ağa was sharply critical of the Islamic religion which pervaded

Azeri society. In his view, Islam was antithetical to the idea of progress (an unusual opinion for a Russian Muslim intellectual to hold before the twentieth century) and was an impediment to the development of the full potential of those governed by its laws and spirit. It nourished ignorance, encouraged intolerance, and fostered injustice; and what was perhaps more detrimental to society, it bred complacency.[17]

Shakhtakhtinskii's negative attitude toward Islam and its role in contemporary life helps to explain his opposition to Jamal ad-Din and the panislamic movement which he espoused.[18] As an advocate of secularization, Mehmed Ağa envisioned a new society that could not be called forth by appeals to anachronistic religious sentiments or presumed bonds cutting across national frontiers. Only the determined effort to break with tradition and substitute the ideology of nationalism for that of religion could lead to a revival of the various Islamic communities and their effective participation in the modern world.

The text follows

According to *Moskovskie Viedomosti*'s Tiflis correspondent, *Kaspii* reported the following a few days ago: 'The well-known Persian patriot and scholar, Shaykh Jamal ad-Din, who has fought the English seizure of Persia, was made prisoner one night in March by a hundred horsemen at the shrine of Shahzadeh Abd al-Azim near Teheran, and was carried off to the mountains. As it now turns out, he was executed there by order of Amin as-Sultan.'

From official Persian sources I know that Shaykh Jamal ad-Din is alive and well and lives at the present time in the city of Kermanshah, on the Turkish border near Baghdad. A year and a half ago, he left St. Petersburg for Persia. I know him very well, having lived [in the Russian capital] while he did. He is an extremely interesting person. Jamal ad-Din is very nearly the only Muslim spiritual leader in the world who has combined a comprehensive scientific education with a thorough knowledge of [both] domestic and international politics and the national development of large and small European and Eastern states.

Shaykh Jamal ad-Din is not, however, a Persian, but is an Afghan who nourishes a deep hatred for Persia, Persians, and all things Persian. Not only is he not a Persian, but he is not even a patriot, [if by the term we mean] one who serves the interests of some country. Jamal ad-Din strives at all times for the opposite: the goal which he seeks is to have countries and people serve his interests and boundless ambitions. Standing head and shoulders above the Muslim society of which he is a member, he developed the idea of establishing his own ruling dynasty in the East. He sees [two ways] to achieve this: either by stimulating a new religio-political movement in the Islamic world, at whose head he himself would be, or by kindling national passions among the European peoples which would prompt a European war for dominance over the East, a war which, so he believes, would make it easy for him to catch fish in muddy water. Hence his incessant travels from one country to another, and hence his expulsion from almost all of the world's states. Jamal ad-Din is an Afghan by nationality; he not only does not hide this fact but even makes his nationality a part of his family name. Neither in Eastern nor in European languages does he sign his name in any way other than as 'The Afghan' Jamal ad-Din. Only three years ago, the very same *Moskovskie Viedomosti* carried news about the arrival in Russia of the Afghan scholar Jamal ad-Din. Both in that newspaper and in *Novoe Vremia* articles were published with the signature of Jamal ad-Din, who called himself, as always, an Afghan. For his intrigue and conspiracies he was expelled from Afghanistan, India, Egypt, France, Tunis, and Turkey. Now the Persians want to do the same, but in spite of their best intentions have been unsuccessful. Their neighbours do not want to accept the Shaykh; he is, they tell the Persians, too good, so keep him for yourselves.

Having followed the Shah to Persia, Jamal ad-Din began to spread revolutionary ideas of a religio-political nature among the people. The Shah and the Shi'ite leaders were outraged and began a campaign of persecution, but the Shaykh hid in the shrine of Shahzadeh Abd al-Azim near Teheran, within which all who hide are considered beyond the reach [of the authorities], since the right of refuge is recognized by those at the shrine. There are a number of such places of refuge in Persia where the homes of several of the most esteemed religious figures are found. They are the only defence against the oppression of the Persian government.

[Thinking himself safe], Jamal ad-Din did not cease to intrigue, but began to arrange revolutionary meetings in the shrine itself. Then the Shah sent two squadrons of the new Persian cavalry trained and commanded by Cossack officers; they managed to seize the Shaykh without much difficulty and carry him out of the shrine. Discipline overcame superstition. Wishing to expel him from Persian territory, the Shah's government sent him under guard to the Turkish border near Baghdad for transfer to the Turkish authorities. This occurred not in March of this year [as reported by Russian newspapers] but in autumn of last year. The Turks, however, flatly refused to accept Jamal ad-Din when he was brought to the border. [As a result], whether he liked it or not, he was settled in a house in the city of Kermanshah by the Persian government. Based on Russian reports, the Constantinople correspondent of *The Times* wrote of [this attempted expulsion] of Jamal ad-Din last year.

Of course, the Shaykh's political cause is doomed to fail. The energy of those who practise Islam and the influence of religious ideas on the Muslim masses have so weakened in our time that the formation of a new Islamic state could not be brought off even if its founder were himself inspired by a deep religious feeling. In this particular case, the necessary condition does not exist at all, for Jamal ad-Din is himself an atheist and does not believe either in Allah or in Muhammad, in whose names he solicits popular support for the creation of a new state that would benefit only him. He fabricates ideas at which he himself laughs. [More than this, one has to ask] whether the general course of world history is such that it is possible to think seriously about the creation of a new Islamic state? Still, all in all, as a scholar, a philosopher, and as a traveller who has observed much, Jamal ad-Din is a very interesting man.

Mokhammed Ağa Shakhtakhtinskii

NOTES

1 Nikki R. Keddie, *Sayyid Jamal ad-Din 'al-Afghani:' A Political Biography* (Berkeley: University of California Press, 1972), p. 4.

2 The official papers of the Ministry of Foreign Affairs, the Ministry of War, and the Ministry of Internal Affairs will surely contain pertinent material. As for private papers, those of M. N. Katkov, N. K. Giers, General N. N.

Obruchev, General O. V. Rikhter, and Count N. P. Ignat'ev, among others, deserve scrutiny if they exist (as some clearly do) and are available.

3 Abd al-Rashid Ibrahim, 'al-Sayyid Jamal ad-Din al-Afghani,' *al-Shubban al-Muslimun*, V (February, 1930), pp. 358–365. The author, who lived from 1856 to 1944, was a major figure among the reformist *ulema* in Russia. His religious training was extensive and included years of *qur'anic* study under scholars in Mecca. After his return to Russia, he became a *mulla* and in 1893 was elected *kadi* at the Muslim Spiritual Assembly in Orenburg. Owing to his position, he was allowed access to all of the private documents of the Assembly, materials which exposed the subservient relationship of the Islamic religious hierarchy to the Russian government. This revelation resulted in Ibrahim's becoming increasingly anti-Russian, an attitude which pervades his polemical tract *Chulpan Yildizi*. He took an active part in Tatar journalism, particularly after the liberalization of the Russian press laws in 1906, by editing or collaborating with such newspapers as *Ülfet* (St. Petersburg), *Al-Tilmiz* (St. Petersburg), and *Beyan al-Hak* (Kazan').

4 A. A., 'Obzor vostochnoi zhurnalistiki,' *Kaspii*, No. 262 (December 4, 1899), p. 2. Born in Azerbaidzhan, Agaev was educated in Tiflis, St. Petersburg, and Paris. He later taught law in his homeland but increasingly turned to journalism as he became caught up in the social and political activities of the Russian Muslims early in this century. In 1908 he left Russia for good and settled in Turkey.

5 'Şeyh Cemalettin ve Muhammed Abdu,' *Şura*, No. 12 (June 15, 1910), pp. 370–372; 'Şeyh Cemalettin,' *Şura*, No. 21 (December 13, 1917), pp. 481–483; No. 22 (December 15, 1917), pp. 497–499 (continued in subsequent issues unavailable to me); 'Al-Sayyid Cemalettin al-Afghani'nin tercüme hali,' *Al-Din v'al-Adab*, No. 4 (May 25, 1906), pp. 120–123. The author of the first two was probably *Şura*'s editor Rizaeddin Fakhreddin.

6 Musa Carulla Bigi, *Islam filosoflari* (Kazan: Tipografiia Kharitonova, n. d.). Well-educated and well-travelled, Bigi (1875–1949) became one of Russia's most famous and controversial Muslim leaders. Like both Abdürreşid Ibrahim and Ahmed Bey Agaev, he participated actively in the tumultuous events affecting the Russian Muslims.

7 Ismail Bey Gasprinskii, untitled article, *Tercüman/Perevodchik*, No. 14 (April 12, 1892), pp. 27–28.

8 Mokhammed Ağa Shakhtakhtinskii, 'Dzhemal-Ed-Din,' *Kaspii*, No. 102 (May 14, 1891), p. 3.

9 K. Zeinalova, 'Neizvestnaia rukopis' M. Shakhtakhtinskogo o reforme alfavita,' *Sovetskaia tiurkologiia*, No. 5 (September–October, 1971), p. 91. In his article entitled 'Mohammed Ağa Schahtakhtinsky,' *Revue du monde musulman*, II, No. 7 (May, 1907), p. 583, L. Bouvat dated his subject's birth, probably erroneously, as June 10, 1848.

10 L. Bouvat, 'Mohammed Ağa Schahtakhtinsky,' pp. 583–584.

11 S. Movlaeva, 'Uchastie M. Shakhtakhtinskogo v gazete *Kaspii*,' *Izvestiia Akademii Nauk Azerbaidzhanskoi SSR*, *Seriia literatury, iazyka i iskusstva*, No. 3 (1969), pp. 31–32 and 36; K. Zeinalova, 'Neizvestnaia rukopis',' p. 91.

12 L. Bouvat, 'Mohammed Ağa Schahtakhtinsky,' p. 584.

13 *Chleny vtoroi Gosudarstvennoi Dumy* (St. Petersburg, 1907), p. 115; *Stenograficheskii otchet zasiedanii vtoroi Gosudarstvennoi Dumy* (St. Petersburg, 1907), I, p. 1594.

14 L. Bouvat, 'Mohammed Ağa Schahtakhtinsky,' p. 584.

15 K. Zeinalova, 'Neizvestnaia rukopis',' pp. 92–93; A. P. Baziiants, 'V. A. Gordlevskii i reforma pis'mennosti tiurkskikh iazykov,' *Sovetskaia tiurkologiia*, No. 5 (1976), p. 76. There is one bizarre note to Shakhtakhtinskii's life. In 1905 the major newspaper in the Russian capital published his obituary. To my knowledge, the notification of Mehmed Aga's 'sudden' and 'tragic' death was never retracted. See S. U-ts., 'Pamiati M. S. Shakhtakhtinskago,' *Sankt-Peterburgskiia Viedomosti*, No. 214 (September 6, 1905), p. 1.

16 See, for example: *Tekmileşmiş müslüman elifbasi* (Tiflis, 1879); 'Shkol'naia zhizn' u musul'man,' *Kavkaz*, Nos. 90, 96, 108, and 121 (1882); *Poiasnitel'naia zapiska o foneticheskoi vostochnoi azbuke Mukhammeda Sultanovicha Shakhtakhtinskago* (Tiflis, 1902); *Khat-i Mehmed Ağa/Shrift Mokhammed-Ağa* (Tiflis, 1903); and numerous articles published in his newspaper *Şark-i Rus*.

17 For Shakhtakhtinskii's views on Islam, see his article 'Zadachi musul'manskoi intelligentsii,' *Baku*, No. 10 (1902).

18 Shakhtakhtinskii's animosity toward panislamism and its proponents as well as his support of the Russian state were noted with approval by one of the participants in a conference meeting in St. Petersburg in 1905 to compose new regulations to govern publishing in Russia. See *Vysochaishe uchrezhdennoe osoboe sovieshchanie dlia sostavleniia novago ustava o pechati* (n. p., 1905), pp. 19–20.

4

Mirza Aqa Khan Kirmani: A Nineteenth Century Persian Nationalist

Mangol Bayat-Philipp

Frantz Fanon, in his *Peau Noire, Masques Blancs*, had written '*la conscience a besoin de se perdre dans la nuit de l'absolu, seule condition pour parvenir à la conscience de soi'*.[1] In the life and thought of Mirza Aqa Khan Kirmani, the nineteenth century Persian revolutionary, we detect a similar, though subconscious, desire to plunge into the darkness of the Absolute in order to emerge with a new, clear-cut image of Iran, the culture and the nation. The resulting self-view bears all the marks of an extremism, generally so characteristic of modern nationalism, which in its best aspects generates a dynamic self-awareness that helps bring about the change necessary to shake off the yoke of the existing socio-political stagnation, and in its worst aspects creates a new breed of fanaticism that is as intransigent, as oppressive and destructive as the one it tries to eliminate.

Abdul Husayn Khan, later known as Mirza Aqa Khan Kirmani, was born in Mashiz, a small village just over 87 kms. west of Kirman city, in 1270 A.H./1853–54 A.D. Both his parents were descendants of illustrious families who could trace their genealogy way back in history. On the paternal side he was son of Abdul Rahim Mashizi, a wealthy landowner affiliated with the Sufi sect Ahl-i haq; grandson of a close companion of Aqa Khan Mahalati, the Ismaili leader who had been governor of the province but had been forced to flee to Bombay; great grandson of a prominent Zoroastrian leader who had converted to Islam.

On the maternal side he was the grandson of a distinguished physician of Kirman; great grandson of a famous jurist and leader of a Sufi order; a direct descendant of an aristocratic physician from Mogul India who was offered an official position in the Safavid court, had settled in Iran and had married a royal Persian princess.[2]

Mirza Aqa Khan could therefore boast of possessing a peculiarly mixed ancestry that included Sufis, Ismailis, Zoroastrians, physicians, jurists and royalty. Consciously or unconsciously, he combined many of the various, often conflicting, traditional traits he had inherited from his forefathers: a philosophical mind that tended to mysticism and freethinking; an interest in law and jurisprudence; a veneration for science and rational knowledge; a great respect for Zoroaster and a deep emotional attachment to pre-Islamic Iran; and, above all, the aristocratic pride of a well-born Persian who holds Arab culture in contempt. He also developed an intense historical consciousness that may or may not have been an obvious result of his own family's long historical background.

Kirmani's education was, in the beginning, typically Persian. Before undertaking the study of philosophy proper, he had first to acquire a thorough knowledge of Persian and Arabic languages and literatures, grammar, rhetoric, logic, mathematics, elements of jurisprudence and theology. Then he went to a well-established teacher with whom he ventured into the hazardous path of metaphysics and philosophy, a study traditionally considered to be the highest intellectual training, and the crown and summit of all knowledge. His teachers were Aqa Sadiq, a disciple of Mulla Hadi Sabzvari, and Hajji Sayyid Javad Kerbala'i who essentially taught him the philosophies of Mulla Sadra, Shaykh Ahmad Ahsa'i and the Bab. Sayyid Javad himself was a noted Babi thinker who became, for a long while at least, Mirza Aqa Khan's chief inspirer and model of perfection to follow. Kirmani also studied elementary French and English with a Zoroastrian teacher, and he acquired a basic knowledge of the ancient Persian languages, Avesta and Pahlavi.

Such an education proved to be a solid background to start with. It was said of him, shortly after he left his native province:

> There was no subject which Mirza Aqa Khan did not know about ... He knew by heart the philosophy of Aristotle ... and Greek thought in

> general ... Mirza Aqa Khan could explain the Koran as if he were a prophet or had got his information from the Commander of the Faithful himself. He had a vast knowledge of the Sunna and hadith, be it Sunni, Shaf'i or Hanafi ... He could carry on a learned conversation on various Shi'i sects and on Babism, and on their different conflicting views.[3]

Yet, once he became acquainted with modern European political and philosophical thought which opened up new perspectives as yet unknown to him, Kirmani decided to reject all knowledge he had previously acquired as 'nonsensical' and 'too poor a meal' for a starving mind. He had an intense craving for knowledge and he set out to pursue his self-education by reading voraciously. The result was a hopeless synthesis of the most disparate philosophical and social ideas which dominated his works. A kind of restless intellectual curiosity characterized his endless quest for novel ideas for he was also a man in pursuit of an ideal, a cause to fight for. When he discovered Babism he invested his hopes in it and became a convert. The Babis seemed to offer him the most potent contemporary Persian manifestation of the longing for change. This, however, did not stop him from seeking elsewhere new ideologies and new faiths. His conversion, therefore, remained superficial.

In 1883, following a heated argument with the governor of Kirman which brought to an end his brief experience as government official, he secretly left Kirman. He was never to return to his birthplace again. He was then just over thirty years of age. He spent two years in Isfahan where he came to frequent a literary circle which used to discuss 'new and progressive ideas', and a few months in Tehran. Throughout this period the governor of Kirman attempted to have him extradited to Kirman, without success. Mirza Aqa Khan finally sought asylum in Istanbul which he reached in 1886. Except for a short trip that took him, during that year, to Cyprus where he met Subhi-Azal and married his daughter, and to Syria and Iraq, for the last ten years of his life he remained in the Ottoman capital. These were ten industrious productive years during which Kirmani wrote, read, studied and, essentially, formulated revolutionary ideas. It was during this period that he became more acquainted with Western thought and began to be considerably influenced by it. He greatly improved his French which he had studied first in

Kirman and then later in Isfahan with some Jesuits. He also studied English and Turkish.

It is impossible to gather exactly what European books he read. We can list with certainty Fénelon's *Télémaque* and Bernardin de Saint Pierre's *Le café de Surat*, since he translated both into Persian. We can also guess from the ideas exposed in his works that he extensively read Descartes, Rousseau, Voltaire, Montesquieu, Spencer and Darwin. He likewise displays a knowledge of eighteenth- and early nineteenth-century socialist and utopian movements. He was also familiar with contemporary European racial theories. He experienced quite an intellectual transformation, and to a large extent we can agree with the following statement:

> He (Kirmani) gave up the imitation of ancient thinkers and turned to Rousseau and Voltaire. He cut his bond to ancient philosophy and adopted materialism and naturalism. He got tired of seeking the spiritual unknown and followed instead the religion of Reason ... In all fields of art and sciences he saw one purpose, social and human progress.[4]

That he genuinely searched for truth, desired to acquire knowledge through reason and had a blind faith in science there is no doubt. It is this natural disposition that made him receptive to European ideas. Hence in the introduction to one of his works he wrote, in a way rather reminiscent of Descartes:

> My aim was to expose the truth of all matters ... impartially ... historically and with the help of rational proof. In reaching my conclusions, I was subject to my personal appraisal. I was thus an interpreter, not an imitator ... I relied on the basic nature of things ... for I found out that the truth of matters cannot be known unless one discovers the chain that links them all together ... I take pride in admitting that it is only after having heard diverse opinions, having mixed with different people, having read books and works of many authors without preconception and never having let my mind loose; after I have walked on my own two feet, looked with my own eyes, using my own mind, and enlightened by my own reason; and just as I had made it a rule not to take anyone's side, having also made it a point not to clash with or spite anyone ... I wrote that work.[5]

He also emphasized the necessity of *doubt* and praised 'those who said that a person's first and foremost duty is to doubt his religion, to demand decisive proofs for it and to go wherever those proofs lead him to'.[6]

In Istanbul Kirmani mixed socially with a group of Persian expatriates, merchants, teachers, writers and poets. His association with the Persian newspaper *Akhtar* which 'was always in each period of its history the lamp of all assemblies of cultivated men and the centre around which rallied the most accomplished and enlightened of the Persian exiles, and was maintained by the literary co-operation of patriotic scholars'[7] gave him the opportunity to enlarge his own circle of friends and acquaintances. For many years he regularly contributed articles on various literary and political subjects. This paper, which had begun its career with the Persian government's blessings, was soon banned in Iran, yet managed to circulate clandestinely. Nasir ud-Din Shah, who used to read it regularly, had come to dislike thoroughly the progressive ideas it contained, and he found Kirmani's articles especially distasteful.[8] It was finally closed down by the Ottoman government in 1895.

Aside from his writings, Kirmani's political action in Istanbul was twofold. On the one hand, he helped Malkam Khan[9] to establish an 'Adamiyyat lodge' in the Turkish capital and to distribute the newspaper *Qanun* among Persian readers; and on the other hand, he collaborated with Afghani[10] in setting up the pan-Islamic movement chiefly among Shi'is. Hence, while his activities with the former were, broadly speaking, secular, with the latter he called for a pan-Muslim revolt against the Persian monarch. His relationship with Malkam was purely based on their correspondence which began in 1890, that is, at the time Malkam began to publish *Qanun*, and ended in 1895 when Kirmani was arrested.[11] They never met personally, whereas he knew Afghani in person since 1892 when the notorious Persian revolutionary came from London to Istanbul at the Sultan's invitation.

These pan-Islamic activities, his noted Babi inclination, his anti-government writings and his open clashes with the then Persian Ambassador to the Porte, Nazim ud-Daula, who proved to be his bitterest enemy, were more and more found distasteful by the Court in Tehran. When one of the 200 letters bearing enthusiastic replies to the pan-Islamic society's call for revolt was intercepted by the Persian Consul in Baghdad and Afghani's conspiracy was then revealed, the order to arrest all persons involved in the plot was issued. Though the Porte at first refused to do so and though Afghani himself was left free, Kirmani and two of his close companions were arrested and sent to Trebizond in 1895. When Mirza Riza Kirmani shot and killed Nasir ud-Din Shah, Kirmani's fate was decisively determined. Since the assassin, an alleged Babi sympathizer, was associated with Afghani and hence with the prisoners, the Persian government found it convenient to charge them all with murder. In July 1896, Kirmani was executed in Tabriz.

Just as Mirza Aqa Khan Kirmani's reading was extensive and disparate, so were his writings.[12] He wrote abundantly but without system. The voluminous disorderly corpus of his works, which included newspaper articles, poems, historical and philosophical treatises, political pamphlets and theological essays, are a trial to anyone who attempts to discover in them a logical sequence of ideas. He claimed to be a Muslim, a Babi, an agnostic philosopher all at one and the same time. For the purpose of our present study we shall limit our discussion to:

1. Kirmani's sharp criticism of his society.
2. His attempt to put the blame for national decay on:
   (a) The Arabs. He displays a violent hatred for them, a hatred that leads him to adopt some of the contemporary European anti-semitic, racist theories.
   (b) Islam, which he rejects as being a religion alien to the Persian's nature and culture.
   (c) The Shi'i ulama.
   (d) The Qajar ruler and his corrupt court.
3. His fierce nationalism which makes him seek Iran's true identity in its pre-Islamic past.
4. The revolutionary solution he offers to cure social ills.

Social Criticism

Throughout his formative years in Iran, Mirza Aqa Khan had suffered from the inadequacy and irrelevance of the traditional education he was given. In all his works he expresses his utter disillusionment with the 'daily meal' which had left him famished and frustrated.

> Any wretched fellow who had drunk this soup remained hungry, poor and distressed.[13]

He assails with scorn the subjects taught in the local schools, claiming that the study of Arabic grammar and vocabulary corrupts the Persian language; the study of *fiqh* and *hadith* reinforces the prevailing spiritual stagnation; the study of *hikmat* and the interpretation of the Koran raise fruitless questions concerning trivial matters.

> What do I gain, I an Iranian, from knowing all about Khalid b. Walid or Yizid b. Mu'awiya? What do I gain by reading all about Ali and his sons or the love and hate of Abbas?[14]

Such learning, he states, makes no solid contribution to the glory of the nation, to the power of the government, to the enrichment of the population. He holds the religious philosophers, such as Mulla Sadra, as well as the ulama of all sects – Shi'i, Shaykhi, Babi – responsible for the nation's intellectual and scientific backwardness. They all have wasted their time dealing with futile 'spiritual matters' and hence have remained ignorant of important matters concerning the world, or even their own country:

> An Armenian school child would surpass the Muslim *alim* in his knowledge of science and foreign languages.[15]

The Persian classical poets are not spared either. He vehemently attacks them for having had a disastrous moral effect on the people:

> The result of their metaphysics and mysticism has been nothing but a crop of brutish idleness and sloth, and the production of religious mendicants and beggars; the result of their odes to roses and nightingales has been nothing but corruption of our young men's morals and the impelling of them toward smooth cheeks and red wine.[16]

For he believed that poetry should primarily have a social and patriotic purpose:

> The proper effect of poetry is the stirring of men's hearts, the moving of their compassion and the quickening of their understanding and thoughts; it must impel the virtues, piety and moderation.

Kirmani's ideal poets are the Europeans who

> ... have brought poetry and the poetic art under so sound a scheme of arrangement and have made their verses so conformable to the laws of logic that they have no other effect than to illuminate men's ideas ... educate them ... inspire them with zeal, patriotism and devotion to their people.[17]

He praises only Firdausi who wrote epics about pre-Islamic Persian legendary heroes.

Thus the author impatiently rejects the Persian cultural heritage as too trivial and useless. Poetry, philosophy, theology, all fields in which the Persians traditionally excelled and which brought world fame to their nation are harshly condemned. It is the 'new sciences' that are important. Hence he complains bitterly that no Persian ever thought of writing a book on physics, chemistry, economy, agriculture, law ... or any subject that promotes 'the progress of humanity'. Consequently,

> while science has enlightened the whole world, Iran still remains in darkness.[18]

Kirmani suggests that the wrong and outmoded Persian system of moral values and beliefs is a direct consequence of a deficient education. He points out the religious fanaticism prevailing among his countrymen. This abject result of ignorance is best illustrated by the Babi episode. Although he defines the Babis as a group of people who rightfully started their movement by 'attempting to shake off the burden of the Arab shari'at and the Shi'i sect' but ended by 'stupidly submitting themselves to the grotesque sayings of the Bab', he nevertheless justifies their faith. He addresses the Muslim audience thus:

> O people! What is their fault? ... What is their crime? ... You believed in Muhammad the Arab, they in Mirza Ali Muhammad the Shirazi. Whatever the former said, the latter also said. One brought the Koran, the other the Bayan. If the one's verse was miraculously revealed in Arabic, the other's was miraculously revealed in Arabic and Persian. What the Jews, Christians and Muslims say, they also say. Either all religions are right and correct, then theirs is also right and correct; or all religions are wrong and lies, then theirs is also wrong and a lie.[19]

And he strongly condemns the bloody massacre of the Babis by the ulama and the street mob. He describes in detail the horrors that publicly took place in Tehran during the reign of terror, following the first attempt on Nasir ud-Din Shah's life: the fierce-looking ulama supervising the scene, the terrifying official executioners, the Dervishes who seemed to take such a cruel and unnatural delight in torturing the 'heretics', the great crowd assembled in the *maydan* to watch, encourage and even participate in the carnage, the shrieks of the women whose passion was unleashed, the whole air of festivity:

> All this to bring to light the blood-thirsty, merciless, cruel, and savage nature of present day Iranians.[20]

Ignorance also breeds superstition, claims Mirza Aqa Khan, who had personally observed its evil results, for his own native city with its numerous saintly shrines and religious sites attracted thousands and thousands of worshippers from all over the country:

> If one wishes to witness a sample of the Persians' misery, one should accompany them to Kerbala or Najaf ... the state of their misery is beyond the power of description.[21]

He criticizes the veneration accorded to the tombs of the Imams and Imamzadas and reveals with great accuracy the abuses of the ulama in charge and the naiveté of the believers who expect and even crave for miracles. The pilgrims spend whatever fortune they possess in this world, endure bad weather and unhealthy surroundings, fall prey to rapacious Ottoman officials and local attendants just to worship a 'few rotten bones in dusty graves'.[22] The author challenges the necessity of pilgrimage to Mecca, one of the pillars of Islam. He asserts that European statistics (in transliterated French) have shown that the performance of this holy ordinance costs the Muslims 100,000,000 tumans a year:

> And what for? ... to go several times around a black stone like crazy people, in the heat of the sun, to kill a thousand poor beasts, and to come back to their country, having lost all their possessions, hungry and barefoot, having gained the title of *hajji* ... I swear by the God of Mecca that, apart from a house, a mosque, a black stone, a burning soil, bitter water, and a handful of lizard-eaters, merciless and rude Arabs, they have seen and understood nothing.[23]

The fortune spent for the upkeep of thousand-year-old tombs all over the nation could be used instead for the building of hospitals, libraries and homes for the aged.

The Persians, laments Kirmani, have lost their power to reason. They believe anything that is said to them without understanding, without thinking, and behave like 'asses and cows'.[24] Another instance of their irrationalism is found in the Shi'i annual custom of mourning the death of the Imams Hasan and Husayn (*azadari*). Mirza Aqa Khan deplores the fact that the believers' energy is misplaced and misused, their complaints misdirected, their attention distracted from the cruel reality of the world. For,

> if those thousands of screams and moans they utter for the Imams are uttered instead for their own miserable conditions, all the injustice and backwardness of their country would have been removed.[25]

Hence the writer here states that the people's grievances, which constitute a powerful potential for rebellion, need to be guided to the right direction.

Kirmani also sees in polygamy and the seclusion of women the root of moral corruption and social problems. Such traditional practices have kept women who (because of their role as first educators of children) hold a vital place in the family and society at large, in a state of ignorance and backwardness. The embittered wives have created at home a tense atmosphere of hostility, rivalry, and cunning. Consequently their influence upon the children has been detrimental, for the latter learn from their earliest years to lie, to cheat and to mistrust one another.[26] Furthermore, the lack of normal relationships between young men and women has encouraged homosexuality.[27] The extreme puritanism and the strict adherence to trivial conventions, such as keeping away from places where there is dancing and music, social etiquette and hypocritical formulas of politeness, traditional costumes, have prevented Persian society from growing normally and efficiently.[28]

And yet, the author argues, the Persians display such pride and conceit which are without any valid foundation:

> Those proud people have no reason to be so, since they are corrupt, cheaters, liars, cruel to the poor and needy, greedy and selfish ... Pride must be earned through service to the country and its people, through good and honest conduct.[29]

In fact, Iran has become a laughing stock in the eyes of the American, European and Japanese nations:

> Whereas the English colonel would never betray his fatherland, not even for a hundred pounds bribery, an Iranian *sartip* would sell his for fifty pounds. Only fear of punishment would prevent him from committing such crimes.[30]

Such a general state of moral corruption, selfishness and lack of patriotism brought about Iran's economic decay. Although the country possesses all the natural resources necessary to develop a prosperous self-sufficient national economy: mountains, forests, rivers, fertile lands, mild climate, and mines of precious metals and stones, it lies barren and wasted. There are no explorers, no efficient experts, no learned scientists to exploit the wealth. There exists no adequate means of communication to facilitate travelling from one part of the country to the other. Hence the Persian merchants import all basic needs for livelihood from abroad. Here the author expresses his fear that 'ignorance has spread so far that even water would soon be brought from Europe'.[31]

Finally, Kirmani angrily denounces the social system which does not promote equality and just laws, and condones unfair distribution of wealth. The Shah and his aristocratic entourage are the obvious target of his criticism:

> Why should one say: I am the Shah, therefore I should possess a vast fortune, many clothes, palaces and gardens, plenty of food ... while a barefoot beggar dressed in rags must starve and sleep on stones? ... Which holy book allows a person to accumulate wealth through illegal and unjust means, such as trade, while a poor worker who sweats all day long has no food, no shelter in compensation for his hard labour.[32]

Mirza Aqa Khan's most fierce and eloquent accusation is directed toward the Arabs whom he holds essentially responsible for Iran's national decay which had started thirteen centuries ago. Although in some of his most lucid, most 'objective' moments, he frankly admits that it was the Sasanid dynastic corruption and bureaucratic chaos as well as the social and economic injustice prevailing at that time that brought military defeat at the hands of the Muslims,[33] he prefers to see in the Arab conquest the root of Iran's problems.

He depicts the Arabs as a handful of ignorant, savage lizard-eaters, bloodthirsty, barefoot, camel riders, desert-dwelling nomads, who, prior to the Prophet's advent, lived from theft, raid and plunder.[34] Muhammad brought the Koran in order to enlighten their minds, refine their mores and customs, organize their political community, and provide them with a sound code of law: in short, to civilize them. Instead, they misunderstood Islam, ignored the Koran's precepts, and, taking up religion as an excuse, were set to satisfy their natural greed and warrior temper by conquering the neighbouring nations.[35] Thus Islam succeeded in unifying them only in times of raiding, killing and stealing, for when it came to sharing the booty, they were at each other's throats. Instead of establishing unity and accord amongst the Muslims, they brought animosity and discord. They shed Muslim blood in fruitless struggles within their own community:

> Ali and Mu'awiya's war, Talha's and Zubayr's rivalry, Aysha's thirst for blood, Fatima's curses, Husayn's exile to Kufa are petty political and personal disputes that had no connection with the holy religion of Islam.[36]

The author then denounces the Arabs' extreme cruelty to the Persians, the slaughtering of those who refused to convert, the destruction of their beautiful monuments, the burning of their books. He blames the Arabs for corruption and degeneration of the once refined, noble and moral nature of the Persian nation as a whole:

> Even though we are no longer ruled by the Arabs, we have still kept their worst characteristic features and have lost our own civilized old habits and customs.[37]

Among these features he mentions false pride, strong animosity and petty feuds among the people, as reflected in the rise of various Persian sects such as the Shaykhi, Usuli, Akhbari, Babi, Bahai, Azali, the habit of killing, and the seclusion of women. The worst consequence of the Arab conquest was, however, the Islamization of Iran. Kirmani states that the Koranic laws, because they were written down by an Arab primarily for Arabs, do not fit the Persians who already had a highly sophisticated civilization of their own and an elaborate political organization. Those rules befit only a 'barbarian nation'.[38] They were designed to raise the Arabs' standard of living, their morals and their beliefs. There was and there will be nothing better for them than the Muhammadan shari'at.[39] The natures of the Arabs and the Persians are as opposite as fire and water, cold and heat; the gap existing between the two is as high as the distance between the earth and the sky.[40] The evil consequences of Islam brought to Iran at the point of the sword are numerous. One result of such an attestation (*tasdiq*) which was made without previous rational judgment, out of sheer fear, is scepticism. For to believe without understanding leads to an exaggerated sense of criticism, doubt, and objection. A second result is imitation. Because the Persians did not understand what they swore to believe in, in a language they could not understand, they did what the others were doing. They lost the habit of thinking for themselves. A third result is the dissimulation (*taqiya* or *kitman*). In order to survive the people had to hide their real thoughts. This habit led to the habit of lying, so much so that the truth is never heard in Iran.[41]

Lastly, Mirza Aqa Khan condemns the Arabs for the heavy Arabization of the Persian language, as well as the adoption of their script which rendered reading and writing difficult:

> The Arabs have not only invaded our religion and government but also our sweet language ... Their destruction of our ancestor's language is worse than our country's ruin, for nothing is remaining from our once glorious nation, since nothing has remained from our beloved language.[42]

Not only did the Persians suffer from the Arab military invasion, not only were they forced to adopt the 'creed of Arabism' (*ayin-i arabiyyat*), not only did they witness the burning of their ancient books and were compelled to study, in an alien language, a 'mixed-up Koran that has no beginning and no end', but also they remained culturally backward, for all Persian studies were entirely neglected ever since.[43]

Thus we see that Kirmani used the Arabs and Islam as a convenient scapegoat for nineteenth century Iran's social, economic, and cultural stagnation, as well as moral degeneration. Such an unjust, grotesque, false and unbelievable accusation brings to the fore the author's extreme chauvinism that blinds him to such a degree that he scornfully dismisses Muslim Iran's thirteen centuries worth of cultural contribution as non-Persian and therefore valueless.

This anti-Arab feeling led him to gulp readily and accept as 'scientific facts' some contemporary European racist theories. Thus he explains that 'some learned people' claim that persistent customs and mores can bring about a total transformation to the physical constitution of a people. One could therefore detect from among a crowd of Persians, Greeks, English, Ethiopians, Sudanese and Arabs who is civilized and who is primitive by their physical features such as the shape of the nose, the colour of the skin, the blood. Here Kirmani implies that the first three nationalities are civilized whereas the last three are not.[44] And he further pursues his racial prejudice, saying,

> Any man can recognize a Jew from the latter's facial form, colour, shape and personal conduct. Any educated person could read in a Jew's physiognomy the 3,000-year-old contempt, abjectness and ugliness. Any scientist with some knowledge in the study of personality would know all about … that nation's stubbornness … cheating, deceitfulness, and hypocrisy.[45]

He attempts to substantiate his argument with 'a scientific proof' by stating that the Jews were made so 'stubborn, hypocritical, revengeful and envious' because nature has created each living being with a means of defence and protection for self-preservation, just as the dog has a heightened sense of smell, or the Siberian bear a thick fur.[46] The author goes on attacking the Jews for their arrogance, conceit, and sense of superiority:

> In spite of the fact that they have been humiliated, and still are, in most nations of the world, they still consider themselves as the noblest elite of the human race.[47]

Finally he denounces Moses as the man responsible for their defects by:

> claiming he was a prophet, with the right to govern and to whom all must pay obedience … Hence the Jewish religion has changed the nation's original nature and given birth to ugly disposition and base character.[48]

Similarly, Kirmani argues, the Persians since the Arab conquest have lost their good looks, their proud and happy faces, their elegant and well-shaped figures because of the acquired low standard of morality, the bad habits, and the feeling of total discouragement.[49]

Along with the Arabs and Islam, Mirza Aqa Khan blames the ulama for their destructive role in the history of the Persian nation and culture:

> This faith, which the Persians were forced to accept at the point of the Arab sword, today is still apparently accepted out of the fear of the ulama's weapon of curse and excommunication. That day fearing the sword, today fearing the pen.[50]

He states that the ulama have created this practice of excommunication, *takfir*, as an instrument for achieving power. The Prophet did not institute such a practice, for Islam was made a simple and easy religion. It was enough to say 'there is no God but God' to be considered as Muslim. Hence the religious leaders have disregarded God's command to judge with justice, equity, and right.[51] Similarly they are guilty of disobeying the Prophet's wishes by declaring the Jews and Christians, whom the Koran considers as 'people of the book', to be 'unclean', *najis*. This foul belief has caused Iran's complete isolation from the non-Muslim world. Such a lack of contact with the outer world and its progress was detrimental to the Muslims.[52] Furthermore, the ignorant mullas, who, in order to consolidate the power of the Safavid dynasty, established Shi'ism in Iran, are responsible for the harmful animosity that was subsequently aroused between the Sunnis and the Shi'is, an animosity that is going to last forever.[53] Kirmani strongly opposes some of the extremist Shi'i practices:

> It is not our duty to deify Ali or to curse the others. We must not see any difference between Ali and Umar, Abu Bakr and Uthman. For there is none, and we cannot elevate Ali to the rank of a prophet.[54]

It is the ulama's ignorance that helped the spread of superstition and faith in erroneous beliefs. For they have corrupted, misinterpreted, and misunderstood the religious precepts:

> While European learned men are busy studying mathematics, sciences, politics, and economics, the rights of man, in an age of socialism and fight for the improvement of conditions of the poor, the Persian ulama are discussing problems of cleanliness and the ascension of the Prophet to Heaven.[55]

Their whole concern is self-enrichment and self-interest. Even their attitude toward God is blasphemous. For they take the

Supreme Being as being a Padishah in need of flatteries who would be gratified if they utter such meaningless addresses as 'we are all under the shadow of your favour'. Kirmani angrily comments that they do not know that God is rich and not in need of his slaves' flattery.[56] And he adds,

> What is left of Islam is only a name empty and dried up. With utter sorrow I warn the ulama that in a few years even the name of Muslims will be taken away from us, and we would then perish as a community.[57]

We observe here, as elsewhere, that the author finds it convenient to identify himself as a Muslim, regardless of his previous un-Islamic statements.

Finally Kirmani charges the secular government with tyranny and cruelty. He claims that ever since the Arab conquest, Iran has been ruled ruthlessly by despots who usurped power in the name of religion and divine right, erroneously pretending to be the descendants and heirs of the Prophet through Ali.[58] The Shahs allowed themselves all rights to dispose of the nation's wealth and of the people's life and property as they pleased. The present king is busy selling his country to the foreigners. He will not be satisfied until

> he has brought affliction to the last Persian left, has handed over all the women to the Russian soldiers, ... and turned the people's ruined houses into stables to be used by the Afghans and the Ottomans.[59]

The attack is also directed against the court officials who share with their sovereign in the responsibility for the nation's ruin.

Nationalism

We now come to discuss the author's subject of despair and love, his greatest obsession, his muse that inspired both a poetic fire and a prophetic fanaticism in him, that unleashed all the passion, hatred and resentment accumulated through the years, namely Iran. That is to say, his own image of Iran. For to him Iran's authentic identity can be sought only in her Zoroastrian past when she was at the zenith of her glory and power, when the neighbouring kings bowed to her mighty emperors, and her soldiers planted her banner in conquered lands. In his search for a worthier identity, Kirmani ends by creating a myth out of the pre-Islamic Iran.

He mentions his country as the 'noble Aryan nation',[60] which belongs to the 'good Aryan people of good extraction'.[61] Zoroastrianism was the religion that best fitted the nature of its inhabitants. Its prophet established a *qanun* that brought about the order and justice necessary for progress and prosperity, because it carefully distributed power among the king, the religious heads, the military forces, and the 'nature of the nation'. It was a law based on four essential pillars: (1) the Shah's rights and the subjects' duty to obey and respect him; (2) the subjects' rights and the Shah's duty to provide them with security and well being; (3) the people's rights and duties towards one another; (4) the religious head's duty to propagate the true religion and guide the faithful to the right path, and prevent idolatry.[62]

Hence Kirmani's claim that ancient Persians led a happy life under the reign of law and justice. Being ruled by the right government and the right religion, they felt secure and not at the mercy of their superiors. The good was rewarded and the bad punished, all according to their deeds. Those who accomplished special services to the society were paid due honour and privileges. Women enjoyed full equality with men. Similarly the people of conquered nations were well treated and the prisoners of war given merciful sentences.[63]

He goes on, stating that the government provided hospitals and orphanages for each town. Good roads and canals were constructed, which expanded trade and agriculture. The Persians then excelled in the arts, engineering and architecture, Persepolis being a good reminder of this past achievement. The rich language which had become universal is another sign of the superiority of Iran's ancient people and civilization over the rest of the world.[64] Further to illustrate the greatness and importance of Iran's culture, he attributes Persian roots to many European and Asian terms. For instance, the old Persian word for god, *div*, is root of the French word *dieu*; the Egyptian royal title *Khediv* is derived from the Persian *Mahadiv*, king of gods. Similarly the Persian word for sun, *ju* or *ja*, is the root of the French words *jour* and *juin*, and of the name Japan, the country where the sun rises.[65]

He sees in Mazdak, whom he highly praises as Mazdak the

pure, the learned Mazdak, the powerful philosopher, the founder of 'just law and righteous creed', who 2,000 years ago laid the foundations of republicanism and égalité (as he transliterates it from the French).[66] The anarchists in France, nihilists in Russia, socialists in England, after 700 years of culture, have barely reached Mazdak's level.[67]

Obviously the author was anxious to paint a glorious picture of ancient Iran. In so doing, he neglected to abide by the 'scientific objectivity' he claimed a historian should follow. He also failed to judge rationally the situation in the past and to come to a conclusion similar to the one he reached in a later work, namely that Iran has always been ruled by despots and its people never enjoyed freedom and equality, for they deified their monarchs.

Furthermore, in his attempt at idealization Mirza Aqa Khan described the old Persian empire as a national entity which, in fact, historically it never was.

Kirmani's grandiose vision of his past renders the present even more bitter. For the past compared to the present is what light is to darkness:

> The name of Iran and Persians in Europe is now in ill repute. They take us for savages and wild beasts. Nobody has any respect for us.[68]

His tone turns lyrically tender, yet full of anguish and resentment as he addresses himself to Iran, which he personifies as a beautiful woman that the ancient Persians honoured, glorified, and adorned, and who was raped by the Arabs:

> O, Iran! Where have all those kings, who adorned you with justice, equity, and munificence, who decorated you with pomp and splendour, gone? From that date when the barbarian, savage, coarse Bedouin Arabs sold your king's daughter in the street and cattle market, you have not seen a bright day, and have lain hid in darkness ...
>
> Alas! What a pity! O, Iran! Where has this great state gone? Where has this opulent glory gone? What happened to this famous power? Where has the divine sovereignty gone? A handful of naked, barefoot, hungry, savage Arabs have come and, for 1285 years, have plunged you into such misery and darkness. Your heavenly soil ruined; your developed cities destroyed; your people ignorant and deprived of all progress of the world, of the blessings of culture and civilization, kept away from the human rights ... Your king is a wild, blood-thirsty despot.[69]

He dreams of the future when his beloved would be rescued and restored to her greatness. And yet, in spite of it all, there is a touch of despair and pessimism as he realizes that this future is so distant:

> Ah! ... It needs such a long life! ... O, Iran! Your happiness is so far away![70]

This despair adds fuel to his passionate hatred for the Arabs. His language becomes more violent as it displays a strong feeling of frustration and humiliation:

> I spit on the Arabs! Shame on those cowards who have attacked such a great state, such a happiness, Iran, which was the signpost of the world, the object of envy for all nations.[71]

How does he think a national restoration could be achieved?

The Revolutionary Solution

To Kirmani only a revolution could bring about the change necessary in such a decadent society. He does not, however, offer any systematic programme. Nor does he propose a sound, consistent ideology. It is therefore very difficult for us to explain, in a clear and concrete fashion, his revolutionary thought. We have merely managed to gather, from among his various works, the political views that suggest a guideline to what he had in mind. Here, once again, we should like to point to already mentioned characteristics of Kirmani's thought, namely the inconsistency and confusion found in his ideas.

We have stated above that Mirza Aqa Khan highly praised Mazdak, the populist revolutionary who had challenged and threatened the Sasanid authority, as a man who wanted to establish in pre-Islamic Iran a republican, egalitarian type of government. In *Ayin-i Skandari*, the author surmises that throughout the long history of Iran, before and after the advent of Islam, no leaders, no movement ever arose to fight for the people's rights. The revolts that occurred were simply 'protests against individuals and not against a prevailing situation'. Similarly, the revolutions that took place were aiming at 'changing the individual governor, or ruler, and not at changing the governmental system'.[72] Mazdak was the only exception, for he believed that each subject had the right to interfere in state affairs and that the government should be entrusted to 'an assembly of national representatives and notables' (*shura-yi muntakhibin va buzur-gan-i qaum*). This 'worthy man' also promoted the idea that 'a nation's progress depended upon freedom of thought and action'.[73] Kirmani claims that had Mazdak succeeded in his time, Iran would have now reached the highest stage of progress and civilization. Unfortunately, the Sasanid Shah crushed the revolt, and thus

> the gate which nature had opened for the people of Iran, and which would have led to endless progress, was forever obstructed.[74]

Hence the Sasanid defeat at the hands of the Arabs was actually history's revenge.

Here, then, we observe that what Kirmani was in fact praising Mazdak for were eighteenth and nineteenth century Western liberal concepts such as human rights, freedom of thought and action, sovereignty of the people, republicanism, national representatives, etc. They were concepts of government which he wished to see established in Iran.

Furthermore, by comparing Persian Mazdakism to the European movements called nihilism, socialism and anarchism,[75] he adds a more radical tone to his political thought. Although in all his works, with the exception of *Hasht Bihisht*, his main Babi writing, he makes flattering references to the revolutionary movements, nowhere does he attempt to define them or explain their respective goals. By referring to them synonymously, he reveals himself to be in fact rather confused and unaware of the real nature, as well as of the significance, of each movement. The only conclusion we can draw from this is that he was merely attracted by their revolutionary aspect which aimed at bringing drastic political and social changes.

For it was drastic social and political changes that Kirmani incessantly called for in his works. In *Sa Maktub*, for instance, he attempts to introduce nineteen French terms, the meaning of which might have seemed revolutionary, to his contemporary Persian readers. A brief review of the choice and definition of these words should clearly illustrate our point:

1. *despote:* defined as a Padishah, and not just any kind of

ruler, who has absolute power over his subjects whom he treats as slaves, deprived of all human rights.

2. *civilization:* 'consists of saving a nation from envy, avarice, and state of savagery, ... barbarism and ignorance; of acquiring full knowledge necessary for progress in life, science and technology; and of improving and spreading humanitarian mores and customs among the people'. The author is then interpreting civilization as a modern, human as well as moral absolute concept that a nation could acquire, and not as the total culture, or the way of life of a people or nation at any period.
3. *littérature:* any kind of composition written in verse or prose.
4. *fanatique:* a person who is religiously so bigoted that he allows the persecution of those who oppose his belief. The term is therefore restricted to the religious connotation.
5. *philosophe:* a rational person who 'attributes the causes of physical laws to nature; who is aware of the deep nature of things; who holds no superstitious beliefs in miracles and in the supernatural power of *Jin*, *Div*, *Pari*, and *Shaytan*; who considers as ignorant those who believe in them; who dismisses the latter as outside the human circle, being inferior even to animals ... There is no being more complete and wiser than the philosophe'. Rationalism is thus seen as the highest and noblest of human virtues.
6. *révolution:* occurs when (a) people, harassed by the despotic rule of the Padishah, dethrone the latter and establish laws suitable to their own happiness, or (b) when people get to understand their religious beliefs rationally, become impatient with the ignorance of the mullahs or popes, throw off the tiresome religious burden, and establish a new law, or a new religion, in accordance to philosophical principles and national nature.
7. *progrès:* a nation's zealous effort to achieve advancement in the sciences and industries, to establish culture, and to eliminate injustice.
8. *poésie:* a composition describing a person, a tribe, or a nation; or stating a problem, or picturing the world of nature in verse and expressing a certain emotion or impression.

9. *patriote:* is a person who, out of love for his country and for the sake of his nation's progress, would not hesitate to sacrifice himself, his wealth, his possessions. He is an honourable person, leader of a society, having given dignity to his nation. The Prophet, for instance, was an Arab who helped the Quraysh tribe and the Arab nation acquire dignity and honour.
10. *changement:* is the happening of a great event in the world, such as Noah's flood; or among a group of people such as the decline of the Roman Empire, the catastrophe of the Mongol invasion ... The author is defining changes as great historical events.
11. *politique:* refers to a state's goals and issues which are profitable to the government as well as the country.
12. *protestantisme:* is the religion in which the individual's duty to worship and obey God's command is substituted by his duty to observe people's rights. 'It is well known in Europe and one can say that its creator and promoter has done a great service to the nation'.
13. *libéré:* is a free man, free in his thinking, and free from religious promises and threats such as hell, heaven, hope, despair, ... He considers as a lie any matter that contradicts the law and cause of nature, even if it is held as true by a whole community, or if recorded in history. He does not believe in tales and sayings that are irrational, not even those attributed to the Prophet himself. He spends all his time in educating and organizing the government, or in establishing progress and culture. He is wise, philosophical, honest and straightforward.
14. *électrique:* widespread power that is of great profitable use in Europe.
15. *penseur:* is a learned philosopher-writer who openly without concealment (*taqiya*) does not hesitate to sacrifice himself for the good of his country. He freely criticizes everything in the newspapers and fearlessly exposes his philosophical ideas. Such a man is greatly honoured in Europe.
16. *charlatan:* a liar, a crook, a selfish, evil man.
17. *parlement:* consists of two assemblies: one composed of deputies elected by the people, and the other composed of

notables of the country. The former discusses new laws, the latter approves them. The Padishah himself has only the right to execute them. He has no power to oppose or interfere with the legislation. He sees himself as an elder servant of the government, and as the affectionate father of the people. He gets his salary from the state treasury, is not allowed a penny more than his due. At the end of the paragraph Kirmani adds:

> I do not believe that the people of the East could conceive or understand such a type of government, since they worship the Padishah as the shadow of God, Son of Heaven.

18. *Pétrarque and Voltaire:* two famous philophers of Europe who have left great literary works. 'Especially Voltaire who fought for the elimination of papal and priestly ideas'.
19. *chimie:* 'a useful science which the ignorant Persians mistake for alchemy'.[76]

Here, then, Kirmani praises political constitutionalism and religious reform. In *Risala-yi Masha Allah* he explicitly calls for a movement within Islam similar to the Protestant revolt within Christianity:

> People should be enlightened and helped to throw the heavy (religious) burden off their shoulders. It is only then that the Muslim religion will emerge in its truth and purity, free from the absurdities that [the ulama] charged her with ... European nations progressed only when they were freed from the influence of pope and priests.[77]

In a letter to Malkam Khan he had actually written that one must:

> ... fight about this Qajar tribe and the stupid mullas ... All their deeds are based on self-interest and nothing in them is trustworthy ... Something must be done to bring into action the clean nature and pure blood of the nation's middle people, the peasants, dignitaries and nobles.[78]

It is interesting to note here Kirmani's attempt to think in terms of a 'united front', that would include people from all classes, as a possible powerful opposition to the ruling government and religious authority. Perhaps he had in mind the early stages of the French revolution when a strong alliance between the nobility, peasantry and bourgeoisie brought about the downfall of the Bourbon monarchy and the Catholic clergy. Most probably, however, he was thinking of the 1891–92 successful resistance to the tobacco concession organized and supported by members of the merchant and religious classes, though the target this time would be to eliminate the power of the ulama.[79]

Such a 'liberation', the author argues, would succeed in turning the people's full attention to 'national problems' and convert their religious fanaticism into patriotic zeal. It would also result in reforming the educational system and promoting the study of meaningful sciences and philosophy. True knowledge would then be widespread, which would lead to national strength. For knowledge, which is the basis of culture and progress, constitutes a powerful barrier difficult for the enemies to cross.[80]

Mirza Aqa Khan similarly explains that since a 'nation's existence depends on the existence of its languages', the Persian language should also be reformed, purified from its unnecessary Arabic terminology and rendered easy to read and to write to combat illiteracy.

> Whereas knowledge is the soul of a human being, language constitutes the body of knowledge.[81]

Language is a nation's unifying factor, its living symbol. We would like to remark here that although Kirmani constantly attacked the Arabic alphabet for being unsuitable to the Persian language, we have not been able to find in any of his works an open call for the adoption of the Latin alphabet.

It is significant that although the author looks back to Iran's pre-Islamic past with great nostalgia and wishes to see it resurrected, it is to modern Europe that he turns in search for a solution. He never fails to refer to it as the model to be followed, as the guide to prosperity, progress and happiness, as the authority to consult, and as the ultimate proof for all his arguments. He prophetically warns his compatriots:

> O ignorant fathers of today! You who are not willing to let your children learn the language of the Europeans and study their sciences because it is *kafr*, soon this ignorance of yours will force them to become the servants and grooms of the Europeans and you will see this abjectness with your own eyes.[82]

Kirmani insists that such a misfortune should at all costs be prevented from happening. It is up to some individuals to take up this ambitious task of reviving a nation, individuals whose great and noble names would be recorded in history with glory. They

> with their force ... would bring about a sudden *changement* in Iran which would cause a revolution. With their *electric(al)* and *literary* power, and with the strength of their ... pen, would liberate the people who are buried alive in their grave of sufferings ... and free them from the grip of the *fanatic(al)* ulama and from the rule of the *despot*.[83]

In his clear and loud call for revolution, Kirmani uses the French terms which he had attempted to introduce to his readers. He obviously considered himself to be his people's educator as well as one of their revolutionary leaders who would direct them straight to the promised era of justice, progress, and happiness.

Conclusion

Mirza Aqa Khan's criticism of nineteenth century Persian society quite adequately depicts the prevailing ills of the time. It also reveals the author's personal feeling of restless discontent and his deep-rooted, passionate strife for a positive fulfillment of happiness. His discontent is with the reality which he finds bitter and unbearable, because it does not conform with his own conception of an ideal society. Iranian reality alienates him and generates in him a mixed feeling of frustration, anger and hatred. The mental formation which had given him so penetrating an insight into the social and intellectual problems of his era at the same time held him back from developing this insight into a coherent theory of social action. He was a highly passionate and committed man more than an abstract thinker. He was also a man with a great quest for heroism, yet he was living in an age of utter mediocrity, the age of Nasir ud-Din Shah: no glorious wars, national humiliation at the hands of foreign enemies, cultural sterility and social stagnation.

He consequently looks for a means to escape and for a substitute gratification which he finds in a mythical past and in a visionary future, both creations of his own mind. He also feels the need for a convenient scapegoat to curse and to condemn for the misery he is suffering, which thus enables him to pour out all the hatred and anger that oppress him. History provides him with the substitute gratification. Unlike James Joyce who had written 'history is a nightmare from which I am trying to awaken', Kirmani found history necessary, even vital, for the shaping of a national self-image. Hence he endeavours to give Iran a Zoroastrian, pre-Islamic identity which appears to him more advantageous and more flattering. In the Arabs and Islam he finds the object to scorn and to blame for Persian decadence. In the Western racist theories of the time, he finds the rationale for the contempt which he heaps on the Arabs, and a positive argument for the glorification of the Persian nation. Finally it is in revolution that he finds a solution for the future.

Paradoxically enough, though it is characteristic of most national movements, the form his opposition takes is, broadly speaking, not a demand for a return to the old system, but a demand for Westernization. We notice a second paradox, which again is common to the European and non-European liberals of that time, in the inconsistency of the ideas he promotes. On the one hand, he calls for human rights, freedom, equality, justice, sovereignty of the people, and on the other, he makes unjust and biased racist statements. Whereas he again and again claims to be rational, he very often passes irrational judgments and displays irrational emotions. He attacks the ulama for their fanaticism and intransigence, yet he reveals himself to be fanatical and intransigent in his views. Though he tries to abolish religion because of its disastrous effects upon society, he actually wishes to establish a new religion, nationalism, that shares many of the former's shortcomings and defects.

Having thus pointed out the negative aspects of Kirmani's national and revolutionary thought, we should like to refer now to the more positive constructive points. The most obvious one is, of course, his great contribution to the awakening of Persian social consciousness. He was one of the first Persians to have not only realized the intellectual and social backwardness of the country, but also to have attempted to find the root of the problem and to have suggested a possible solution. Unlike his contemporary statesmen and fellow revolutionaries, he had the great courage openly to denounce the Muslim institutions, the political regime, and the educational system as the real causes for the national stagnation. The solution he offers therefore aims at more than mere 'window dressing'. For he demands a radical, profound change within the entire social structure and system of values and beliefs. The revolution he calls for he correctly sees as a moral necessity, as springing out of the dire needs of the society and not as a mere tradition borrowed from the West.

In spite of his own personal failure to abide by them consistently, his call for modern, rational, scientific concepts and principles was a healthy sound to hear. He genuinely wished to see Iran modernize and its people enjoy better living conditions and a better intellectual, more creative atmosphere.

LIST OF WORKS

Kitab-i Rizvan (Book of Paradise)

It is his first work, started at the age of twenty-five while still in Kirman, continued in Isfahan, and completed in Istanbul in 1304/1886–87, though later on he kept adding material to it. Written in imitation of Sa'di's *Gulistan*, it contains proverbs, sayings, anecdotes, poems, and biographical notes. The University of Tehran Central Library has a microfilm copy of the original MS belonging to Dr Mujtaba Minovi, Professor at the School of Theology, University of Tehran.

Kitab-i Rihan (Book of Wind)

His last work, written in Trebizond a few months before his death, not completed. It is essentially a critique of Persian literature in general and a call for a new genre of *littérature engagée.* Original MS belongs also to Mr Minovi, with a microfilmed copy at the University Library.

Salarnama

An epic in verse in imitation of Firdausi's *Shahnama*, relating the history of pre-Islamic Persia. The last part contains an essay on literary criticism and a few patriotic poems. It was written and completed in Trebizond in 1895. A second volume was added to it, written by a former companion of his, Shaykh Ahmad Adib Kirmani, relating the history of Islamic Iran. Both volumes were published in 1937, the last part of Volume One having been omitted. Nazim ul-Islam had published this omitted part in his *Tarikh-i Bidari-yi Iraniyan*.

Ayin-i skandari

Another history of pre-Islamic Iran, from the earliest time to the rise of Islam. First started in 1889, it was most probably finished two years later in 1891. It was published in 1947.

Sa Maktub and **Sad Khitaba**

Volume One and Two of a work in which the author, following nineteenth century European socio-anthropological as well as natural science theories, has attempted to study the history and society of Iran. It is in the form of letters written by a fictional prince Kamal ud-Daula, a Persian living in India, to another fictional prince Jalal ud-Daula of Persia. In spite of the titles, Volume One is in fact one letter and Volume Two consists of forty-two letters. *Sa Maktub* follows quite closely Fath Ali-Akhundzada's own book with the same title, with some major differences, though. We have been unable to determine the date of this work. E. G. Browne states that *Sa Maktub* was written 1280/1863–64, but he is mistaking it for Fath Ali Akhundzada's work of the same title. At that time, Kirmani was barely ten years old. We assume that he wrote it while he was in Istanbul, for the references to European scholars and writers, to their theories and to some European terminologies, reveal a fair knowledge of Western studies. It is a knowledge that he acquired essentially during his stay in the Ottoman capital. A manuscript copy of Volume Two is found in Browne's collection, Cambridge University library. Mrs Nikki R. Keddie, Professor at the University of California at Los Angeles, has a handwritten copy of Volume One.

Tarikh-i Shanzhman-i Iran (History of changes in Iran)

A critical essay on the impact of historical events. Only eighteen pages of it are available. It was most probably written in Trebizond, for at one section he refers to the time 'when I was in Istanbul'. I have not been able to see this work.

Takvin va Tashri (Book of genesis and holy law)

A philosophical essay, heavily influenced by Western natural scientists and empirical theories. It is not dated, but again we assume that it was written in Istanbul. Handwritten copy of the MS is in the possession of Mr Qasimi.

Qahva Khana-yi Surat, Ya Haftad ud-Dau Millat

A short essay, mostly based on a direct translation of Bernadin de Saint Pierre's *Café de Surat*, to which Kirmani added some of his own ideas. It is a critique of the fanaticism and narrow-mindedness of all religions and sects. It was meant to be a preface for *Hikmat-i Nazari*, but was separately published in Berlin, 1964.

Hikmat-i Nazari

A Babi metaphysical treatise inspired by Western and Muslim philosophical and theological concepts, ancient, classical and modern. Not dated. MS belongs to Mr. Qasimi.

Hasht Bihisht

It is supposed to be the second volume to the preceding work, dealing with Babi practical concepts and ordinances. Both volumes were written in collaboration with Shaykh Ahmad Ruhi in Istanbul. Although the authors state in the introduction that both volumes attempt to expound and analyze Babi religious and philosophical concepts, they have in fact added ideas inspired from Western modern secular thought. Though undated, we know it was written in Istanbul and finished sometime in 1892. Browne, in *Materials for the Study of the Babi Religion*, mentions the fact that he had just received a recently completed manuscript of *Hasht Bihisht* in that same year. Furthermore, the last chapter of that book refers to Baha'ullah's death 'a few months ago' and to the subsequent rivalry between his successors. The Bahai leader died in May 1892. It was printed in Tehran in 1958, but had to be circulated secretly.

Risala-yi Insha Allah Masha Allah

A short pamphlet criticizing both Sunni and Shi'i ulama for their fruitless and pedantic, scholarly endeavours. It was written in Istanbul in Rajab 1310/ January 1893. There is a handwritten copy of the MS in the Browne Collection, University of Cambridge Library.

Translation of Fénelon's Télémaque

Not completed.

Articles for Akhtar

He contributed from the No. 37, fifteenth year to No. 11, sixteenth year. The title of his column was *Dar Fan-i Guftan va nivishtan* (On the Art of Speech and Writing).

NOTES

1. F. Fanon, *Peau Noire, Masques Blancs*, Paris, 1952, p. 128.
2. For a more detailed biography see F. Adamiyat, *Andishaha-yi Mirza Aqa Khan Kirmani*, Tehran, 1967. (From here on cited as *Andishaha-yi* ..., and my own dissertation, chapter 3.)
3. This praise is attributed to Shaykh ur-Ra'is, a Qajar liberal and learned prince whom Kirmani first met in Meshhad, then later in Istanbul. Shaykh ur-Ra'is was a follower of Afghani's pan-Islamism. See the introduction to Mirza Aqa Khan Kirmani, *Haftad ud-Dau Millat*, Berlin, 1964, p. 67.
4. *Andishaha-yi* ..., p. 32.
5. Mirza Aqa Khan Kirmani, *Takvin va Tashri*, unpublished handwritten manuscript in possession of Mr Ali Muhammad Qasimi, Director of the Bank Kar, Tehran.
6. *Ibid.*
7. E. G. Browne, *Persian Press and Poetry*, Cambridge, 1912, p. 17.
8. Yahya Daulat Abadi, *Hayat-i Yahya*, Tehran, 1957, Vol. 1, p. 125.
9. Mirza Malkam Khan Nizam ud-Daula (1833–1908) was a Persian reform-minded political adviser at the Court of Nasir ud-Din Shah and long-time Ambassador in London until he lost royal favour and settled in the British capital where he published, from 1890–1896, *Qanun*, a revolutionary Persian newspaper. Heavily influenced by Auguste Comte's 'Religion de l'humanité' and freemasonry, he sought to organize a secret society with various lodges in Iran and abroad which would propagate his own socio-religious philosophy 'Adamiyyat' (humanity).

   See my own thesis, chapter 2. See Muhit Tabataba'i, *Majmu'a-yi athar-i Mirza Malkam Khan*, Tehran, 1327. See Hashim Rabi'zada, *Kulliyat-i*

Malkam Khan, Tehran, 1325. See Fereydun Adamiyat, *Fikr-i Azadi*, Tehran, 1340.

Cambridge University library, the E. G. Browne collection, has a copy of all issues of *Qanun.*

10. Jamal ud-Din Asadabadi known as Afghani (d. 1897), a famous Persian revolutionary who unsuccessfully sought to establish to rally all Muslim subjects of the world around a pan-Islamic nation which would then be strong enough to countercheck the increasing Western encroachment in Muslim lands. See Nikki R. Keddie, *Islamic Response to Imperialism*, Berkeley and Los Angeles, 1969; *Sayyid Jamal ad-Din Afghani: A Political Biography*, Berkeley and Los Angeles, 1972; 'Religion and Irreligion in early Iranian nationalism', *Comparative Studies in Society and History*, Vol. IV, No. 3, April 1962. See Homa Pakdaman, *Jamal ed-Din Assad Abadi dit Afghani*, Paris, 1969. See Sadr Vasiqi, *Sayyid Jamal ud-Din Husayni: Payaguzar-i Nuhzatha-yi Islami*, Tehran, 1348. See Elie Kedourie, *Afghani and Abduh*, London, 1966; and other numerous books and articles on the subject listed in the bibliographies of the above-mentioned books.
11. The whole correspondence is now found in the Bibliothèque Nationale, Paris, Manuscrits Orientaux, Archive du Prince Malkom Khan, Suppléments Persans, 1996, Folios Nos. 60–167. University of Tehran library has a xerox copy of it.
12. See the complete list of Kirmani's works following the footnotes.
13. *Sa Maktub*, p. 45.
14. *Sad Khitaba*, no. 27.
15. *Sa Maktub*, p. 10.
16. Translated by E. G. Browne, *Modern Press and Poetry in Persia*, Cambridge, 1924, p. XXXIV.
17. *Ibid.*, p. XXXV.
18. *Sa Maktub*, p. 16.
19. *Ibid.*, p. 112.
20. *Ibid.*
21. *Ibid.*, p. 77.
22. *Ibid.*, p. 79.
23. *Ibid.*, p. 80.
24. *Sad Khitaba*, no. 24.
25. *Ibid.*, no. 31.
26. *Ibid.*, no. 32.
27. *Ibid.*, no. 34.
28. *Ibid.*
29. *Ibid.*, no. 26.
30. *Ibid.*, no. 25.
31. *Ibid.*, no. 3–4.
32. *Ibid.*, no. 20.
33. *Ayin-i Skandari*, p. 169; ad *Sad Khitaba*, nos 6, 18, 20.
34. *Sad Khitaba*, no. 15.
35. *Sa Maktub*, pp. 24–26.
36. *Ibid.*, p. 35.

37. *Sad Khitaba*, no. 28.
38. *Ibid.*, no. 27.
39. *Sa Maktub*, p. 21.
40. *Sad Khitaba*, no. 32.
41. *Ibid.*, no. 24.
42. *Sa Maktub*, p. 164.
43. *Ibid.*, p. 88.
44. *Ibid.*, pp. 39–40.
45. *Ibid.*, p. 97.
46. *Ibid.*, p. 98.
47. *Ibid.*, p. 105.
48. *Ibid.*, p. 106.
49. *Ibid.*, p. 40.
50. *Ibid.*, p. 74.
51. *Ibid.*, p. 30.
52. *Ibid.*, p. 29.
53. *Ibid.*, p. 53.
54. *Sad Khitaba*, no. 24.
55. *Ibid.*, no. 37.
56. *Risala-yi Insha Allah Masha Allah*, p. 7.
57. *Ibid.*, p. 21.
58. *Sa Maktub*, p. 43.
59. *Sad Khitaba*, no. 41.
60. *Sa Maktub*, p. 88.
61. *Salarnama*, p. 12.
62. *Sad Khitaba*, no. 17.
63. *Sa Maktub*, pp. 6–9.
64. *Sad Khitaba*, no. 1.
65. *Ibid.*, no. 6.
66. Mazdak was the founder of a religious sect in Iran which had great political influence during the years 488–531 A.D. The best known feature of his teaching was the endeavour to remove every cause of covetousness and discord among men, and thus to purify religion, by making women and possessions common property. The reigning Persian monarch of the time had adopted the sect and even had made arrangements for putting its teaching into practice. There were also numerous conversions among the upper classes and among the common people. The movement thus became a remarkable force and permeated all the machinery of government. Its growing power, however, provoked a *coup d'état* in the palace, and the king was dethroned and imprisoned. Mazdak and his followers were invited to the court by the new king on the pretext that a theological dispute was to be held, and they were massacred en masse. Surviving Mazdakis were persecuted, and their books burned. Mazdakism and its reforms which aimed at establishing a more egalitarian and more humanitarian society were often interpreted by scholars, including Kirmani, as essentially a social movement similar to the modern social communism.
67. *Sa Maktub*, p. 88.
68. *Ibid.*, p. 15.

69. *Ibid.*, pp. 10–11.
70. *Ibid.*, p. 14.
71. *Ibid.*, p. 17.
72. *Ayin-i Skandari*, p. 160.
73. *Ibid.*, p. 165.
74. *Ibid.*, p. 169.
75. *Salarnama*, p. 120; *Sad Khitaba*, no. 6; *Sa Maktub*, p. 88.
76. *Sa Maktub*, pp. 1–6.
77. *Risala-yi Masha Allah*, pp. 21–22.
78. Letter to Malkam Khan dated 12 Rabi'al awwal, 1311/23 September 1893.
79. Nevertheless, this antagonism and mistrust of the ulama did not prevent the young rebel from seeing their potential usefulness once they fought on the right side. For he did not fail to appreciate their indispensable role in fomenting the spirit of revolt during the period of the Tobacco Affair. In an undated leter to Malkam he admitted this and added that one should not miss the opportunity, and 'as long as the ulama are in a dancing mood', one must make use of it.
80. *Sad Khitaba*, no. 16.
81. *Sa Maktub*, p. 161.
82. *Sad Khitaba*, no. 39.
83. *Sa Maktub*, p. 169.

5

Kasravi: The Integrative Nationalist of Iran

Ervand Abrahamian

National Integration

'Political Modernization' has become a sponge term. For some it has soaked up the process of building such centralized institutions as state bureaucracies, standing armies, and disciplined political parties. For others it is closely related to the breakdown of regionally independent agrarian economies into highly interdependent industrial economies. And yet for others, it is synonomous with the transformation of traditional cultures where subjects owe allegiance primarily to their parochial groups, and view themselves as distinctly detached from the central authorities, into modern cultures where citizens owe allegiance to the state, consider it their natural right and even civic duty to participate in public affairs, and feel that their political system – whether democratic or totalitarian – should have deep roots in the social system.

But in whatever specific way 'political modernization' is used, it is invariably associated with the general process of national integration: the integration of traditional decentralized administrations into centralized modern state bureaucracies; the integration of agrarian economies where there are few direct links between the regional units into industrial economies where these units are fused into one unitary and directly linked social system; the integration of rulers and ruled through institutions that stretch from the centre to various areas and layers at the periphery; the integration of exclusive bonds – such as to clans, tribes, religious sects, and regional groups – into more inclusive ties to the nation; and the integration of multi-cultural, multi-tribal, multi-lingual empires into new nation-states often, if not always, with one political ideology, one culture, one language, and one national identity.[1]

Although as early as the nineteenth century two such different minds as Marx and Durkheim both wrote on the transformation of independent agrarian units into inter-dependent industrial societies, it was not until quite recently that social scientists have focused their attention on the problem of political unification. This revival of interest is reflected in Clifford Geertz's much quoted article 'The Integrative Revolution: Primordial Sentiments and Civil Politics in the New States' which first appeared nine years ago in a collection of essays entitled *Old Societies and New Nations: The Quest for Modernity in Asia and Africa.*[2] In this work Geertz showed how newly independent countries were invariably confronted by the agonizing problem of reconciling traditional affiliations – such as ties to tribes, regions, religions, languages, and ethnic groups – into modern nation-states demanding the political allegiances of all their citizens. He concluded that this was one of the major 'revolutions' facing the emerging states of Africa and Asia.

The concept of political unification has also been used in a somewhat different fashion by Leonard Binder in his articles 'Egypt: The Integrative Revolution' and 'National Integration and Political Development'.[3] While for Geertz national integration means the aggregation of communal groups into nations, for Binder it signifies the closing of the wide gap between elites and masses through the building of new national values and state institutions.

Binder's use of the term 'national integration' is derived predominantly from the study of Egypt where the traditional elites had almost nothing in common with the masses. And Geertz's conclusions are formulated mostly from the experiences of the newly independent African states created in the aftermath of Western decolonization. Yet their general observations are applicable to Iran in spite of the obvious considerations that Iran is not a 'new state' – its history reaches back over two thousand

and five hundred years, and Shi'ism had been a common bond between the rulers and the ruled since the sixteenth century. They are applicable because, in spite of history and religion, the country in the nineteenth century was in many ways a typically unintegrated society: it was divided horizontally into a ruling court with no organizational roots among the population: and the population itself was fragmented vertically into a number of distinct sectarian, linguistic, and tribal communities.

The Iranian population – estimated at about eight million at the end of the nineteenth century[4] – was divided into a Shi'i majority; a significant Sunni minority of tribal Kurds, Arabs, Baluchis and Turkmans; and small urban concentrations of non-Muslims, such as Armenians, Assyrians, Jews, Zoroastrians, Bahayis, and Azalis. Moreover, the Shi'i majority itself was fragmented into smaller groups, especially in the Ni'mati and Haydari factions and into the Mutashari, Shaykhi, and Karimkhani sects.

Iran was also a mosaic of languages. The population of the central plateau, which totalled less than half the country, was predominantly Persian with an intermingling of Qashqayis, Arabs and Bakhtiyaris. The west and southwest were a mixture of settled, semi-settled, and unsettled Kurds, Lurs, Bakhtiyaris, Arabs, and Mamsamis. The southeast was mostly Baluchi. The northwest was Azari with scattered settlements of Kurds, Shahsavans, Armenians, and Assyrians. The peasantry in the Caspian provinces spoke their own Iranian dialects of Gilaki, Talashi, and Mazandarani. And the population of the northwest was an amalgam of Persians, Kurds, Shahsavans, Afshars, Turkmans, and Timurs.

Much of Iranian history was a history of communal struggles: tribe against tribe, sect against sect, faction against faction, region against region. The dynasties were able to survive these conflicts – at least, for some periods of time – both by taking advantage of existing communalism and by remaining aloof from the social system. The Shahs accepted group rivalry, and invariably encouraged it, as long as this rivalry was directed at other groups and not at the central authorities: rebels were brought to heel not by a standing army nor by a large bureaucracy – for the elites had neither – but by rival communities anxious to enforce the royal writ against their own local enemies. The kings often tolerated religious minorities and unorthodox sects as long as all paid their taxes and accepted the divine right of kings: the aim was to obtain outward obedience, not inward conviction; to make holes in men's pockets, not in their minds. The central governments delegated much of the day-to-day administration of the provinces to regional authorities as long as they were willing to mobilize their followers at times of emergency: the intention was to achieve a limited degree of political security and conformity, not an unlimited measure of administrative uniformity. And the Qajar monarchs, speaking in their own dialect of Turkish with their own tribesmen and in court Persian with their royal administrators, would have viewed linguistic diversity – had they ever contemplated the subject – as a permanent and unalterable fact of life imposed on man by God.

Increasing contact with Europe at the beginning of the twentieth century undermined this traditional relationship between state and society. The old basis of legitimacy – the divine right of kings – was gradually replaced by the concepts of elective institutions, representative governments, and inalienable rights of man. Secularism gradually eroded the political influence of Shi'ism which had served as a narrow but useful bridge spanning the wide gulf between the governors and the governed. The traditional aloofness of the political system from the social system became unacceptable as citizens viewed the government not as a distant court uninvolved in society, but, on the contrary, as the vanguard of economic and social modernization. And the old tolerant attitude toward cultural heterogeneity was gradually supplanted by an intolerant crusade for national homogeneity: tribal nomadism became associated with rural gangsterism, regional autonomy with administrative anarchy, communal variety with political incompatibility, and linguistic diversity with oriental inefficiency.

Iranian intellectuals, on the whole, were aware of the general problem of transforming their unintegrated society into an integrated nation-state. But they all – with one major exception – failed to direct their attention to the problem as a whole. They tended either to dismiss it offhand as one of the many difficulties confronting the country, or else to concentrate on one part of the problem, ignoring the other parts: to focus on class conflicts, forgetting the various communal cleavages fragmenting the population; to discuss the official religious minorities, oblivious to the many unofficial sects and factions within the Shi'i majority; to denounce the tribes, disregarding the other social organizations dividing the country; to advocate the elimination of the visible linguistic minorities, such as the Azaris and the Arabs, unaware of the less visible but equally large marginal-inguistic minorities such as the Gilakis and Mazandranis; and to propose reforms in order to bridge the cultural abyss between the modernized elite and the traditional masses, invariably overlooking the many gaps existing among the various groups in the masses.[5]

The one major exception was Ahmad Kasravi, the most controversial of all modern Iranian intellectuals. To some he was the 'theorist' of modernization.[6] To others he was a 'dangerous iconoclast' who was eventually and justly murdered for trying to destroy the foundations of traditional authority. For many he was the leading historian of the reform movement. To a few he used history both as a grab bag to peddle his theories, and as a weapon with which he carried out character assassinations of his opponents. For some he was a true *philosophe*, 'single-handedly bringing an age of reason and enlightenment to Iran'. For others he was a *mulla* in modern dress, attempting to replace the old superstitions with his own 'highly confused dogma'. He was considered a broad-minded internationalist, a 'humanist' concerned with the problems of the world; or again, a narrow-minded nationalist, a xenophobe who wanted to purge all foreign words from the Persian language. Whereas some saw in him a 'petit bourgeois idealist', an idealogue for the propertied classes, and an apologist for military dictatorship, at the same time others saw in him a 'militant constitutionalist', an uncompromising enemy of the political elite, and a subversive radical whose writings offered a half-way house to many intellectuals as they moved from their Shi'i backgrounds toward the revolutionary socialist movement.

Although most of these descriptions contain an element of the truth, none defines the essence of Kasravi. For his chief concern was neither religion nor irreligion, neither democracy nor dictatorship, neither the preservation nor the overthrow of the establishment, but, far more important to him, the transformation of unintegrated traditional Iran into what he hoped would be an integrated modern Iran. He was, in fact, with all his shortcomings and contradictions, the only intellectual who even tried to tackle the problem of national integration in Iran.

Kasravi's Life: Encounters with Social Cleavages

Kasravi's short autobiography, *Zindigani-yi Man*, reads like a series of painful encounters with the divisions splintering Iran.[7] He was born in 1890 into a middle-class Azari-speaking family in Hukmavar, a poor agricultural district on the outskirts of Tabriz. His mother, illiterate and unconcerned about the world outside her household, came from a peasant background. But his father's father had financed the building of the local mosque and the family continued to serve as the spiritual guides of the orthodox Mutashari community in Hukmavar. However, Kasravi's father, Mir Qasim, was somewhat of a controversial figure.[8] He could not resist denouncing mullas who lived off the charity of their congregations. He persistently tried to dissuade people from going on pilgrimages and performing religious ceremonies at home, arguing that such expenditures were wrong as long as 'relatives and neighbours needed assistance'.[9] He criticized any rituals, sermons, and 'historical misinterpretations' that could inflame old antagonism between Sunnis and Shi'is.[10] And locally more significant, he tried to bridge the gap between the Mutasharis, Shaykhis, and Karimkhanis in Tabriz:

> These conflicts between the three communities had started in the reign of Fath 'Ali Shah, when they often reached the point of bloodshed. In my father's time they rarely reached that point, but they remained one of the main problems in the country. The communities segregated themselves from each other: they prayed, studied and lived separately: they refused to intermarry: and, on the whole, they did all they could to keep alive their ancient animosities. But my father, even though he was a member of the leading Mutashari family in Hukmavar, tried his best to be friends with Shaykhis and Karimkhanis ... I often heard him say that these conflicts had been created by foreigners.[11]

These unorthodox views had unfortunate repercussions. The mother's side of the family drifted away: 'They were the sort who regularly performed ceremonies at home and who went on pilgrimages to Karbala at least once every three years'.[12] And politically more unfortunate, the local Mutasharis began to harass them because of his father's associations with the Shaykhis:

> One day an unpleasant incident occurred which we always remembered with sorrow. The young and dashing nephew of Hajji Muhammad – the leading Shaykhi in Hukmavar – accosted a Mutashari lady in the Tabriz bazaar. The Mutasharis immediately used this as a pretext to inflame communalism. And because my father was a friend of the young man, Mutashari thugs threatened him as he returned home from work that evening. The following day, they broke into our home dragging him off to the Crown Prince for punishment. This incident blew into a full-scale conflict, with the Tabriz *Shaykh al-Islam* representing the Shaykhis and the *Mujtahid* supporting the interests of the Mutasharis. And the crisis did not blow over until Tenran intervened. But by that time a family feud had begun between us and the Hajji Muhammad.[13]

Although Kasravi's father was unconventional in his social attitudes, he was very conventional in the upbringing of his son. He named him after his elder brother, Mir Ahmad, who had died on his way home from the seminary in Najaf to take up the spiritual leadership of the local Mutashari congregation. He forbade him to play with the neighbourhood urchins. He educated him to fill the gap left by his uncle's death, even forcing him to go through the 'painful' ritual of head-shaving before starting the *maktab* school.[14] And his last words on his death bed were: 'My son must continue his education, because there must always be a scholar in our family. But he must never live as a parasite, like other mullas'.[15]

Kasravi had finished only the *maktab* when his father died, but circumstances forced him to disregard this final testament. The rug market in Europe had collapsed, ruining their family carpet business in Tabriz. There was no *madrasah* school in the vicinity. And he became increasingly aware that education in his traditional society was a one-way passage into clerical ranks, a destination he had no desire to reach.[16] Consequently, he gave up his studies and found employment in the Tabriz bazaar helping manage a carpet business. For three years he successfully supported his mother and younger brothers until his father's old friends, by constant pressure and generous offers of financial help, persuaded him to enrol in a newly opened *madrasah* in Tabriz.

The constitutional revolution of 1905 broke out while Kasravi was studying at this school. He wrote in his memoirs that he was immediately attracted by the concern of the reformers for the 'progress of the people and the future enlightenment of the country'.[17] But he also confessed that he kept his sympathies hidden, because his mother's family and his Mutashari community in Hukmavar were staunch conservatives.[18] He shut himself up in the house with a collection of books, only occasionally venturing out to watch his environment torn by a bloody civil war. In Tabriz he observed the royalists entrenched in the lower class Mutashari districts of Davachi and Sarkhab, and the constitutionalists barricaded in the more middle class Shaykhi and Armenian precincts of Nubar, Khiaban, and Amir Khizi.[19] And he heard from friends how other cities in Iran were increasingly splintered by either similar Shaykhi-Mutashari sects or old Haydari-Ni'mati rivalries: 'One of the regrettable themes in Iranian history has been this factionalism between Haydaris and Ni'matis. We did not know exactly how these two rival groups came into existence, but we do know that since the sixteenth century and even during the constitutional revolution they divided many of the cities into antagonistic districts.'[20]

The civil war had ended by the time Kasravi graduated from the *madrasah*. At first he tried to go into business in the bazaar but family friends again pressured him into religion, arguing that Hukmavar needed a competent mulla and that they had not educated him all these years so that he would become a mere tradesman: 'If you wanted to become a merchant why did you bother to study?'[21] This was to be the last time that social pressures determined his final decision. In his maiden sermon he shocked the audience by not preaching in the usual Arabic, which only the very few educated Azaris could understand. He spent a great deal of time reading books in Turkish and Arabic on European astronomy, because the West, unlike the East, could calculate accurately the actual movement of the stars. He later remarked in his memoirs that 'it was astronomy that attracted me to Western knowledge'.[22] He sent his younger brother to study modern subjects in a new secular school. He outraged his parishioners by not wearing the conventional attire of the mullas, such as a long cloak, a large turban, green shoes, white trousers, and an unkempt beard. Instead he wore simple shoes, short scarfs, machine-woven socks, and, perhaps more unusual, glasses for his weak eyes. And politically more dangerous, he openly criticized the conservative Mutashari *uluma* for taking advantage of the Russian occupation in 1911 to settle old scores with their liberal Shaykhi opponents. In later years he described how he had forced himself to watch the barbarous executions of these liberal martyrs so that he would never forget the 'savagery' of the bigoted mullas.[23] These unorthodox habits and unreserved attitudes had obvious consequences. The local population of Hukmavar began to look upon him as 'an imitator of foreigners', 'a Babi sympathizer', or perhaps even 'a secret unbeliever'. And their increasing hostility finally persuaded him to give up preaching in the mosque and to become instead a teacher of Arabic in the American missionary school in Tabriz. In return for Arabic he received English lessons so that he could pursue his interests in the 'new knowledge' of the West.

At the American school Kasravi encountered another form of communalism. The student body, which, for some time, had been divided socially into Christians, Shi'is, and Ali-Ilahi – a Shi'i sect that raised the martyr Ali to the same level as the prophet Muhammad – became factionalized politically into three warring groups as a result of the World War. The Shi'is were sympathetic to the Central Powers, especially to Germany. The Armenians and Assyrians supported whole-heartedly the Allies, particularly the Russians. And the Ali-Ilahis refused to take sides in a European war which they felt was no concern of theirs. Although Kasravi was contemptuous of these disputes, he was unwillingly and by default dragged into them. And he escaped a severe beating at the hands of the Christians only by the timely intervention of the city law enforcement authorities. Depressed by this incident and feeling that his presence could spark off similar unpleasant incidents, he resigned from the faculty.

For a short while he was unemployed – making use of his time writing a textbook on how to learn Arabic – until the Ministry of Education, opening its first secondary school in Azarbayjan, hired him as an instructor of Arabic. He had been teaching there for a few short months when the Russian Revolution disintegrated the Tsarist army in northern Iran. As the regiments melted away, the reformers in Azarbayjan revived their secular Democratic Party, took over the administration of Tabriz, and began to cast threatening eyes on those who had collaborated with the

Russians. In Hukmavar, conservatives who had previously quarantined Kasravi as an 'undesirable liberal' now sought his protection and influence among the city Democrats. He willingly gave them this assistance, believing that 'bygones must remain bygones.'[24] And in the severe famine of 1918, when religious leaders in Hukmavar refused to distribute state food to the poor because they considered such grain as 'unclean', he, remembering his family's moral responsibility to the community, organized the Democratic Party's local food relief committee. He noted in his memoirs that he helped the destitute at a time when they needed his assistance, knowing well that their hostility would return as soon as the crisis ended.

This prediction was fulfilled sooner than expected. Before the famine was over, northern Iran was invaded by the Ottomans who immediately helped the religious conservatives to form an Ittihad-i Islam Party against the Democrats, and encouraged Azari separatists to demand the independence of Azarbayjan. Kasravi, fearing for his life in Hukmavar, especially now that his conservative mother was dead, moved to a more liberal and prosperous district within the city walls of Tabriz. This move, however, proved unnecessary, for within a few months the Ottomans were forced to retreat. And as they evacuated Azarbayjan, the local Democrats, headed by Shaykh Muhammad Khiabani, took over the administration of the whole province. Although Kasravi had great admiration for Khiabani – especially for his eloquent speeches delivered at the Shaykhi mosque in the precinct of Khiaban during the constitutional revolution, and for his role in the formation of the Democratic Party in the national Majlis – he had major differences of policy with him over communal issues. Kasravi opposed Khiabani's decision to eliminate old enemies, convinced that this would keep alive the Shyakhi-Mutashari conflicts. He spoke out against Khiabani's separatist drift: the changing of their organization's name from the Democratic Party branch in Azarbayjan to the Democratic Party of Azarbayjan; the recruitment into the party of the Azari journalists who had earlier supported the Ottoman demand for Azarbayjan independence; the establishment of a provincial council challenging the authority of the central government; and, as a last straw, the declaration of independence for the Republic of Azadistan. Kasravi, finding himself at the head of a small minority within the Democrats in Tabriz, with his life threatened and his followers in prison, decided to flee for the safety of Tehran.

In the capital Kasravi joined the Ministry of Justice. As a trouble-shooter for this ministry, he travelled extensively during the next ten years, between 1920 and 1930. Returning to Azarbayjan in the wake of Khiabani's defeat, he found the tribes up in arms, while Kurds, Armenians and Assyrians fought for their own states on the shores of Lake Urmia. Visiting Mazandaran soon after the collapse of the separatist movement led by Mirza Kuchik Khan, he discovered a new aspect of the communal problem. He found that the local population spoke neither Persian nor Turkish, and, therefore, to communicate with them in court proceedings he had to learn their Mazandarani dialect. 'It was the first time I had encountered one of these marginal-linguistic groups. In fact, it was the very first time I had even been aware of their existence in Iran.'[25] And arriving in Khuzistan at a time when the region was virtually autonomous, he experienced again, at first hand, the disruptions caused by communalism. Shaykh Khaz'al, the leading Arab chieftain, had rallied the Arab tribes, had usurped the functions normally performed by the ministries, and was now threatening to declare the independence of Khuzistan. Moreover, the local Persian minority was sharply divided into Haydari-Ni'mati factions, while the Arab majority – even though exploited by the Shaykh – felt itself 'an integral part of the Arab nation'.[26] Kasravi did his best to preserve what little remained of the Ministry of Justice, until the commander-in-chief of the army, Riza Khan, defeated the Arab tribes and re-established the authority of the central government. This victory, however, brought Kasravi into a head-on collision with the army officers, especially with the Governor General, who, while 'plundering the province in order to line his own pockets', was usurping the constitutional jurisdiction of civilian courts with unconstitutional military tribunals.[27] Finding that the Prime Minister favoured the army over the Ministry of Justice, Kasravi resigned his post in Khuzistan and returned to Tehran.

The Ministry was unable to reassign him directly to another position. So he spent the next few months synthesizing the information he had collected in the southwest on tribalism and religious factionalism into a book entitled *Tarikh-i Pansad Salah-*

i Khuzistan (Five Hundred Year History of Khuzistan). By the time he finished this work he was appointed High Inspector for special disputes. This post kept him mostly in the capital, occasionally taking him to the provinces to solve especially difficult cases. One category of such cases were land disputes between neighbouring villages. He wrote in his memoirs: 'One group of peasants would claim a piece of land. Another group would put in a counterclaim. And invariably these conflicts would result in bloodshed.'[28] As High Inspector, Kasravi gained a reputation for toughness, hard work, incorruptibility, and courage. It was this last trait that ended his career in the ministry. Riza Khan, the commander-in-chief who conquered Khuzistan, had deposed the Qajar dynasty in 1925 and had crowned himself Riza Shah. Having obtained full power, he proceeded to modernize the country, while, at the same time, stabilizing his own position in the true traditional fashion – by accumulating landed estates for his own family. This he did mainly by reclaiming for himself villages that had previously belonged to the Qajars, but which sales and gifts had alienated to private citizens generations earlier. In retaliation against such reclamations, a number of evicted farmers in Mazandaran took their case to Kasravi. And Kasravi, refusing to be intimidated like other judges and believing strongly that land should belong to those who cultivated it, decided in favour of the farmers and against the Shah.[29] Not unexpectedly, the government soon pressured him to resign from the judiciary.

From the time Kasravi lost his government salary in 1930 until his assassination in 1946, he earned a living partly as a private attorney in Tehran and partly as a lecturer of jurisprudence in the Law College.[30] But most of these sixteen years were devoted to the unrelenting mission of attempting to formulate and propagate an ideology which he hoped would transform Iran from an unintegrated society into an integrated modern state. In these years, especially after the relaxation of censorship following Riza Shah's abdication in 1941, Kasravi published over fifty books, booklets, and pamphlets. Many of them dealt, either directly or indirectly, with the theme of national integration. He discussed the problem of class divisions mainly in *Aiyin* (The Creed), *Dadgah* (Court of Justice), *Afsaran-i Ma* (Our Officers), *Sar Navisht-i Iran Chah Khvad Bud?* (What Will Be the Fate of

Iran?), *Dar Rah-i Siyasat* (In Politics), *Kar va Pishah va Pul* (Work, Trade, and Money), and *Dawlat Bayad Bah Ma Pasakh Dahad* (The Government Must Give Us an Answer). He focused on the question of communalism in *Shi'igari* (Shi'i-playing), *Sufigari* (Sufi-playing), *Bahayigari* (Baha'i-playing), *Dar Piramvan-i Islam* (Concerning Islam), *Davari* (Judgment), *Zabani-i Farsi* (The Persian Language), and *Hafiz Chah Mi-Guyad?* (What Does Hafiz Say?). His general ideology was summarized in editorials, articles, and notes written for his journal *Payman* (The Promise), which appeared regularly every month between 1933 and 1942; in his daily newspaper *Parcham* (The Flag), which was published during the war and was superseded first by the weekly *Parcham-i Haftegi* (The Weekly Flag) and later by the monthly *Parcham*; and in a series of such short books as *Din va Jahan* (The World and Ideology), *Inqilab Chist?* (What Is Revolution?), *Farhang Chist?* (What Is Education?), *Dar Piramvan-i Adabiyat* (Concerning Literature), *Dar Piramvan-i Ruman* (Concerning Fiction), *Dar Piramvan-i Khurd* (Concerning Wisdom), *Zaban-i Pak* (A Pure Language), *Imruz Chah Bayad Kard?* (What Must Be Done Today?), and *Varjavand Bunyad* (Worthy Foundations). Moreover, many of his other works also dealt indirectly with the question of national integration. For example, he admitted that he had written his popular history of Iran – *Tarikh-i Mashrutah-i Iran* (History of the Iranian Constitution) and *Tarikh-i Hijdah Salah-i Azarbayjan* (Eighteen Year History of Azarbayjan) – with three main aims in mind: to show that the destiny of Azarbayjan lay with the rest of Iran; to illustrate how the reform movement had been damaged seriously by internal conflicts; and to prove that the constitutional revolution of 1905 had in the long run failed because it had been unable to eliminate the various divisions splintering the general population.[31]

Kasravi's Ideology of Solidarism

'Man,' according to Kasravi, 'is born with an inherent desire to progress.'[32] This creates two very different types of struggle in the world: the struggle of man against nature to improve the human condition; and the struggle of man against man to improve his personal condition.[33] The former is beneficial since it tends to integrate and solidify individuals into society. But the latter is harmful because it dissolves society into an amorphous mass of isolated and conflicting individuals.[34]

The struggle of man against man was predominant in the natural condition of humanity. Families – separated from each other by dialects, by such geographical barriers as deserts, jungles, and mountains, and by the constant competition for scarce resources – came in contact only to rob each other of 'their wives, children, and few material belongings.'[35] Fearing to be an easy prey if they settled, families were on the constant move from hiding place to hiding place. Thus, life was poor, solitary, nasty, brutish, short, and nomadic.

The desire for progress, however, took man out of this state of nature into civil society.[36] Groups of families began to coalesce in order to work together against the elements: to grow crops, raise cattle, irrigate land, mine, manufacture, and trade their wares.[37] Eventually, common languages and urban societies came into existence. Kasravi often stressed that the English word 'civilization', derived from the Latin 'civil', originally meant not merely the ability to manufacture, but, far more important, the capacity to live harmoniously in one place.[38] He, therefore, coined a new Persian term *shahrigari* (city-living), to contrast it with *biyabangari* (wilderness-living), and to be interchangeable with the Arabic word *tamaddun* (civilization).[39]

But paradoxically, as societies developed their struggle against nature, they inevitably became fragmented by the division of labour.[40] And with the increasing division of labour, the old struggle of man against man gradually seeped back into society, turning into a torrent during the process of industrialization, when wealth was consolidated, in a few hands, when injustice and inequality reached new proportions, and when modern means of violence and mass communication were invented:

> Although such inventions as the telegraph, telephone, and steam engine are wonderful in that they help man in his battle against backwardness, they also have the harmful effect of intensifying conflict between individuals. Take for example the railway. In former ages, a farmer, isolated in his own small village, was in competition only with those in his immediate vicinity. But in the modern age, the railway has placed him in constant competition with millions of other farmers throughout the width and breadth of the whole country.[41]

This reintroduction of conflict into society was the source of all evil.[42] It disrupted mankind's march toward human progress.[43] It caused internal and international wars.[44] It diseased the body-politic, preventing some organs from performing their functions, hindering the growth of others, and eventually terminating in death.[45] Without social strife the world would be an 'earthly paradise', for only one per cent of its problems were caused by the natural environment. The other ninety-nine per cent had their origin in man's conflict with his fellow man.[46]

Since civil society was intrinsically departmentalized by division of labour, some superior force was needed to join the various parts into a larger whole. This force was *din* (a term used to denote more than the usual meaning 'religion'), an ideology that effectively integrated the individual into a nation, instilling in him social consciousness, cultural ethos, and values oriented toward the public good:

> My use of the term *din* is different from those of others. I use it to describe an ideology that teaches people the true meaning of life and gives them a practical code of ethics. For example, what is the real function of the division of labour? Its purpose is not to give licence to the various occupations to make as much money as possible at the expense of others. On the contrary, its real purpose is to permit each profession to perform the duties necessary for the prosperity of the whole society. When groups and individuals have a code of ethics they are able to live in harmony. And living in harmony, they are able to pursue the main goal of struggling against nature.[47]

For Kasravi, only true ideologies – not coercive powers, nor laws nor state institutions – could hold together a mass of conflicting groups and individuals into a collective nation. The state institutions were merely instruments implementing the goals of an ideology, they were not the creators of that ideology.[48] Laws, policemen, and prisons simply punished those who harmed society, they did not bring into existence societies. And government organizations could at most protect the citizen from internal and external enemies, they could not, in any real way, bind an amorphous mass of clashing wills into a coherent and organic solidarity.

Islam, in its original form, had been a genuine ideology, for it had effectively solidified, at least for an extensive period of time, a large number of separate tribes, towns, regions, and peoples –

each with their own petty and rival pagan gods – into a broad Muslim Empire with One Omnipotent God. But over the years, Islam had lost its internal cohesiveness, first dividing into the Sunni and the Shi'i branches, with each later subdividing into numerous competing factions. There was, therefore, no longer a true Muslim ideology (*din*) in the contemporary world. There were, instead, a large number of small Muslim sects (*kish*). And as long as each Islamic state was factionalized by these rival sects, it was unable to achieve the internal co-operation necessary to wage the all-important struggle for national progress.[49]

Kasravi's View of Iran

Kasravi, like most of his contemporaries, saw nothing but backwardness in Iran: poverty and economic backwardness; ignorance and social backwardness; and sharp fluctuations from despotic stability to chaotic instability, a sure sign of political backwardness. But unlike his contemporaries, he refused to accept the stock explanations for this deplorable state of affairs. He argued against the racial theory – advocated by antisemitic writers – that the country's problems had their origin in the Arab invasions, by pointing out the obvious fact that Iran had been independent of the Arabs since the third century after Muhammad.[50] He criticized the liberal view that despotism had been the main factor in retarding development by claiming that the period of 'democracy' from 1905 until 1925 had produced little progress, but, on the contrary, had resulted in the absolutism of Riza Shah.[51] And he dismissed as paranoia the popularly held belief that Western Machiavellianism lurked behind Iran's misfortunes. Such claims, according to him, were unsubstantiated by facts and the actual behaviour of European states.[52] He even commented that his father, in insisting that foreigners were responsible for religious factionalism, was showing his 'ignorance' of national and international politics.[53]

Kasravi's own explanation why his environment remained backward was direct: the country was underdeveloped because it was fragmented into conflicting groups.[54] The imperialists had not created the various religious sects: they had merely manipulated what they had found in existence.[55] The Arabs had not rammed their culture down the throats of Iranians: on the contrary, the population had willingly accepted Islam; and in the first centuries it had consistently failed to unite behind rebels who had tried to overthrow the Arabs.[56] The economy was poor not because it lacked natural resources, but because the occupational groups refused to co-operate in the true fashion of the division of labour.[57] And Riza Shah had not suddenly appeared from the 'primitive jungles of Africa', but had risen up from the indigenous population.[58] In fact, during the twenty year period when the masses had been able to elect their own representatives, they had constantly 'voted' for 'divisive politicians', thus paving the way for Riza Shah's rise to power:

> We all know that Iran is backward. Today most Iranians with a grain of intelligence are saddened by this situation. And their grief is justifiable, because our country was at one time a great empire while now it is a weak and small state. What lies at the root of this drastic decline? At the beginning of this century, reformers could answer that the main culprits were the despots who had a vested interest in keeping their subjects ignorant and unenlightened. But after twenty years of constitutional government, we cannot, in good conscience, give the same answer. For we know that the main blame rests not with the rulers but with the ruled. Yes, the chief reason of underdevelopment in Iran, perhaps in most eastern countries, is disunity among the masses.[59]
>
> ... The worst calamity that can befall a nation is disunity. A people who share a common territory and live together should never be divided into rival factions. Contemporary Iran is a good example of a nation that has not heeded this warning – it is now suffering from the worst miseries of backwardness.[60]
>
> ... The famous heroes of modern Iran – Amir Kabir, Sipasalar, Amin al-Dawlah, Malcolm Khan, Tabattabai, Khurasani, Tehrani, Shaykh al-Islam, Kuchik Khan, Khiabani, and Taqi Khan – all, without exception, failed to achieve any lasting reforms because they were unable to grasp this fundamental fact – that the population is torn apart into rival groups.[61]

Rivalry was caused by divisive ideas – by conflicting theories (*andishah-ha-yi zid-i ham*), misleading concepts (*andishah-ha-yi gumrah*), absurd visions (*andishah-ha-yi bi-huvdah*), clashing assumptions (*andishah-ha-yi guvnaguvn*), corrupt sentiments (*andishah-ha-yi aluvdah*) and disharmonious ideas (*ikhtalaf-i aqiydah*). As Kasravi stated repeatedly and often monotonously:

'Iran is backward because false ideas and corrupt sentiments have divided the population into conflicting groups'.[62]

The ideas and sentiments Kasravi considered disruptive fall into four categories: the sectarian religious creeds; the linguistic ties; the tribal affiliations; and the class divisions that separated the governors from the governed, the rich from the poor, the 'educated elite from the uneducated masses':[63]

> One of the worst maladies afflicting Iran is factionalism. Factionalism caused by religious sectarianism: I can count fourteen separate sects in existence, each of them with their own goals and interests. Factionalism caused by tribal and linguistic differences: there are at least eight linguistic groups, each of them rival and competitor with the others. But these are only the more obvious cleavages, for there are other less obvious ones. For example, there is the factionalism caused by the wide gulf between classes – between the western educated and the traditional masses, between the city and the countryside, between the young and the old generations.[64]

Of these four categories, Kasravi directed much of his attention at the religious sects, which he often enumerated to a total of fourteen: Sunnis, Sufis, Shaykhis, Mutasharis, Karimkhanis, Bahayis, Azalis, Ali-Ilahis, Jews, Armenians, Assyrians, Zoroastrians, 'dialectical materialists', and the followers of Greek philosophy. Although he had theological and metaphysical criticisms of each of the fourteen, his main objection to all of them was that they were 'states within the state':

> We have listed fourteen sects in Iran. This means fourteen separate states, fourteen separate goals, fourteen separate interests. Some readers may not deem this as very important, but it does mean that the population is divided into segregated communities, all with their own leaders and followers, all viewing the government as an antagonistic force, all reluctant to pay taxes, and all considering themselves apart from the rest of the nation. They live in this land, taking advantage of its benefits, but they refuse to behave as responsible citizens of the state.[65]

Shi'ism received the brunt of his attacks. It was a 'perversion whose origin lay neither in ethics nor in theological issues, but in a sordid struggle for dynastic power'.[66] It hindered historical progress because it refused to accept the notion that man, by his own efforts, could improve society.[67] It had proved not to be a true ideology (*din*) by the simple test that it had fractured into a number of small sects (*kish*).[68] It disrupted the country by insisting that its own laws should be enforced on the rest of the population.[69] Worst of all, it fostered anti-state attitudes. It differentiated sharply between the government (*dawlat*) and the people (*millat*); discouraged the faithful from serving in the armed forces, working in the ministries, and paying their taxes to the 'unclean' treasury. Instead it encouraged them to pray to a supra-national authority and to waste national wealth on unnecessary pilgrimages to foreign shrines. And, worst of all, it preached an anti-democratic political theory, claiming that sovereignty resided in the Imams not in the people:[70]

> Shi'ism and democracy are two contradictory forces. According to the former, the authority to rule resides in the Imam and his *uluma*. But according to the latter, it rests with the people and their representatives. Some Shi'i theologians, however, try to brush away this contradiction by arguing that democracy really means the rule of the majority and that the majority in Iran desire the guidance of the *uluma*. But this line of argument has two main fallacies. First, it ignores a fundamental principle in democracy – that no group, such as mullas, can claim special privileges. Second, it confuses true democracy, which is representative government, with majority rule, forgetting that if democracy meant the rule of the majority then Iran should have not obtained a constitution, since at the time of the revolution the bulk of the population – especially the peasantry and the lower classes – wanted royal despotism.[71]

Kasravi's critique of tribalism was less elaborate since his reading public shared an inherent prejudice against the nomadic way of life. The tribes were a 'disruptive element', rushing to arms whenever the central government showed the slightest signs of weakness.[72] They still lived in the 'state of nature', terrorizing, plundering, and murdering their more developed neighbours.[73] Economically they were unproductive, wasting time travelling from their winter to summer quarters.[74] And, most important of all, they were petty kingdoms with their own internal autonomy:

> My objection to the tribes is not limited to the fact that they are predominantly nomadic, but that they retain their exclusive social organizations. Each tribe considers itself separate from the rest of the population, refusing to recognize the authority of the central government, ignoring the administration of the national ministries,

and obeying only the commands of their own hereditary chieftains. One cannot but label such groups as enemies of the people.[75]

His opposition to the linguistic minorities started in the early days of the constitutional revolution, when the Shah had tried to sow dissension among the reformers by cultivating differences between Persian and Turkish-speaking liberals in Tehran.[76] This opposition was reinforced when the Ottomans tried to exploit Azari sentiments in Tabriz. Soon after the First World War, he attacked these separatists in a short book entitled *Zaban-i Azari: Ya Zaban-i Bastan-i Azarbayjan* (The Azari Language: Or the Ancient Language of Azarbayjan). Here he claimed that the people of Azarbayjan had originally spoken pure Azari – the Turkish words being introduced later by the Seljuks – and, therefore, their real attachment was not to Turkish but to ancient Azari, which had ceased to exist except in a few isolated villages. His opposition to the linguistic minorities, however, became more vocal during the Second World War, when the Soviets supported Azari grievances against the central government. They argued that since Azarbayjan had its own distinct language, it constituted a genuine nation (*millat*), and, consequently, had the inalienable right to form its own provincial government within the framework of the Iranian state and to use its own language in schools, offices, and law courts. Kasravi vehemently denounced such ideas on two main grounds. First, they opened up a whole Pandora's box of evils; 'If the Turkish-speakers gain these privileges, other minorities – such as the Arabs, Kurds, Gilakis, Mazandaranis, and so on – have equal claims to demand the same concessions. And if they gain them, what will remain of Iranian sovereignty?'[77] Second, he believed that linguistic diversity was inherently disruptive, arguing that: 'These languages are all good, but their existence within one state causes dissension. It is always best to have one common language in a nation.'[78] He dismissed counter-arguments that some countries, such as Belgium and Switzerland, prospered with more than one language, by retorting that Iran was neither Belgium nor Switzerland. Moreover, there was no reason why Iran should imitate the 'mistakes' of others.[79]

Kasravi directed most of his attacks at the linguistic and religious conflicts, but his first main book – *Aiyin*, – published in 1932 – was aimed at the theory of class struggle popularized by a group of Marxist intellectuals headed by Dr Taqi Arani. Although Kasravi admired Arani's intellect, and defended his group at their political trials in 1938, he attacked their theories persistently, especially after 1941 when they rallied a large segment of the intelligentsia and the urban working class into the communist Tudah Party. For Kasravi, Marxism – with such conflict-provoking concepts as 'life is a constant battle for survival', 'capitalism is exploitation', and the 'past is a history of class struggles' – destroyed social unity by dividing each nation along class lines: 'Civilization means the ability to live harmoniously. Barbarism, on the other hand, means the lack of harmony. Socialist parties in Europe, in appealing to the masses with Marxist propaganda, are splintering their nations into competing classes, and so are threatening to revive a new age of barbarism.'[80]

Kasravi's remedy for curing the malady was as simple as his diagnosis of the disease. It was to replace disharmony with harmony, disunity with unity, and diversity with uniformity. He hoped to supplant class conflict with occupational collaboration;[81] to replace the minority languages with Persian 'purified' of its Arabic and Turkish words;[82] to transform the heterogeneous nomads into a homogeneous farming population;[83] and to supersede religious sectarianism by social solidarism where all would feel themselves an integral part of the nation:

> What is patriotism (*mihan parasti*)? Some complain, how can one love a piece of land – a village, a hill, or a field. Others claim that all men are the same, therefore we should not distinguish between the citizens of one country and the citizens of another country. And some people believe that love for a nation is a new form of paganism, distracting man from his true goal, God. But all these objections fail to understand the true meaning of nationalism. I repeat what I have often said: nationalism means the original contract for unity which individuals sign when they agree to constitute a nation. When twenty million people, sharing the same territory, form a nation, they are, in fact, agreeing to work together to improve their environment, to share jointly the hardships as well as the rewards, the grief as well as the happiness involved. For example, if there is an outbreak of tribal banditry in Kirman, the inhabitants of Azarbayjan, Khuzistan, and Gilan should willingly send help and should not shrug their shoulders and say 'it has nothing to do with me'.[84]

The strategy he advocated for attaining the goal of solidarity covered two areas: social reforms alleviating the objective differences between the various groups; and, more important, cultural reforms replacing subnational sentiments with a strong feeling of national consciousness. The former could be accomplished directly through the political system. But the latter had to be achieved indirectly through education transforming the social system.

Riza Shah's social reforms won Kasravi's approval, especially the abolition of such 'feudal' titles as *ilkhan*, *saltanah*, and *dawlah*; the elimination of local privileges, customs, and costumes; the expulsion of the *mullas* from public life; the secularization of law; the granting of certain rights to women;[85] the creation of a modern army and a new administrative structure; and the forced settlement of some of the nomadic tribes.[86] After Riza Shah's abdication, Kasravi pressed ahead for more improvements, particularly improvements that would narrow the gulf between the classes. He advocated laws limiting wealth, so that individuals would be neither too rich nor too poor:[87] new factories were to be owned not by a few industrialists but by many 'small capitalists' with joint-stock holdings.[88] He opposed state ownership because he believed that citizens had a 'natural' right to private property.[89] 'Parasites' who did not perform necessary functions in society – such as gamblers, romantic novelists, obscurantist poets, fortune-tellers, snake-charmers, passion-play actors, prayer-writers, and petty usurers – were to be outlawed by the state.[90] Villages were to be distributed among the peasantry, because moderate equality was desirable and 'land should belong to those who till it'.[91] And the political power of the ruling elite was to be destroyed:

> A small selfish inbred elite has been monopolizing all power in our country for the last sixty years. Only its members can become ministers, under-secretaries, generals, and heads of departments. They oppose progress, abhor the idea that we can catch up with others, and hope to perpetuate the present unfortunate condition, with the central government weak, the tribes up in arms, the ministries unable to enforce legislation, the people distrustful of the state, the majilis a picture of ridicule, and the mullas preaching false ideas to the public.[92] ... This elite is powerful and well interconnected. Its members are not only in the ministries but also in all fields of public life. They have not

just appeared recently, but were in power during the days of Qajar despotism, during the constitutional revolution, during the years after the revolution, during Riza Shah's reign, and now during our own time. *If we do not cut their roots they will always remain in power*. (His own stress.)[93]

The phrase 'cut their roots', however, did not mean a violent revolution. He explained its meaning in three polemics directed at contemporaries who advocated seizure of power: 'What Must Be Done Today', 'Why We Are Not Politicians', and in a collection of essays compiled under the title *Inqilab Chist?* (What Is Revolution?). Here he argued that radicals who hoped to achieve major social reforms through a violent seizure of political power would inevitably fail. They would fail because it would be impossible to unite the existing rival groups into an effective mass movement. The street riots of November 1942 had proved this: 'While some demonstrated against the government and others came out in support of the government, youngsters shouted communist slogans, mullas demanded the return of the *shari'a* and the poor plundered stores and bakeries'.[94] Even in the unlikely event that revolutionaries were able to bypass this hurdle and carry through a successful *putsch*, their victory would be hollow, for the real problem of the country – factionalism among the masses – would remain. The seizure of power and the decreeing of legislation were useless as long as the people remained divided by 'corrupt' ideas:

> We stress that we must first and foremost deal with the problem of corruption in the masses and only later turn to other issues. For example, the distribution of villages is meaningless unless the peasant who receives land knows the ethics of life and the ability to work with fellow citizens. If he is unable to co-operate with others, land reform will merely create new problems.[95]

Thus, for Kasravi a true revolutionary in his environment was not someone who attacked the elite with slogans calling for the seizure of power, but someone who gradually undermined the elite by reforming the attitudes of the public:

> If we desire to remedy the ills of Iran in a statesman-like fashion, we must focus our attention on the source of the malady – the masses. We must save the people from corrupting ideas, instil in them a love for their country, arouse in them the instinct for social progress, teach

them to make personal sacrifices for this collective goal, and unite them into a national consciousness.[96]

Public education, therefore, became the *deus ex machina* for Kasravi. The expansion of state lycées and literacy classes, together with the closing of parochial schools and community printing presses, would gradually replace minority dialects with one dominant language – Persian: 'The minorities must understand that diversity causes disunity and disunity prevents progress. In order to improve the condition of all, including their own, they must give up their own languages and adopt Persian.'[97] The reading of Iranian history would teach the people their national heritage and the harmful effects of religious sectarianism: 'The sects know all about the petty squabbles that created them, but they know nothing about the major calamities that have struck our country, such as the Mongol invasions. The teaching of our national history must replace the sectarian interpretations of the past.'[98] Such instruction, moreover, would convince all that they are an integral part of the nation and that racial and linguistic diversity is a relatively recent phenomenon introduced into the country by Turkic incursions.[99] The encouragement of literacy and scientific knowledge would undermine the power of the reactionary mullas for it would eliminate ignorance and popular superstitions.[100] Professional training would yield doctors, engineers, geologists and other modern professional skills needed to harness the forces of nature.[101] Proper upbringing of children would produce a new generation of citizens conscious of their responsibilities and aware of their duties in a constitutional democracy.[102] It would 'erase' class conflicts by showing each occupational group its true role in the division of labour;[103] narrow the gap between the elite and the masses by pointing out the necessary activities performed by the state, such as law and order, public administration, and social guidance;[104] and safeguard against the dangers of man fighting against man by stressing the essential need for unity in order to wage the important war against nature:

> Readers often write agreeing with us that the way out of our backwardness is through national unity. Everyone seems to realize now the advantages of eliminating internal conflicts, but many still do not realize that national unity can result only through ideological

> unity. Those who sincerely desire this unity must teach others the need to eradicate the false ideas that cause divisiveness in Iran. We must concentrate our efforts on exposing the fallacies and harmful effects of these divisive ideas.[105]

Strict censorship and the burning of such 'unhealthy' works as Sufi poetry, romantic novels, and religious mumbojumbo could prevent the public from being led astray.[106] 'Healthy' books – accurate histories, scientific studies, and, by implication, his own works – could guide the masses onto the right road to 'national salvation'.[107] Hierarchical and 'feudal' concepts could be gradually eroded by careful choice of vocabulary, especially by the avoidance of such obsolete but popular expressions as *sarkar* (esquire), *jinab* (Your Excellency), *hazrat* (Your Highness), *bandah* (bondsman), *ghulam* (slave), and *chakar-i khanahzadah* (household servant).[108] Moreover, a purge of the vocabulary would eliminate the confusing terms introduced into Persian from foreign languages, especially from Arabic and Turkish.[109] The word *millat* was a case in point.[110] In Arabic it originally meant a 'religious community', but during the constitutional revolution it was widely and mistakenly used in Iran to denote the French term '*nation*'. Consequently, Iranians continued to confuse the secular concept of the modern state with the traditional notion of the religious community. Accordingly, the obvious way out of the difficulty was to replace the Arabic *millat* with the Persian term *mardum* (people). For Kasravi only by supplanting unclear alien expressions with clear Persian vocabulary would the intellectuals be able to instil the feeling of national solidarity among the people.

Kasravi and Gökalp

There are striking similarities between Kasravi and Gökalp, his better-known and older contemporary in Turkey. Both were leading theorists of social solidarism in their respective countries, having been born in mixed border regions, living through old communal conflicts, and devoting their intellectual energies to submerging these communal groups into new nation-states. Both took the daring step – in the case of Kasravi it proved to be fatal – of considering Islam as a 'historical phenomenon' which, like other major religions, had in its own time united diverse communities into one *Umma* but which could no longer function as the main cement of social solidarity. Both considered this cement to be neither laws nor institutions but a social consciousness instilled in the public through mass education. They, therefore, became first and foremost educationalists who perceived the 'revolution' not as the overthrow of the establishment but as the transformation of public values. To achieve this transformation, they gathered around themselves devoted disciples and eventually became highly intolerant of rival teachings. This intolerance was more marked in Kasravi because he – unlike Gökalp and Durkheim – saw occupational specialization produced by the modern division of labour not as a new social link, but, on the contrary, as an added threat toward social dissolution. Only total ideological uniformity could prevent final dissolution. And both were anxious to distinguish between being modernizers – which they were – and Westernizers, which they did not consider themselves to be: they were keen to adopt the technical aspects of the West, especially the means of developing the economy, but they were also equally keen to keep out the cultural aspects of the West which they deemed harmful to social solidarity, such as the liberal stress on individualism, the socialist theory of the class struggle, and the anarchist concept of the state as an 'unnecessary evil'. Since Kasravi was well-read in contemporary Turkish political thought, one is tempted to suspect that at least some of his ideas were inspired by Gökalp. These suspicions, however, cannot be proved, for he constantly claimed that 'all his theories were original', frequently accused other writers of snobbery for quoting Western philosophers, and he himself consistently abstained from citing any foreign sources.[111]

In spite of these striking similarities, there is one major difference in the political thought of the two theorists, reflecting the main contract in the social structure of their respective countries. Gökalp, living in a state that was comparatively homogeneous after 1921, was able to adopt a Western concept of the nation – the concept that a nation was formed of a people with a common culture, especially with a common language. He elaborated enough on this theme that three separate books have appeared in the West either discussing or translating his articles on Turkish nationalism: Uriel Heyd's *Foundations of Turkish*

Nationalism: The Life and Teachings of Ziya Gökalp (London, 1950); Niyazi Berkes' *Turkish Nationalism and Western Civilization: Selected Essays of Ziya Gökalp* (New York, 1959); and most recently, Robert Devereux's *Ziya Gökalp: The Principles of Turkism* (Leiden, 1968). One would search in vain through Kasravi's prolific writings to find a single article on Iranian nationalism. As he admitted late in his career, 'I have never written on the theory of nationalism'.[112] The nearest he came to formulating such a theory was his passing statement that a people residing in one state – irrespective of race, creed, or language – by virtue of living in one geographical area had signed the original contract to work together harmoniously as one nation.[113] According to Gökalp, this stress on geography was a false premise – the same false premise made by the Ottomanists – for only a common culture, especially language, could provide the fundamental basis of a nation. He, therefore, concluded that the neighbouring state of Iran was formed of not one nation but of three distinct nations: Persian, Turkish, and Kurdish-speakers. While this linguistic diversity inhibited Kasravi from formulating a theory of what Iranian nationalism had been in the past and what it was in the present, it also encouraged him to discuss at length what it would be in future if only the public accepted his teachings: an integrated and unified nation with one language, one culture, one central authority, one political religion, and, most important of all, one clear goal of modernization. Kasravi, therefore, was not a theorist of Iranian nationalism but a theorist of national integration in Iran.

Kasravi's Failure

Kasravi's strategy for implementing his programme of modernization involved four consecutive stages: first, the inspiration of a group of faithful followers; second, the organization of these disciples into a structured association; third, the conversion of the national intelligentsia through the publications of this association; and fourth, the dissemination of the new doctrine among the masses by the converted intelligentsia. The campaign would begin as a teaching group. It would expand into an intellectual movement. And it would end with the successful proselytization of the general public.

The first stage was initiated in the 1930s when Kasravi attracted a number of disciples around his monthly journal *Payman*, but the second stage was delayed by Riza Shah's prohibition of all independent organizations. This obstacle, however, was removed by the change in regime in 1941. Kasravi immediately announced the formation of the Azadigan Society, with its own printing house and its daily newspaper *Parcham*. As the first issues stressed, the aim of the Society was to wage a crusade to supplant the old fourteen sects of Iran with the new ideology of unity. When one sceptical reader asked, 'What if you merely create a fifteenth sect?', Kasravi retorted confidently that his ideology would win because it was based on present-day realities.[114] History, however, has proved the reader's scepticism justified, and Kasravi's self-confidence unjustified.

No doubt some of Kasravi's works – especially his historical and anti-clerical writings – greatly influenced contemporaries, but his theory, as a whole, failed to ignite an enthusiastic spark. In fact, his strategy never reached the third stage. The Azadigan Society, even at its height in 1945, attracted no more than a few thousand members, mostly drawn from the ranks of teachers, office workers, and high-school students. And a year later when the fundamentalist Shi'i party – the *Fida'iyyan-i Islam* – murdered Kasravi, the Society, instead of being in the midst of the community leading a national crusade, was isolated from most segments of the population and was the target of a rising religious crusade. Preachers were ascending their pulpits to denounce its publications as 'heretical' and its leader as 'the most notorious enemy of Islam'. Opponents were spreading the rumour that its book-burning sessions included the holy Koran. Violent mobs were attacking its members and club-houses. And the group had become the victim of a political alliance between the government elite and the religious elite, at a time when the former was seeking the support of the latter: the royalist Speaker of the Majlis, Sayyid Muhammad Sadiq Tabatabai, had publicly accused Kasravi of advocating 'anti-Islamic views'; the conservative Premier Sadr, who had presided over the executions of liberals in the constitutional revolution, had brought formal charges against him for propagating 'heretical ideas'; the Tehran police had released a fanatic who made an unsuccessful attempt on his life in late 1945; and a High Military Tribunal a few months later acquitted the two members of the *Fida'iyyan-i Islam* who eventually succeeded in assassinating him. Symbolically, his body remained unburied for a number of days because no religious authority would perform the funeral rites. In the years after the assassination, the Azadigan Society – at times divided, frequently persecuted, and invariably isolated – continued to linger on as a small discussion group, its size a pitiful memorial to Kasravi's failure. He had hoped to lead a national crusade to eliminate sub-national factions, in the end he had only created a new faction.

Kasravi's ultimate failure was partly due to his refusal to compromise with expediency – he had a strategy without any political tactics – and partly due to the persistent survival of traditional sentiments, thus, paradoxically, illustrating the truth of his original proposition that the population was fragmented by sub-national factions. Unintegrated communities, with their social affiliations, survived his ideology of national integration; religious and tribal bonds, with their ingrained roots, failed to melt away when confronted by his arguments for uniformity; and class consciousness, with its interest groups, persisted in spite of his schemes of social solidarism. Trumpet blasts against all sectarianism were unable to bring down the ancient religious walls, but, simultaneously, the same blasts alienated him both from his inherited community and from the minorities who hoped to weaken the Shi'i majority. Militant anti-clericalism naturally antagonized the faithful, but, at the same time, he provoked raised eye-brows among fellow-secularists with his preaching manner, dogmatic intolerance, claims of founding a new *din*, and the worship of his disciples for him as a modern *Payghambar* (prophet). At one point he found it necessary publicly to deny that he was a *mulla* in civilian clothing.[115] His policy of integration through eradication offended those non-Persian intellectuals who were conscious of their cultural identity. But, the proposal to purge Persian of mystic poetry and foreign words – a proposal that would have destroyed classical literature – also antagonized the Persian intellectuals. Even members of the communist intelligentsia found the book-burning sessions of Hafiz as too much to stomach.[116] Periodic denunciations of the elite as 'corrupt' and of Riza Shah as 'tyrannical' made him appear in the eyes of the upper class as a dangerous hothead. His insistence, often in the same breath, that the masses were also 'corrupt', that Riza Shah had initiated some beneficial reforms, and that the theory of the class struggle in history was a 'divisive myth', gained him the notoriety in radical circles of being an apologist for the ruling class. Even his policy of revolution through education lost him potential friends: impatient reformers felt that politics could not wait for the 'awakening' of the masses: and more patient reformers soon realized that if they were to attract large segments of the population they would have to compromise some of their modern and secular ideas with the traditional and religious sentiments of the masses.[117] Consequently, few contemporary radicals found their way into his Azadigan Society. And in more recent years, even fewer radicals have been attracted by Kasravi's ideology of unity through uniformity, mainly because they have gradually reached the conclusion that unity is more likely to be achieved through economic integration than through forced acculturation.[118]

NOTES

1. For a general discussion of the subject of national integration and political modernization see: M. Weiner, 'Political Integration and Political Development,' *Annals of the American Academy of Political & Social Science*, No. 358 (March 1965), pp. 52–64; D. Rustow, *A World of Nations* (Washington, DC, 1967); and A. Organski, *Stages of Political Development* (New York, 1967).
2. C. Geertz, 'The Integrative Revolution', *Old Societies and New Nations* (Edited by Geertz) (New York, 1963), pp. 105–57.
3. L. Binder, 'Egypt: The Integrative Revolution', *Political Culture and Political Development* (Edited by L. Pye and S. Verba) (Princeton, 1969), pp. 396–449; 'National Integration and Political Development', *American Political Science Review*, Vol. LVIII, No. 3 (September 1964), pp. 622–31.
4. There are, of course, no accurate statistics for the population in the nineteenth century. Sir John Malcolm, writing in the first half of the century, estimated it at about six million. *The History of Persia* (London, 1829), Vol. II, p. 372. Lord Curzon, at the end of the century, 'hazarded' a guess of nine million. *Persia and the Persian Question* (London, 1892), Vol. II, p. 492. R. Watson, in mid-century, placed it anywhere between five and ten millions. *A History of Persia* (London, 1866), p. 2.
5. The well-known writer Muhammad Jamalzadeh is a good case in point. In a short work entitled 'Persian is Sugar' in his collection of essays *Yiki Bud, Yiki Nabud* (Once Upon a Time), he paints a vivid and frustrating picture of how Westernized intellectuals, because they have absorbed so many foreign words, are unable to communicate with the common people. The

message of the short story is that the intelligentsia, in order to reform society, must write in simple Persian. But nowhere does the author indicate that even if they accepted his advice, they would still be confronted with a public large sections of which spoke languages other than Persian.

6. For various assessments of Kasravi, see: W. Staley, 'The Intellectual Development of Ahmad Kasravi', (unpublished Ph.D. dissertation, Princeton, 1966); J. Elder, 'The Spiritual and Moral Situation in Iran', *Muslim World*, Vol. XXVIII, No. 3, (November 1948), pp. 100–07; P. Shahriyari and M. Ni'matullahi, *Ahmad Kasravi* (Tehran, 1947); M. Azadah, *Chahra Kasravi-ra Kushtand?* (Why Did They Kill Kasravi?) (Tehran, 1946); J. Siyar, 'The World Outlook of Kasravi', *Dunya*, Vol. II (Autumn, 1964), pp. 85–91; F. Kazemzadeh, 'Iranian Historiography', in *Historians of the Middle East* (Edited by B. Lewis and P. Holt) (London, 1962), pp. 430–34; and Society of Azadigan, *Sukhranrani-ha-yi Haftagi* (Weekly Talks) (Tehran, n.d.).
7. A. Kasravi, *Zindigani-yi Man* (My Life) (Second Edition, Tehran, 1946). This edition also contains the two sequels to his memoirs: *Dah Sal dar Adliyah* (Ten Years in the Ministry of Justice) and *Chara az Adliyah birun Amadam* (Why I Left the Ministry of Justice).
8. In Azarbayjan families claiming descent from the Prophet use the title *mir* while in most other parts of Iran they use another Arabic term, *sayyid*.
9. Kasravi, *Zindigani-yi Man*, p. 12.
10. *Ibid.*, p. 11.
11. *Ibid.*, p. 13. The quotes from Kasravi are all free rather than literal translations.
12. *Ibid.*, p. 23.
13. *Ibid.*, pp. 14–15. Kasravi did not explain this intriguing sentence in his memoirs, but in his history of the constitutional revolution he wrote that Hajji Muhammad hated his family because one of his cousins had accosted a Shayki lady soon after the incident in the bazaar. *Tarikh-i Mashrutah-i Iran* (History of the Iranian Constitution) (Fifth Edition, Tehran, 1961), pp. 759–62.
14. Kasravi commented that one of the first memories he had was this 'painful experience': 'The barbarous fashion of shaving the head was unknown in early Islam. It was started by the Sufis, who, in order to show that they were unconcerned with worldly matters, sheared their hair, but soon the fashion spread among the common people, and consequently, the Sufis decided not to shave their heads. In the days when the people had long hair, the Sufis wanted to have no hair. And in the days when the people had no hair, the Sufis wanted to have long hair. In my own time in Azarbayjan, the mullas, *sayyids*, merchants, bazaaris, and some farmers had shaven heads. If anyone from these groups disregarded the custom, he was reproached by the others, denounced as a libertine, and his testimony was even refused in court. Meanwhile, soldiers, *lutis*, courtiers, and some peasants had long locks at the back of their heads. Since my father was from a long line of *sayyids*, I was forced to go through the painful and repetitive ritual of having my scalp shredded.' *Ibid.*, pp. 6–7.

15. *Ibid.*, p. 21.
16. *Ibid.*, p. 26.
17. *Ibid.*, p. 31.
18. *Ibid.*, p. 33. There was probably another reason why he did not participate. The reformers in Hakmavar were led by Hajji Muhammad, the head of the Shaykhi community and now the staunch enemy of the Kasravi family.
19. Kasravi, *Tarikh-i Mashrutah-'i Iran*, pp. 393–99, 492–94.
20. *Ibid.*, pp. 192–93.
21. Kasravi, *Zindigani-yi Man*, p. 40.
22. *Ibid.*, p. 43.
23. *Ibid.*, p. 46.
24. *Ibid.*, p. 78.
25. *Ibid.*, p. 132.
26. *Ibid.*, p. 193.
27. *Ibid.*, pp. 227–28.
28. *Ibid.*, p. 301.
29. *Ibid.*, p. 320.
30. In private life Kasravi continued to clash with the power structure. He caused a minor scandal in the College when he failed a student he had caught cheating. The student happened to be the son of an influential dignitary: 'To have passed him would have been unfair to the others, especially to the poorer students from the provinces who had made personal sacrifices to come to college.' Kasravi's Defence, *Parcham*, September 10, 1942. And he unwittingly caused a political scandal when a Soviet Iranologist translated a book on linguistics Kasravi had published years earlier. Although this book had no political content, the police arrested and investigated him to discover why a Russian would reprint his work. Staley, *op. cit.*, p. 20.
31. Kasravi, 'Again Concerning Azarbayjan,' *Parcham*, December 6, 1942.
32. Kasravi, 'A Message to European and American Intellectuals,' *Parcham*, September 28–October 16, 1942.
33. Kasravi, *Din va Jahan* (The World and Ideology) (Third Edition, Tehran, 1957), pp. 10–13.
34. Kasravi, 'Concerning How to Understand the World,' *Payman*, Vol. VII, No. 2 (July 1941), pp. 120–27.
35. Kasravi, *Din va Jahan*, pp. 10–13; 'A Message to European and American Intellectuals', *op. cit.*; and *Aiyin* (The Creed) (First Edition, Tehran, 1932), p. 65.
36. *Ibid.*
37. Kasravi, 'Concerning How to Understand the World,' *op. cit.*
38. Kasravi, 'What is the True Meaning of Tamadun?' *Payman*, Vol. III, No. 5 (May 1935), pp. 290–96.
39. Kasravi, *Varjavand Bunyad* (Worthy Foundations) (Third Edition, Tehran, 1957), pp. 86–92.
40. Kasravi, 'Farming As a Source of Life,' *Payman*, Vol. IV, No. 2, (June 1937), pp. 73–80; and 'A Message to European and American Intellectuals,' *op. cit.*

41. Kasravi, 'Concerning How to Understand the World,' *op. cit.* He, however, strongly took issue with Gandhi over the proposal that man should live without machines. For Kasravi, man needed machines in his struggle against nature. 'A Glance at India,' *Parcham*, August 19, 1942.
42. Kasravi, *Aiyin*, p. 105.
43. Kasravi, *Din va Jahan*, pp. 10–14.
44. Kasravi, *Varjavand-i Bunyad*, p. 35.
45. Kasravi, 'Islam and Iran,' *Payman*, Vol. I, No. 8 (February 1933), pp. 9–14; and 'The State Is Like a Human Body,' *Parcham*, April 20, 1942.
46. Kasravi, *Aiyin*, pp. 8–9.
47. Kasravi, 'A Message to European and American Intellectuals,' *op. cit.* For his definition of *din*, see 'Ideology and Politics,' *Payman*, Vol. VII, No. 8 (April 1942), pp. 527–49. Here he attacks the western view of secularism – that politics and *din* should be separated: 'The former guides the state. The latter guides the people's way of life. And both should have the same goal of social harmony.'
48. Kasravi, 'The Division of Labour,' *Parcham*, April 2–6, 1942.
49. Kasravi, *Din va Jahan*, pp. 28–37; and 'Payman's Message on How to Save the Nation,' *Payman*, Vol. III, No. 6 (June 1936), pp. 346–50.
50. Kasravi, 'Iran and Islam,' *op. cit.*; and *Zaban-i Farsi* (The Persian Language) (Third Edition, Tehran, 1955), pp. 3–5.
51. Kasravi, *Dadgah* (The Court of Justice) (Third Edition, Tehran, 1957), pp. 4–6; and 'What Must Be Done Today, *Payman*, Vol. VII, No. 4 (August 1941), pp. 242–43.
52. Kasravi (published anonymously), *Sar navisht-i Iran Chah Khvad Bud?* (What will Be the Fate of Iran) (First Edition, Tehran, 1945), pp. 17–21.
53. Kasravi, *Zindigani-yi Man*, p. 14. In one place, however, Kasravi contradicts himself and agrees with his father. He argues that the Great Powers will use all means possible to expand their influence, including the manipulation of religious sects. This, he claims, explains why Western scholars are so interested in such sects as Sufism and Western politicians are so concerned in religious freedom for minorities. *Dar Piramvan-i Islam* (Concerning Islam) (Fourth Edition, Tehran, 1963), pp. 5–10.
54. Kasravi, 'It All Has Its Origin in the People,' *Parcham*, February 9, 1942.
55. Kasravi, *Sar navisht-i Iran Chah Khvad Bud?*, pp. 17–21.
56. Kasravi, 'Iran and Islam,' *op. cit.*; and *Zaban-i Farsi*, pp. 3–5.
57. Kasravi, 'The Division of Labour,' *op. cit.*
58. Kasravi, 'A Short History,' *Parcham*, February 29–March 3, 1942; and 'What Must Be Done Today,' *op. cit.*
59. Kasravi, 'The Chief Cause of Backwardness in Iran,' *Parcham*, April 27, 1942.
60. Kasravi, Iran and Islam,' *op. cit.*, p. 10.
61. Kasravi, 'Corruption among the Masses,' *Parcham-i Haftegi*, April 15, 1944.
62. Kasravi, *Dar Rah-i Siyasat* (In Politics) (First Edition, Tehran, 1945), p. 32.
63. *Ibid.*, p. 98.

64. Kasravi, 'A Short History,' *op. cit.*
65. Kasravi, 'What Must Be Done Today,' *op. cit.*
66. Kasravi, 'The Shi'i Perversion,' *Payman*, Vol. VII, No. 10 (May 1942), pp. 546–60.
67. Kasravi, *Dadgah*, p. 10.
68. Kasravi, *Din va Jahan*, pp. 28–31.
69. Kasravi, 'An Unnecessary Uproar,' *Parcham*, April 1945.
70. Kasravi, 'A Message to the Mullas of Tabriz,' *Parcham*, November 2, 1942; and 'Why We Are Not Politicians,' *Payman*, Vol. VII, No. 9 (May 1942), pp. 579–87.
71. Kasravi, 'An Unnecessary Uproar,' *op. cit.*
72. Kasravi, 'Fars and the Qashqayis,' *Parcham*, April 2, 1942.
73. Kasravi, *Din va Jahan*, pp. 22–23.
74. Kasravi, 'The Tribes,' *Parcham-i Haftagi*, April 25, 1944.
75. Kasravi, *Dar Rah-i Siyasat*, p. 50.
76. Kasravi, *Tarikh-i Mashrutah-i Iran*, p. 481.
77. Kasravi, *Sar navisht-i Iran Chah Khvad Bud?*, p. 51.
78. Kasravi, 'Concerning Languages,' *Parcham-i Haftagi*, April 22, 1944.
79. Kasravi, 'Concerning Azarbayjan,' *Payman*, Vol. VII, No. 7 (March 1942), pp. 474–88. His opposition to the linguistic minorities led him to distort his autobiography in one place. In describing how he refused to preach in Arabic, he avoided mentioning that he substituted Azari. Staley, *op. cit.*, p. 95.
80. Kasravi, 'How to Obtain Genuine National Independence,' *Parcham*, April 8, 1942.
81. Kasravi, 'The State Is Like the Human Body,' *op. cit.*
82. Kasravi, 'Let Us Struggle to Eliminate Turkish,' *Payman*, Vol. III, No. 11 (January 1937), pp. 685–88.
83. Kasravi, 'What Is Wealth,' *Parcham*, March 30, 1942.
84. *Ibid.*
85. Although Kasravi supported women's rights on the question of polygamy, the veil, and entry into such occupations as medicine, dentistry, and teaching, he adamantly opposed the principle of equality between the sexes and their entry into law, politics, and government service. His opposition was based on the following premises: the 'natural' place of woman was in the home, 'cooking', 'sewing', 'raising children,' and 'pleasing their husbands'; such professions would 'corrupt' women because they would bring out harmful competitive instincts; their entry into such fields would take away jobs from men; and their presence in offices would 'distract' men from their work. Modern writers tend to mention Kasvari's progressive views on the question while ignoring his highly conservative attitudes. For Kasvari's writings on the issue, see, 'Our Mothers and Sisters', *Payman*, Vol. IV, No. 2 (February 1935), pp. 318–33; and 'God Created Man to Work', *Parcham*, April 19, 1942.
86. For Kasvari's balance sheet of Riza Shah's successes and failures, see 'They Originated from the Masses,' *Parcham*, February 9, 1942; 'The Source of Instability Must Be Eliminated,' *Parcham*, February 23, 1942; and 'Concerning Riza Shah and His Activities,' *Parcham*, June 25, 1942.

87. Kasravi, *Dar Rah-i Siyasat*, p. 84.
88. Kasravi, 'What Are We Saying,' *Payman*, Vol. II, No. 1 (January 1935), pp. 3–10.
89. *Ibid.*
90. Kasravi, 'The Division of Labour,' *op. cit.*
91. Kasravi, *Din va Jahan*, p. 20; and 'A Message to European and American Intellectuals,' *op. cit.*
92. Kasravi, *Afsaran-i Ma* (Our Officers) (First Edition, Tehran, 1945), pp. 25–26.
93. Kasravi, *Dadgah*, p. 44.
94. Kasravi, *Inqilab Chist?* (What Is Revolution) (First Edition, Tehran, 1945), p. 11.
95. Kasravi, *Din va Jahan*, p. 61.
96. Kasravi, 'Why We Are Not Politicians,' *op. cit.*, p. 581.
97. Kasravi, *Dar Rah-i Siyasat*, p. 45.
98. Kasravi, 'A People Must Have Both a Road and a Guide,' *Payman*, Vol. VI, No. 7 (September, 1940), p. 420.
99. Kasravi, *Sar navisht-i Iran Chah Khvad Bud?*, p. 62.
100. Kasravi, 'Education,' *Parcham*, September 11–15, 1942.
101. *Ibid.*
102. *Ibid.*
103. Kasravi, 'The Division of Labour,' *op. cit.*
104. Kasravi, 'What Must Be Done Today,' *op. cit.*
105. Kasravi, 'Unity Is Dependent on Unity of Thought,' *Parcham*, March 9, 1942.
106. Kasravi, 'The Harmful Effects of Poetry,' *Parcham*, April 21–22, 1942; and 'One of the False Theories', *Parcham*, May 17, 1942.
107. Kasravi, 'A People Must Have Both a Road and a Guide', *op. cit.*; 'How to Become Good', *Parcham*, January 30, 1942; and 'We Must Understand the Meaning of Constitutionalism', *Parcham*, February 1, 1942.
108. Kasravi, 'False Titles', *Payman*, Vol. I, No. 1 (November 1933), pp. 17–20.
109. Kasravi, *Zaban-i Farsi*, pp. 30–40.
110. Kasravi, 'New Mistakes', *Payman*, Vol. I, No. 3 (March 1934), pp. 3–5.
111. Kasravi, 'I have taken Nothing from Others,' *Parcham*, April 10, 1942. The only direct tie between Kasravi and Gökalp seems to be the periodical title *Payman*. Early in the century, Gökalp had edited and published some of his important articles in a journal with that name. And Kasravi used the same name when he began publishing his own monthly journal in 1933.
112. Kasravi, 'A People Must Have Both a Road and a Guide,' *op. cit.*
113. Kasravi, 'What is Wealth?', *op. cit.*
114. Cited in *Parcham-i Haftegi*, April 22, 1944.
115. Kasravi, *Dadgah*, p. 27.
116. E. Tabari, 'Concerning Persian Literature,' and A. Qasimi, 'Concerning Hafiz,' *Mardum*, Vol. III, No. 1 (September 1948), pp. 3–16, 57–68.
117. Kasravi often denounced the Tudah Party for not waging a more militant campaign against Islam, and, at times, criticized it for allying with

segments of the anti-government *'uluma'*. *Dar Rah-i Siyasat* and *Sar navisht-i Iran Chah Khvad Bud?*

118. This is best seen in the changing attitudes of Iranian Marxists towards linguistic minorities: in 1924, Arani had argued for the Persianization of the provinces, especially of his native Azarbayjan ['Azarbayjan: A Vital Issue for Iran,' *Farangistan*, Vol. I, No. 5 (September 1924), pp. 247–53]; now, in 1972, the three main Marxist groups – the Tudah, the Revolutionary Tudah, and the Azarbayjani Democratic parties – are supporting the cultural rights of the linguistic minorities in Iran.

6

The Iranian Heritage in the Eyes of the Contemporary Poet Midhi Akhavan Salis (M. Omid)*

Sorour S. Soroudi

'Persia must, outwardly and inwardly, in body and spirit, become *Farangi* (European)'.[1] Although not always formulated so explicitly, this view was a characteristic response of Iranian intellectuals when they first became acquainted with Europe. Dazzled by the prosperity of Western civilization and dejected by the conditions of their own society, they lost confidence in themselves and were ready to give up almost everything – with the exception of the Persian language[2] – in order to become European. Since then, however, Iranian intellectuals have come a long way in their evaluation of both Western civilization and their own national heritage. A better acquaintance with European culture, recent social and cultural crises in Western societies, and the impact of westernization on different aspects of Iranian society in the last century, have drastically changed their views on this issue. Nowadays one can easily notice an increasing awareness among some Iranian intellectuals that modernization, although inevitable, need not entail adoption of all aspects of Western society and its cultural values. A major factor at the root of this awareness is the increasing fear of losing their national identity, of becoming uprooted – a fear widely shared and a major factor in determining their attitude towards Iran's national heritage. However, Iranians differ in evaluation of their cultural and

* This article was written before the recent events in Iran.

historical deposit and are not of the same mind as to what should be done in order to preserve their national identity.

In this paper I shall examine the views of the contemporary poet Mihdi Akhavan Salis (M. Omid, b. 1928) on this vital issue. This examination will be based on poetic works as well as other published writings of the poet, and will consist of two parts. In the first part I will present his general views concerning Iran's heritage, and will then examine some specific issues in the light of those general views.

Omid is today an outspoken supporter of the view that blames foreigners, mainly the Arabs, for Iran's present predicament, and proposes restoration of and emphasis on pure Iranian elements, Iran's pre-Islamic heritage. This conflict, based on the dichotomy of Iranian and non-Iranian, brought to open realization in the Shu'ubi movement of the early Islamic period (eighth and ninth centuries), had manifested itself following Iran's traumatic encounter with the West in the nineteenth century. It served as a soothing response to one of the painful questions posed by this encounter: what went wrong in the history of Iran that caused her deterioration? In responding to this question some chose the way of laying the blame, at least partly, at the door of others, in this case the Arabs who had in the seventh century destroyed the Iranian empire. As in other societies which had faced similar problems, this response was intended not only to provide a shelter against frustrating realities, but also to restore confidence in the Iranians' ability to rebuild their society.[3]

Omid's non-poetic expression of his views concerning Iran's past heritage is mostly included in the 'afterword' of one of the collections of his poetry published in 1965.[4] However, his opinions in this regard had been formed previously and have found expression in many of his poetic works as well. The earliest poems of Omid available in print belong to the years 1947–48 and do not contain anti-Arab or anti-Islamic sentiments. On the contrary, we encounter occasional lines respectfully mentioning or alluding to Muslim religious leaders:

> Do not believe, without forty years of asceticism
> One can, unduly, become Muhammad the apostle.[5]

The young poet appears to have absorbed the religious atmosphere of his home town, the holy city of Mashhad, where he was raised in an observant Muslim family. In the following years, however, Omid develops strong sentiments in favour of ancient Iranian culture and against foreign influence in both past and present-day Iran. This development seems to be related, at least partly, to his growing social consciousness, the first signs of which are found in the early poems of the Mashhad period.[7] His move to the capital city of Tehran in 1948 and his involvement in public activities strengthened his social consciousness. At first this is expressed in slogan-laden poems which are concerned with present problems and do not relate to specific events in Iran's past:

Lessons of history have granted me glad tidings:
The arm of capital will lose its power.
Flushed with the wine of victory, says Omid:
Labourer will become the manifestation of human ideals.[8]

The oil crisis of 1950–53 and Iran's powerlessness to repel foreign inroads created much frustration among the young, active generation of Omid's time. It is at this time that the first signs of condemning foreigners for Iran's predicament appear in Omid's works. These first expressions bear a personal colouring and focus on his home province of Khurasan and the town of Mashhad. As the site of the shrine of Imam Riza (Ali ibn Musa al-Riza, the eighth Shi'ite Imam, 770–813), Mashhad, the capital of Khurasan, is a major pilgrimage city where people's social and economic activities were, and to some extent still are, concentrated around the Imam's mausoleum compound. The poet, whose secular tendencies had developed during his stay in Tehran, revisits Mashhad and is greatly disconcerted by certain social phenomena he observes in the vicinity of the shrine: a 'ten year old woman' used as 'trading capital', the many poor and invalid swarming round the shrine for their livelihood, the hypocritical sheikhs who exploit the people, and the general condition of people's lives.[9] He connects the negative aspects of the life of his fellow Mashhadies with the religious character of the city and indirectly holds Islam responsible for them. His love for music (he played *tar* in his youth) and his liking for wine 'both forbidden in this religion [Islam] like any other thing of beauty',[10] intensify his anti-religious sentiments and he depicts the city of Mashhad and the province of Khurasan as a graveyard and elaborates:

Again have I fallen in Khurasan, the deathful
As the enemy's desire: stagnant, silent, sorrowful.
Where permitted are theft, oppression and conceit,
And forbidden liberty, music and wine.[11]

Gradually, as social and political developments add to the poet's frustration, idealization of pre-Islamic Iran appears in his writings alongside of condemnation of foreign influence. Omid draws a symbolic comparison between the disfavoured Mashhad of today and the ancient, idealized city of Tus, next to whose ruins the Muslim city was built. His conclusion is:

I am from Tus and a devotee of Zardusht
Neither an Arab, nor a Turk, or anyone of this sort.[12]

Ancient Khurasan, for which Tus stands as a symbol, is believed to have been a primary centre of Iranian culture including Zoroastrianism. It was also a main centre of the eighth and ninth century Iranian uprising against Arab occupation, the centre of the first independent Iranian dynasties in the ninth century, and the hotbed of Iranian cultural renaissance at that time. Omid's pride in Khurasan, 'the eye-light of the land of Iran',[13] is shared by others as well.[14] However much at times the poet crosses the border of moderation by downgrading other parts of the country,[15] it may be asserted that his great concern with Khurasan projects his loving care for Iran in general. Indeed the comparison he draws earlier between Tus and Mashhad is later drawn between ancient Iran and the foreign enemy in general. His picture is black and white in the sense of the Zoroastrian dualistic principle of light and darkness represented by Ahura Mazda and Ahriman. Everything connected with ancient Iran and Iranian culture is pure, bright and beautiful, whereas foreign elements, especially of Arab origin, are impure and destructive:

This [Arab] Ahriman has plundered and still doth he
Has destroyed, swallowed up and still doth he
Whatever good, pleasant, and beautiful,
Whatever pure, whatever Ahuraic.[16]

Likewise, the message of Islam was nothing but

False lights ...
Caravan of dead flames in the lagoon –
On the sacred face of the mihrab. ...

Whereas

We are
Conquerors of History's fortresses of glory,
Witnesses of each century's cities of splendour,
We are
Survivors of the sad innocence of the epochs.
We are
Narrators of cheerful and sweet tales,
Stories of the clear sky,
Flowing light, water,
Cool breeze, earth.
Stories of the most delightful message
From the limpidity of life's luminous brook.[17]

Omid himself seems aware of the unreal nature of this flight into the past. Remembrance and glorification of the past are, in some of his works, set in the framework of a wishful, almost delirious dreamworld – as in the above poem – from which the poet awakens to merciless reality. In other cases flight into the past is the strong yearning of a refugee, who in the end arrives at bolted doors, or a wandering, hopeless prince whose shining spring dries up and whose luminous fire is extinguished by wind.[18]

However, recourse to the past takes place in a later stage of Omid's life and appears to be connected with his disillusionment with contemporary events and ideological organizations, and the unfulfilment of his aspirations in the social and political domains. For practical solutions Omid at first turns neither to the Zoroastrian message nor the social order of ancient Iran, nor even to the *Mazdakite* reforms. He adopts the ideology of Karl Marx and like many other young men of his time joins the ranks of the communist *Tudeh* party. For a few years in the early fifties he is engaged in public activities until he is imprisoned following the defeat of the party in 1953. This was for him the beginning of a cold and sombre period duly reflected in many poems of the collection *Zimistan* (Winter).[19] In these and later poems one can trace Omid's great disappointment with the *Tudeh* party which proved to be for him another false light:

This is a night, yes, a horrible night;
Yet there was no day beyond the hill either.[20]

Before reaching the stage where he projects his ideals on to the historical and legendary images of ancient Iran rather than relinquish these ideals, Omid retreats into a mournful mood whose poetic fruits are agonized elegies also filled with ancient Iranian images and concepts. For instance, according to the Zoroastrian dual principle of light and darkness, he symbolizes the prosperous, idealized past as 'the golden rare palace of the charming morn', and contrasts it with the present frustrating reality:

With its nights bright like day,
Its rigid, dark days like the night at the depth of the legend.[21]

The legendary hero Rustam, the symbol of the glorified past, who could rectify this 'crooked-faced' reality, is dead, and the poet's wishful thinking of no avail.[22] Even recourse to ancient heritage, at first at least, proves fruitless, as reflected in his celebrated poem, *The Story of the Petrified Kingdom*.[23] The hero, prince of a kingdom petrified by a spell, is the Zoroastrian eschatological figure Bahram-i Varjavand who is destined to restore Iran's prosperity and expel all foreigners from the land as preparation for the coming of the Messiah Sushiyant. But the prince is now a defeated, desperate person, tired even of singing elegies and bemoaning his fate, for his kingdom which

Once was the guiding light of the world
An ever blooming spring. ...
Is now a loath-land, nesting disgust,
Mourning, its festivity.[24]

As a last attempt to remove the spell he is advised by magic pigeons to wash off the dust of centuries of depression in a 'bright, clear spring', to whole-heartedly worship Ahura Mazda and the seven Amshaspands (Zoroastrian archangels), to kindle a fire and sincerely pray to it. ... For 'he has fallen only off his steed and not his [noble] origin'. The prince performs all these rites but fails to raise up the people, to bring about the hoped for rebirth. Frustrated, Omid goes so far as to damn his beloved land which he likens to a garden which has not been rejuvenated by grafting:

For thy swift mourning, O shameless garden,
When thou art eternally gone with the wind,

> May all clouds of anger everywhere be pregnant with tears of hate,
> Like my silence shedding clouds of envy.
>
> O you barren trees, hidden roots in debaucherous soil!
> One single worthy bud can sprout not on your body round.
> O you handful of leaves, fouled warp, fouled woof!
> Remembrance of dustful droughts,
> No rain will ever be able to wash you.[25]

Do these lines indicate that the poet had lost hope for a fruitful grafting as in neighbouring gardens? Did he doubt the ability of his people and his national heritage to respond to the challenge of time? Were the trees barren because of an inherent fault, because of fruitless years of drought, or because someone had 'stopped up the bright sacred springs and dried up the sea into a desert'?[26] The elegiac poems may be the expression of doubt which overpowered the poet, or perhaps the cry of a frustrated soul who is unwilling to put up with reality as it is but is unable to act in order to change it.

Disillusioned on every side, Omid develops a mystic hope, according to his own testimony, 'expecting a miracle, a new prophetic mission, a new revelation'.[27] And since his expectations do not come true, he takes upon himself the mission of bringing about an inner, individual salvation. The nature and direction of this salvation are determined by Omid's previous experience, his ideals, and the existing conditions of society. He decides to adapt the national, pre-Islamic heritage to the needs of the present time. To this purpose he reconciles the prophet Zoroaster with the socialist reformer of the Sassanid period, Mazdak[28] and brings them together under one roof with Buddha and Mani. In his own words:

> In short, my dear, I have reconciled Zardusht with Mazdak. Economy, sociology and society's substructure [according to] Mazdak; ethics, metaphysical beliefs, and beautiful legendary and mythical structures [as in the] Zoroastrian; asceticism and some moral instructions according to Buddha and Mani; *vas-salam* (that is it). With such noble, great and intelligent zendik as I know in our own vicinity, there is no need to go out of Iranian and Avistan realm ... to be accused of Russia [Lenin] and Prussia [Marx]. ... Indeed, one does not talk of the licentious, unrestrained Mazdak that the shameless, lying Arab has introduced to us by his historians and flatterers; and not the Zardusht, the Buddha, and the Mani that have been presented

> to us wrongly, through lies; but the wise, noble, high-minded Mazdak, the seeker of equality ... the real Mazdak who is quite moral-minded and chaste, and so too [concerning] Zardusht, Mani, and Buddha.[29]

Thus the Mazdushtian[30] (Mazdak and Zardusht combined) message is born, a message whose principles are propounded in a sort of 'new Avista', a collection of poems and articles named *Az In Avista* (*From This Avista*), the harvest of the years of seclusion and despair. To formulate this new message the poet had to cross the borders of the 'Avistan realm', but he is apparently content to have remained in the 'Indo-Iranian' realm, ignoring the important Christian Semitic influence on Mani's doctrines.

However, neither Mani nor Buddha nor even Zoroaster, important as he is, are the key figures in Omid's Mazdushtian message. The key figure is Mazdak; far more than being the prophet of a new religious message, Mazdusht represents a social ideal:

> [By this message] I do not mean all those childish grimaces and ridiculous, stupid religious businesses about principal doctrines and minor precepts of religion (*usul va furu'-i din*) or things of this sort. Religion in its vulgar meaning ... is not today ... a major question; it is not a question at all, except for politicians and ... priests and *akhunds* (Muslim priests) who want to exploit. ... What is important is for today's man to be acquainted through human and social insight with the truth of a free and noble life, to look a bit farther than his nose. Understanding and friendship of souls, welfare and tranquillity for all, justice, generosity and human love, the useful and beautiful toils of men; these are the sacred and the noble, these are the things which give value to life ... nothing else.[31]

Omid rejects the portraits of Mazdak and Zardusht as drawn up by 'Arab historians'[32], but neither are the portraits he draws exact replicas of those historical figures. Omid's Mazdak as reincarnated in Mazdusht is a projection of the aspirations of a man facing the problems of a society faltering to reach the twentieth century. If Omid declares Mazdak 'the most victorious man of history'[33] despite his tragic end, it is because he symbolizes the struggle for the social order which the poet desires. This consciousness of the necessity to fight social evils and Omid's proclivity towards whatever is Iranian, seem to lie at the core of the *bi'sa* (rebirth) which he hopes will some day take place in the heart of every free-minded man and woman.[34] Relying on his own clues, however, one sees that Omid himself does not consider his Mazdushtian message, taken at its face value, able to provide a formula to solve the complicated problems of our time. He is very vague and general about this message, leaving the 'operative rules' to be worked out by coming generations, and he admits, seriously or not, that his Mazdushtian message is a 'half-witted' aspiration, the result of a free, wandering imagination.[35] Omid himself, the only believer in Mazdusht, does not seem to have found the tranquillity, the search for which had driven him in the first place to unite Mazdak and Zardusht. On the contrary, the darkness is deeper now and the poet can tell of his fears only to his own shadow:

Beware, O shadow! the road has turned darker.
No longer the hand and the wall
No longer the wall and the friend.
Now on me rely, O me, O friend, but
Beware, for on this side horror lurks
And on that side, monster of dismay
And from none any affection for us.
O shadow! my heart suddenly withered,
Would that we knew
What star suddenly died.[36]

Seen from this angle Omid's *New Avista* is an elaboration of his dreamland, an attempt to expand and beautify the shelter to which he retreats more frequently as time passes. This shelter serves others as well, for Omid's poetry enjoys great popularity in educated circles whose members find their own fears, frustrations and aspirations reflected in his poems. The question is whether they share his partiality for whatever is Iranian and his holding foreigners, especially the Arabs, responsible for all the evils of society. Views of this kind enjoy considerable following among some intellectuals. However, the specific question on Omid's proclivities in this regard cannot receive documented answer. The only criticism known to me that has been levelled publicly against Omid in this respect has been expressed by Riza Barahini who maintains that such nationalistic views and Omid's talk of 'greater Iran'[37] can only serve the cause of Western imperialism.[38] In his response Omid denies having any territorial or political claims in mind when he talks of 'greater Iran' or the limits of *Iraniyat*

(Iranianism) and explains that his opinions bear only cultural significance. He deplores the lack of cultural unity and cultural access among different parts of what he calls 'the Avistan realm' and accuses Western imperialism for having created this situation. Omid is quite aware, however, of the contradiction of drawing borders for a 'greater Iran' and at the same time aspiring to the 'Mazdushtian' ideology which wishes to share everything among all human beings. He therefore qualifies his position by explaining that this border-drawing is valid until such time that 'all borders in the world would be eliminated and human beings would become mature. ...'[39]

Whatever the real significance of such views, it should be pointed out that, unlike some other Iranian poets who have also reacted to the disquieting realities of their country by praising the pre-Islamic period,[40] Omid does not emphasize the military power or political grandeur of the Acheamanids and the Sassanids, and kings or military leaders of the past, with two exceptions, do not win his attention. The most outstanding of these exceptions is the legendary national hero Rustam who has been turned by Omid into a multifaceted symbol of the Iranian national heritage.[41]

Omid's evaluation of Iranian culture is based on pre-judgments. Only seldom does he criticize anything connected with pre-Islamic Iran and very seldom is he willing to concede that there has been any positive Islamic influence on Iranian culture. For example, he criticizes the fanatic Zoroastrian religious leaders who opposed the Mazdakite reforms and brought about the massacre of the social-minded Mazdak and a group of his followers;[42] and he remarks positively on the Sufi (mystic) literature and concedes that 'this universal view [of Sufi poets] has perhaps been influenced to some extent by Islamic culture which has been influenced in turn from without. ...'[43] From where, he does not specify, but probably refers to an Iranian or Indo-Iranian source.

The question, therefore, is how does Omid view the great Persian culture of the Islamic era. His point of departure is shared by many of his compatriots who nevertheless express greater appreciation for Islam than he does. To use the words of Jalal Al-Ahmad: 'Islam became Islam only when it reached the settlements between Tigris and Euphrates [then the political and cultural centre of the Sassanid empire] and before that was nothing but the *jahiliyat* [paganism and ignorance] and the *badaviyat* [beduinism] of the Arabs'.[44] Omid himself, commenting on the contemporary problem of 'brain drain', expatiates:

> Previously the Arabs stole our great and precious minds – history testifies that the most exalted cultural and philosophical creations of Arabs and Islam, the loftiest verses in the Arabs' book of glories were created by Iranians – then the Moguls and now the Farangis [do the same]. Alas![45]

Even if one does not agree with such unequivocal statements, one can hardly deny the crucial influence exerted by Iranians on the formation and development of Islamic culture, so that even with his pre-judgments Omid might accept the Persian-Islamic culture as an integral part of the Iranian creation. Yet, those very pre-judgments, although not they alone, determine his more specific evaluations of this culture.

Omid holds in general that '... Iranian culture and art, particularly music and poetry, are one of the ancient pillars ... and great oceans of human intellection and reflection. ...'[46] Yet in his writing he discusses at length only the poetry of the Islamic period, his main field of interest. Clearly he cherishes the classical poetic heritage; but he has reservations as well. In the course of his discussion on modern Persian poetry he compares this poetry with the classical tradition and states that

> Our poetry in the last millenium was tightly shackled by several chains and bonds ... most of which were the result of imitating Arabic methods. Among others, *Arabic poetic metres*, of course with some changes and differences, have in general been accepted in our poetry too; particularly the bond of equal length of hemistitches which was removed by Nima [Yushij].[47]

Omid too relinquishes the principle of equal hemistitches, but he is unwilling, as Nima was not, to give up the basic metric feet of the classical poetry. Three years after the above statement he declares:

> ... I am of the opinion that the *'aruz* metrics is not, contrary to what is known, Arabic at all. I think that even Khalil ibn Ahmad's *'aruz* system was based on the metres of pre-Islamic Iran and was borrowed from musical scales of that period. For they say that this Khalil ibn Ahmad was an Iranian prince ... and no doubt was familiar

> with music players and music scales. ... The conclusion is that these metres are perfected forms of [those] old metres, syllabic metres for instance or other sorts.[48]

Similar arguments have been put forward by other Iranians who rely on the highly developed musical tradition of ancient Iran as compared with the not so impressive musical tradition of the pre-Islamic Arabs.[49] However, we know too little about pre-Islamic Iranian poetry to be able to reach clear-cut conclusions concerning the origin of the *'aruz* metric system, an issue still much disputed.

Omid continues his discussion:

> Most of our poetic forms and genres such as *qasidah* (ode), *qit'ah* (poetic fragment) and others have been also borrowed from Arabs. Of course here too some changes have been introduced, but in [our] modern poetry we have come closer to free native and local [dialectic?] forms, particularly some pre-Islamic forms.[50]

Local (folkloric) traditions form one of the sources on which Nima drew to create his new poetics. Some scholars tend to believe that these traditions are related to pre-Islamic poetry.[51] But the same dearth of evidence prevents conclusive comparison with pre-Islamic forms. The important point is, however, that Omid still avails himself of some of those classical forms, even though he has long since adopted free verse as his main form of poetic expression.[52] On more than one occasion he has defended the works he has written, and still writes, in classical vein and classical forms and has asserted that any form, classical or modern, may be used provided it suits the needs of a given poem. 'For the main thing,' he says, 'is the thought and the content, form comes next'.[53] Elsewhere he comments that some classical forms such as *ghazal* (short lyrical ode), *masnavi* (rhyming couplet), *ruba'i* (quatrain), and *du-baiti* (a kind of quatrain) are used more frequently [by modernist poets] because they are more flexible and simpler and thus closer to modern moderation.[54] It is puzzling, however, that he does not comment on the probable Iranian origin of some of these classical forms.[55]

Omid also criticizes the rhetorical system of classical poetry. He maintains that this system, also borrowed from Arabic poetry and modified by Persians, denies to the hearer, with few exceptions, the natural poetic pleasure and replaces it with unnatural *badi'i* (of rhetorical artifices) pleasure. This ailment has been passed on to Persian poetry from Arabic.[56] On the other hand:

> Today's poetry possesses, if any, only that very simple, downright poetic pleasure, not the *badi'i* pleasure; that is to say, it has returned to the pure, pleasant epochs of the pre-Islamic poetic world before it was polluted with Arabic methods.[57]

The examples Omid provides of 'simple poetic pleasure' are taken from the works of two poets of the Islamic period with proclivity for folkloric poetry.[58] He does not provide any example of pre-Islamic poetry, perhaps for scarcity of extant sources, even though he bases his arguments on those very sources. Moreover, it seems hardly necessary to point out, particularly to the well-versed poet himself, that not all Persian poetic works of today (by which he apparently means the school of Nima) are characterized by what he calls 'simple poetic pleasure'.

Omid expresses unequivocal opinions concerning the mythical and legendary background of Persian classical poetry. He decries what he calls the domination of Semitic-Arabic-Islamic myths and legends in most of the poetic works of the past millenium and considers one of the characteristics of modern poetry its liberation from these myths. He calls for a revival of pre-Islamic myths and legends, 'to grant justice to a grand world of beauty and felicity. ... a grand, wondrous, forgotten world of our own Aryan ancestors'.[59] Omid himself has revived many of those forgotten myths and legends in his poems, mainly in those of an epic type.[60] In so doing he aims not only 'to make amends' for the neglect of the classical period, but also, it seems, to stir the young generation to national and social consciousness through the symbols he creates. However, here also the Islamic influence is so deeply rooted in Iranian culture that the poet himself continues to employ poetic images based on Semitic-Islamic legends.[61]

The Persian language is perhaps the most important issue for Omid in this context. We should bear in mind that from a mere literary point of view, aside from content, language forms the most sensitive element in Omid's poetic creation. His mastery of Persian on all its levels and in all its nuances is universally acknowledged. In his early poems he followed the classical style, then experimented in Nimaian language, and finally developed a distinct style of his own which exerted considerable influence on the younger generation of poets.[62] In creating this style he has tried:

> to graft the healthy nerves and veins of a neat current language – whose solid skeleton and living cells belong to the days past – upon the blood, the feeling, and the tempo of today in so far as I am able to carry out such medical mediation.[63]

He has been quite successful in carrying out this mission in the course of which he has, expectedly, been attracted by Iranian elements, forgotten or rarely used words of Persian root, especially those of the Khurasani school of poetry and prose: 'the best Persian language'.[64] Omid has displayed a remarkable ability in juxtaposing archaic terms and colloquial expressions of today, although he has been criticized for excessive use of archaic words.[65] The other side of Omid's attraction to Persian words is his aversion for words of Arabic origin as he explains in a parenthetic sentence:

> I do not know why already at the beginning of my acquaintance with literature I did not like the word *vaqqad*. It had a stressed and unpleasant *vaq*. Even when I learned its meaning [radiant, fiery] my dislike lasted. How more pleasant sounding are our own Persian *darakhshan*, *rawshan*, *furuzan* ... like all other Persian [words] whose Arabic synonyms are unfortunately more commonly used. ...[66]

However, treasures of Iranian culture documented in Persian are too dear to Omid to allow such 'puristic' sentiments to influence his final judgment. Persian is considered by him, and many others,[67] as the main factor in preserving the Iranian national identity. Persian is the *national* language. Omid defends it and repeatedly calls for precision in its employment. He decries the predominance of the Tehrani dialect which does not differentiate in the use of *'illat* (cause, reason), *mawjib* (cause, motive), *ba'is* (motive, incentive), *dalil* (proof), *sabab* (cause, reason), and *angizah* (motivation). 'If our national language is so rich and extensive that it contains all these words in itself ... why should we not be precise in its use?'[68]

There is no doubt that Omid is well aware of the fact that five out of the six words he mentions are *Arabic* words. The reason for such a concessive approach on his part is quite clear: fear of uprootedness. For should Persian be 'purified' of its naturalized

Arabic elements, as has so many times been suggested and even attempted,[69] coming generations will be severed from their past. This is explicitly expressed by Omid when he talks of the new Turkish alphabet, no doubt bearing in mind similar proposals to change the Persian (Arabic) alphabet:[70]

> I believe that what counts is having roots in earth, in human earth. For instance strange tendencies and recent developments have turned Turkey into a rootless country; especially the change in their alphabet. After passing through the meagre and not so valuable culture and literature [created] during the past thirty to forty years, the present generation of Turkey will reach the gate of the grand library of ancient Turkish, Persian, Arabic, and generally *Islamic* culture. But today's generation cannot enter that library because its alphabet is foreign. The roots of the nation are only thirty or forty years deep; roots should be deep, not hair-like. ...[71]

Our presentation so far suggests that Omid's evaluation of the Iranian heritage is influenced by two main factors: his strong dislike for overwhelming foreign influence, especially Arabic and Islamic influence; and his desire to preserve this heritage and to strengthen the national consciousness. He does not basically oppose mutual influences among different cultures:

> As far as historical evidence ... demonstrates, no healthy borrowing which is based on sound principles and proper understanding has ever been harmful to any civilization. The basis of civilization is perhaps this very spiritual transaction.[72]

The poet does not explain what he means by 'healthy borrowing'. I would venture that he is not willing in such 'spiritual transaction' to give up the dominant national character of his culture. Here lies perhaps another reason for Omid's ambivalent approach towards the legacy of Islamic Iran. Despite reservations enumerated above, he approves of Persian language and literature – and of Persian art and music – for their original character has been substantially preserved despite the foreign influence. On the other hand, he opposes Islam as a religion because here the foreign element has prevailed. Indeed, Islam itself, and Shi'a Islam in particular, have absorbed many Iranian elements, but to him they remain basically foreign.

Omid is aware, however, that no matter how strong his desire may be, he is not able to undo the results of an event in the distant past of Iran. He is now concerned mainly to repel the new and more dangerous invasion of the West:

> So great is the Farangi oppression that we say,
> Blessed be the Arab invasion and the Tartar attack.[73]

Thus there appear two levels in Omid's approach to Iranian culture: the historical level with the clear dichotomy of pre-Islamic and Islamic, is the first level. The pre-Islamic is beautified and idealized to suit the poet's aspirations and to help him formulate his defeated but not forgotten ideals as yearning for a 'return to the paternal home'. On the road to that unattainable goal one may even indulge in wishful dreams and excessive xenophobic sentiments against seventh and eighth century foreign oppressors in order to release the pent up anger of frequent frustrations in the present daily struggle.

The second, the level of the contemporary, is a struggle not between Iranian and Arab elements, but between the whole cultural legacy of Iran and the massive material, social and cultural onslaught of the West, a source of great concern for many Iranians.[74] Here we meet a more realistic Omid, one who is willing to make concessions even to the Arabic-Islamic elements for the sake of preserving the national heritage and preventing uprootedness in the face of this new enemy. That is why he opposes all those who have made the West their Mecca without being adequately acquainted with their own culture or other great Asian cultures. For in his opinion, 'Asia is the inheritor of loftiest thoughts, most tender sentiments, and highest spiritual summits'.[75]

To help achieve his goal, Omid defends the Iranian tradition as a whole but at the same time tries to strengthen the national character of the tradition by reviving the cultural and historical memory of his compatriots, mainly the memory of pre-Islamic times where lie the nation's deep roots. This is clearly reflected in an essay he wrote for youngsters about Firdawsi and *Shahnamah*. There he defines Shahnamah as the 'identity card of the nationality, glory, and greatness of ancient Iran and Iranians' and argues:

> It is true that Shahnamah is the book of Iran's past ... but this very past can be a future-builder as well. This duty began the very first day the book was handed to the people by Firdawsi. ... The vitality and

> the continuous glory of Shahnamah testify that it has carried out this duty properly and will continue to do so.[76]

Thus, Omid wishes to block the flood of Western influence by reviving ancient traditions, by providing substitute values for those which were lost following the first encounter with the dangerously charming West. But he does not sound optimistic. His concern in this regard is expressed in a couple of poems (written in 1968) in which the confrontation of Iranian tradition and Western onslaught forms the main theme. In the first poem, called 'khan-i hashtum' (The eighth adventure),[77] the *naqqal*, the traditional storyteller who is none but the poet himself,[78] symbolizes the national heritage. The audience are the clients of the *qahvah-khanah*, the traditional tea-house, one of the main scenes of *Shahnamah-khvani*, the semi-dramatic declamation of Shahnamah stories. The storyteller, depicted as a Khurasani villager, 'an ancient reminder of the good old days', considers himself 'narrator of forgotten stories'. For a moment, threatening and in hate, he points his staff westward to chastize perhaps the West for its deceitful ways, and contemptuously towards the East, perhaps for its having surrendered so easily. Then in a painful voice he relates the tragic death of Rustam, the national hero who frequently defended Iran against foreign invasions. Now the danger is mainly spiritual and Rustam is turned into a symbolic guardian of Iran's past tradition. The narrator, sobbing, relates how Rustam is sacrificed by his own treacherous step-brother[79] who represents those Iranians who have completely given themselves up to Western influence, facilitating from within the destructive inroads of the West. In the original Shahnamah story Rustam succeeds at the moment before his death in avenging himself by killing his step-brother. But in the present poem Omid changes this detail and grants the step-brother a complete victory. Rustam 'the supporting pillar and the hope of Iran' did not avenge himself:

> The story goes that …
> He [Rustam] could also have, had he so wished,
> Opened his sixty arched noose
> Thrown it up, on some tree, some stone,
> And climbed up.
> And if you ask truthfully, I tell you truthfully

That the story tells the truth
But. …[80]

The reason for the change and the addition is provided in the second poem called 'Adamak' (Puppet-man), a sequel to the first poem. The scene is the same tea-house and the audience is the same, but the event takes place 'a year or so' later. The popular storyteller of the first poem is now sitting in a corner of the tea-house, sad, depressed, dejected; he has been replaced by 'the magic *box*, [television], the gift of Farang, born of European father and Yankee mother'.[81] The audience, all ears, listens to the 'box' which continuously spreads deceit, rattles lies, and declares the death of Rustam and of all his household:

The hero of the legends has died with the legends.
Since a long time ago, a very long time
The fire of legend has died out.
Dear kids, nice kids!
Rejoice in the living hero.
Listen to us, the past is dead.
Rejoice in the present, the future.
O you lovers of the dead!
Now *we* are the life, *we* are the living
We, whom you watch, whom you know
We, about whom they talk, about whom you read.
And you lovers of heroic acts!
We are Sam-i Nairam, and Zal
Rustam-i Dastan, and the gallant Suhrab
We are Faramarz and Burzu
And the renowned Shahriyar too.[82]

The old truthful narrator,
Silent, tired of these lies, of this ado,
Is about to leave, alone,
His corner of envy in the old tea-house.
By a finger top whose past weeps over its present
And whose present trembles over its future –
The remembrance of his hate and rage
Takes shape on the steamy window:
The figure of a puppet-man, with a fluid body.
I do not know
Whether the window puppet-man, in that shape
Is the figure of that magic glib-tongued
Or those who listen to him, all ears.[83]

The unawareness of people, the deceitful but enticing ways of the foreign invader, and the cooperation of treacherous insiders, combined together have created conditions in which the symbolic Rustam dies without avenging himself or trying to release himself from the trap set for him by his step-brother. For even if he should come out of the ditch, there is nothing left for him to guard; the 'box' has defeated the traditional storyteller.

It is perhaps this feeling of hopelessness that drives the poet to depict his son, called Zardusht, as the 'crucified Zoroaster'.[84] Omid himself identifies with that image intending to suggest, perhaps, that Zoroaster as a symbol of ancient Iran is crucified in his own land, by his own people.

NOTES

1. Editorial of *Kavah* (by Sayyid Hasan Taqizadah), new series, I, 1 (1920), p. 2. Later on Taqizadah regretted his extremist stand; see his *Akhz-i Tamaddun-i Khariji* (Tehran, 1950?), p. 9.
2. *Kavah*, *op. cit.*, p. 2.
3. Strong anti-Arab and anti-Islamic views were first expressed by the nineteenth century writer Mirza Fath Ali Akhundzadah (1812–1878); see Firaidun Adamiyat, *Andishaha-yi Mirza Fath Ali Akhundzadah*, (Tehran: Khvarazmi 1349), pp. 109–136, 186–237. Anti-Arab and/or anti-Islamic sentiments have been since expressed by quite a few Iranian literati among whom one may mention Mirza Aqa Khan Kirmani (d. 1896), Abulqasim 'Arif (d. 1933), Muhammad Taqi Bahar (Malik al-Shu'ara, d. 1951), Sadiq Hidayat (d. 1951), Ibrahim Pur-Davud (d. 1969), and Sadiq Chubaq (b. 1916). Idealization of the past and xenophobic sentiments have been a characteristic response of all Islamic peoples who have gone through the same trial of humiliation in the face of Western influence; see G. E. von Grunebaum, *Modern Islam: The Search for Cultural Identity* (New York: Vantage Books 1964), particularly chapters v–vii.
4. Mihdi Akhavan Salis (M. Omid), *Az In Avista*. In this paper I will quote the second printing (Tehran: Murvarid 1349/1970).
5. Mihdi Akhavan Salis (M. Omid), *Arghanun*, second printing (Tehran: Murvarid 1348/1969), p. 42; for more examples see pp. 115–116, 286.
6. According to Omid's own testimony his father was an observant Muslim who prayed regularly; see his *Bihtarin Omid* (Tehran: Rawzan 1348/1969), p. 28.
7. Mihdi Akhavan Salis (M. Omid), *Zimistan*, third printing (Tehran: Murvarid 1348/1969), pp. 37–39.
8. *Arghanun*, p. 32; see also pp. 42, 120, 123, 242.

9. *Zimistan*, pp. 71–74.
10. Mihdi Akhavan Salis (M. Omid), *Pa'iz dar Zindan* (Tehran: Rawzan 1348/1969), p. 81; the poem from which this line has been taken was written in later years, but its content corresponds to and explains the earlier example quoted in the text. It should also be noted that music is not expressly forbidden by Islam itself but is quite unfavourably looked upon by Islamic pious tradition. In ancient Iran, on the other hand, music was much appreciated and formed a main vehicle for artistic expression.
11. *Zimistan*, p. 70; the terms Omid uses for 'forbidden' and 'permitted' are the Muslim religious expressions *halal* and *haram*.
12. *Arghanun*, p. 126.
13. *Ibid*., p. 261.
14. See for instance, Muhammad Taqi Bahar (Malik al-Shu'ara), *Divan* (Tehran: Amir Kabir 1344–45/1965–66), vol. I, p. 631; vol. II, pp. 72, 491. However, Bahar, although also a xenophobe and anti-Arab, does not share Omid's anti-Islamic sentiments and is quite moderate in his local patriotism for Khurasan.
15. See for instance *Az In Avista*, p. 190. Omid's local patriotism has been criticized by Riza Barahini in his *Tala dar Mis*, second printing (Tehran: Zaman 1347/1968), pp. 418–419, 423–425.
16. *Az In Avista*, p. 228; see also pp. 17–18, 24–25; also *Arghanun*, p. 188; also *Pa'iz*, pp. 66–67, 81.
17. Mihdi Akhavan Salis (M. Omid), *Akhar-i Shahnamah*, third printing (Tehran: Murvarid 1348/1969), pp. 79, 83; the adjective 'sacred' apparently bears ironic significance.
18. Respectively *Zimistan*, pp. 146–147, and *Az In Avista*, p. 24.
19. *Zimistan*, pp. 111–113, 152–153, 120–121 for examples.
20. *Akhar-i Shahnamah*, p. 21; see also *Arghanun*, pp. 33, 34; *Zimistan*, pp. 12, 123, 133, 154–156.
21. *Akhar-i Shahnamah*, p. 80; the previous line is on p. 86.
22. *Ibid*., pp. 84–85.
23. *Az In Avista*, pp. 14–25.
24. *Ibid*., p. 21.
25. *Ibid*., p. 94; see also pp. 14–25, 154–155. In a poem written a few months later he calls himself 'the elegist of my dead homeland', *Arghanun*, p. 70.
26. *Az In Avista*, p. 90.
27. *Ibid*., pp. 154–155.
28. The Zoroastrian establishment of the Sassanid period vehemently opposed Mazdak and his doctrines and brought about the massacre of a large number of Mazdakites including Mazdak himself. Omid believes that some day Mazdak will be rehabilitated in a new trial; *Az In Avista*, p. 227. Omid is not the first to display interest in the Mazdakite movement. One of the many historical novels published in the first decades of the twentieth century is called *Damgustaran ya Intiqam-khahan-i Mazdak* (Trap-setters or the Avengers of Mazdak). This novel is known to have been written by San'tizadah Kirmani; however, Firaidun Adamiyat has recently suggested that the original writer of the book is the nineteenth century revolutionary thinker Mirza Aqa Khan Kirmani who was executed in 1896; see

Adamiyat, *Andishaha-yi, Mirza Aqa Khan Kirmani* (Tehran: Tahuri 1346/1967), pp. 55 ff. For more examples of pro-Mazdakite sentiments see Abulqasim 'Arif, *Divan* (Berlin: Mashriqi 1924), p. 204.

29. *Az In Avista*, p. 155.
30. I use the adjective Mazdushtian on the basis of the name *Mazdusht* coined by the poet himself; *Pa'iz dar Zindan*, p. 11.
31. *Az In Avista*, p. 155.
32. Omid's criticism of Arab historians is unfounded, for their writings on this and other Iranian subjects of pre-Islamic times are based on sources written by Iranians themselves; these sources were not for the most part favourable towards the Mazdakite movement.
33. *Az In Avista*, p. 157. Riza Barahini criticizes Omid for this statement apparently on the supposition that the poet refers to the historical Mazdak; see his *Tala dar Mis*, p. 422. Omid's local patriotism leads him to accept Nishapur (in Khurasan) as Mazdak's birthplace with no hesitation; Iranian sources, however, have mentioned several sites in different parts of the country as the reformer's birthplace; see Otakar Klima, *Mazdak, Geschichte 2.30Einen Sozialen Bewegung im Sassanidschern Persien* (Praha 1957), pp. 159 ff.
34. *Az In Avista*, p. 157.
35. *Ibid.*, p. 157.
36. *Ibid.*, pp. 105–106.
37. *Ibid.*, p. 161.
38. *Tala dar Mis*, pp. 418–421.
39. *Az In Avista*, pp. 164–168. The approximate borders of the Avistan Iran in Omid's view stretch to the Volga in the north, Jaxartes and Oxus in the north-east, the middle of the Black Sea in the north-west, Tigris and Euphrates in the west, and Sind in the south-east; *Ibid.*, p. 161.
40. See for instance Mirzadah 'Ishqi, *Kulliyat-i Musavvar*, ed. by Mushir Salimi, fourth printing (Tehran: Amir Kabir 1342/1963), pp. 233–237.
41. For an example of Rustam's symbolic position in Omid's poetry see below, p. 148. The only military leader of interest to Omid is the Afshar king *Nadir* (1735–1747). In the poem 'Nadir or Alexander' the imprisoned poet expresses the following wish:

    Omid, another Nadir will not appear,
    O that another Alexander would.
    (*Akhar-i Shahnamah*, p. 25).
42. *Az In Avista*, p. 227.
43. Cyrus Tahbaz, ed., *Daftarha-yi Zamanah*, special issue on M. Omid (Tehran, 1968), p. 55.
44. Jalal Al-Ahmad, *Gharb-zadagi* (Tehran, n.d.), p. 17.
45. *Zimistan*, p. 163.
46. *Az In Avista*, p. 165.
47. *Ibid.*, p. 213. Nima Yushij (1895–1959) is the founder of modern Persian poetry; italics are mine.
48. *Daftarha*, p. 39.
49. See for instance Muhammad Taqi Bahar, *Tarikh-i Tatavvur-i Shi'r-i Farsi*, ed. Taqi Binish (Tehran 1955), pp. 14–19. Bahar relies on Taha Husain and other Arab writers in denying the authenticity of pre-Islamic Arabic poetry.

50. *Az In Avista*, p. 213.
51. See Parviz N. Khanlari, *Vazn-i Shi'r-i Farsi* (Tehran: Bunyad-i Farhang 1965), pp. 73–74.
52. For a recent example of his classical writing see *Yaghma*, XXVII, 4 (1975), p. 194.
53. *Bihtarin Omid*, pp. 36–46.
54. *Daftarha*, p. 4.
55. For instance *masnavi*, *ruba'i*, and *du-baiti*; see Jan Rypka and others, *History of Iranian Literature* (Dordrecht 1968), pp. 96, 98.
56. *Az In Avista*, p. 214.
57. *Ibid.*, p. 219.
58. *Ibid.*, p. 216; the poets are Shahid Balkhi (d. 936?) and Baba Tahir (d. 1055?).
59. *Ibid.*, p. 222.
60. Outstanding examples are 'Akhar-i Shahnamah' (The Ending of the Shahnamah) in *Akhar-i Shanamah*, pp. 79–86, and 'Qissah-yi shahr-i sangistan' (The Story of the Petrified Kingdom) in *Az In Avista*, pp. 14–25.
61. For a detailed discussion of this subject see my 'Myth and legend as a key to reality and vision in the works of Mihdi Akhavan Salis (M. Omid)', *Asian and African Studies*, vol. XII, no. 3, pp. 84–107.
62. The notable among them are the poets Muhammad Riza Shafi'i (M. Sirishk), and Isma'il Khu'i in his early works.
63. *Daftarha*, p. 36.
64. *Ibid.*, p. 16.
65. *Tala dar Mis*, p. 641; see also, Jalal Al-Ahmad, *Arzyabi-yi Shitabzadah*, second printing (Tehran: Zaman 1343/1964), p. 26.
66. *Arghanun*, p. 307.
67. See for instance Sayyid Fakhr al-Din Shadman, *Taskhir-i Tamaddun-i Farangi* (Tehran: 1326/1947), p. 1; also *Andishah va Hunar*, special issue on Jalal Al-Ahmad, vol. V, no. 4 (1964), p. 399.
68. *Az In Avista*, p. 197.
69. The nineteenth century poet Yaghma used pure Persian in his correspondence and so did the prince Jalal al-Dawlah in writing his history of Iranian kings. In the twentieth century Ahmad Kasravi (d. 1945) has been the most zealous advocate of this movement.
70. The Arabic-Persian script has been mentioned by Akhunzadah as one of the reasons for Iran's backwardness; see Adamiyat's *Andishaha-yi Akhunzadah*, pp. 69–107.
71. *Daftarha*, pp. 66–67. Italics are mine.
72. Mihdi Akhavan Salis (M. Omid), *Majmu'ah-yi Maqalat*, vol. I (Mashad: Tus 1970), p. 172.
73. *Arghanun*, p. 185.
74. See the sources quoted in note 67.
75. *Daftarha*, p. 55.
76. Mihdi Akhavan Salis, *Avardah-and ki* ... (Tehran: Kanun-i Parvarish-i Fikri 1975), p. 5.
77. *Pa'iz dar Zindan*, pp. 54–65; the title of the poem is based on Rustam's famous *haft-khan* (seven adventures) in the Shahnamah.

78. Mas, the name by which the storyteller is called, is formed of the initials of the poet's name, Mihdi Akhavan Salis.
79. According to the Shahnamah Rustam was trapped by his step-brother Shaghad who dug a ditch on the path where the hero galloped on his famous steed Rakhsh.
80. *Pa'iz dar Zindan*, p. 65; dots are the poet's, ending the last line of the original.
81. *Ibid.*, pp. 66–67.
82. All the heroes mentioned are Rustam's ancestors and descendants.
83. *Pa'iz dar Zindan*, pp. 68–70; italics are mine.
84. *Ibid.*, pp. 102–103; his two other sons are called Tus and Mazdak.

7

Shi'ism in Contemporary Iranian Politics: The Case of Ali Shari'ati*

Mangol Bayat-Philipp

This paper is essentially a study of a current Iranian intellectual's crisis of identity. The three-generation old trial of religion versus secularism, which began with the simultaneous rise of nationalism and modernism at the turn of the century, now more than ever constitutes a disruptive obstacle to the development of a definite unifying national ideology. The process of secularization itself is following a steady path, and the life of the majority of the population is being affected by it. It is not necessarily accompanied by a dramatic rejection, or defence, of religious traditions and values. Though there are no statistical data available to substantiate this point, one can nevertheless safely assume that their faith is still basically undisturbed. They do not question the validity of its truth, nor the relevance of its teaching today. The battle, like most ideological battles, is being fought at the level of a small circle of decision and opinion makers, lay or clerical, and the still, relatively speaking, small though rapidly growing number of educated people.

The issue is rendered more complex by the fact that it is not a clear cut fight between the traditional, religious, clerical partisans on the one hand, and the modern secular state and its defendants on the other. The emergence of lay religious ideologists in the contemporary Iranian political scene, of whom Ali Shari'ati is perhaps the most important example, is adding a new dimension

* This paper was written before the 1978–79 events in Iran.

to it. Through their education and professional occupation, they are different from, and more often than not opposed to, the traditionally oriented *ulama*. They are twentieth century *embourgeoisé* modernists, both secularist and secularized, and, whether they wish to admit it or not, westernized, hence intellectually alienated from the average Iranian as well. And yet, their national consciousness expresses itself with a vehement attack on the westernizing, secularizing elements in the society. In their search for an 'authentic' self-definition which would challenge that of their opponents, they turn to Shi'i Islam. They choose to speak to, and on behalf of, the newly educated, increasingly self-aware, mainly urban middle and lower middle classes. Their message touches the raw nerve of some of those profoundly pious youths who are so eager to become 'modern', and yet remain faithful to their traditional system of values and beliefs. Youths who, in the process, are not yet uprooted but are disoriented enough to seek the guidance and above all the reassurance offered to them by those educated modern and yet Muslim lay preachers.[1]

In his works, Shari'ati never doubts or even questions the Islamic faith itself, nor the Shi'i dogma. His task is essentially to combat the traditional method of teaching and of understanding it.

> If we are Muslims, if we are Shi'is, and believe in the Islamic and Shi'i precepts, and yet those precepts have had no positive results upon our lives, it is obvious that we have to doubt our understanding of them. For we all believe that it is not possible for a nation to be Muslim, to believe in Ali and his way, and yet to gain no benefit from such a belief.[2]

He dismisses both the 'old-fashioned' way of 'believing without thinking', and the 'religious modernist' attempt to prove scientifically the validity of Shi'i principles. He tells his audience, 'those who have the strength and the courage to listen to and understand new ideas', that the most relevant question a Muslim should ask himself today is not whether each religious concept is rational or irrational, compatible or incompatible with science; but rather what is its usefulness and its worth to the society in which he lives. 'The belief in the Imamate must be useful to this world in order to bring result in the other world', he emphatically asserts.[3] Hence he calls for an 'Islamic Protestantism', similar to the one Northern Europe experienced in the sixteenth century, to help make Islam once more a 'positive social force that would abolish the Dark Ages and usher in the Age of the Renaissance.'[4] Its most immediate aim should be to purify religion from its foreign elements brought about through the centuries by despotic régimes, élite cultures, class distinctions, self-interest of power-seeking groups,[5] and by some ignorant *ulama* and superstitious 'so-called pious' parents;[6] in order to return to the 'original Islam of fourteen centuries ago.'[7] It is not, he claims, a matter of rethinking the religion, but of understanding the 'true spirit of the original Islam', and of rendering the Qoran readable again.[8] 'Too many of the not so obscure verses of the Qoran were rendered obscure by the *ulama* who attributed to them an esoteric meaning which was not there in the first place.'[9]

Shari'ati's aim, however, is not so much to reform as it is to emphasize the potentially radical notions inherent in some basic Shi'i concepts. For 'true Islam' is Imami Shi'ism, the 'religion of protest', of holy war and of martyrdom. It is important, he writes, to arouse the ignorant people and to infuse into them that 'true spirit' of revolt 'against the major spiritual, social and traditional obstacles to progress.'[10] *Ijtihad*, the search for the most correct understanding of the religious dogma by the qualified learned men, the *mujtahids*, he defines as the 'heavy responsibility of all Shi'i individuals, ... an independent responsible research done, not for an academic institution or for a publication, but for people, to show them the right path, and to keep religion alive and relevant to the changing conditions and the exigencies of time.'[11] Religious dogma, he explains again and again, follows a development parallel to social and scientific progress,[12] without, however, altering its basic precepts.[13].

Although he does not totally dismiss the role of the *ulama* as the legitimate leaders of religion, Shari'ati nevertheless holds them responsible for misleading and keeping the masses in ignorance of their true faith. Islam, he argues, unlike other religions, relates to all aspects of man's life. But some 'ignorant and irresponsible *ulama*' have, through the centuries, neglected their duties and narrowed down their science, which is interdisciplinary, to the highly specialized field of jurisprudence. The historical, sociological and political implications of the

Qoranic revelation have thus been either obscured or entirely overlooked. Those *ulama*, he states, are not 'learned people' in the true comprehensive meaning of the term. On the other hand, they are not the representatives of the Imam, for they have neither been appointed by him, nor elected by the people.[14] Shari'ati draws the conclusion that it is possible for an educated person to understand Islam better, live and think in a more Muslim way than an *alim*, or a mystic, or a philosopher, or a jurist.[15] In fact, he says, only qualified specialists can methodologically analyze religious concepts and hence scientifically reach the true meaning of the Qoran.[16] His-own position, a non-theologian by training, as a legitimate interpreter of religion he takes to be fully justified.[17]

Ultimately, Shari'ati believes that the task of reforming Shi'ism, and hence Shi'i society itself, can only be undertaken by the *raushanfikr*, a term commonly used for intellectual, but to which he adds a slightly different meaning. Denouncing the educated élite 'who now form a small, exclusive, aristocratic circle', living in an ivory tower, uprooted, aloof and detached from the masses, he chooses to differentiate a *raushanfikr*, 'a man endowed with an enlightened mind', from the professional thinker, the *mutafikir*, since the one is not necessarily the other as well.[18] Like most of his contemporary fellow Iranian intellectuals, Shari'ati professes a firm faith in the *raushanfikr* as leader. Depicting him as the 'torchbearer', the 'scout',[19] and, in stronger terms, 'the antithesis of oppression and darkness, ... for he is light',[20] in one of his works he goes so far as to compare the *raushanfikr*'s task to that of earlier prophets. For he gives birth to new social movements, even new cultures.[21] Slightly deviating from his statements elsewhere that only 'qualified specialists' can analyse the religious dogma, Shari'ati here claims that the *raushanfikr* does not have to be a highly educated man, nor does he have to be a scientist. For he discovers the truth, whereas the latter discovers facts. His qualification lies in his own consciousness and in his awareness of the problems of his society.[22] If not born from among the people, his feelings and his concern are nevertheless close to the masses. But he is different from the masses, for he belongs to, and forms, a class of his own. And yet, again unlike the scientist, his world view is not, and should not be, universal. He is bound to and by his own social milieu.[23] Shari'ati vehemently attacks what he calls the Western *raushanfikr-sazi* for the East which manufactures intellectuals who are *assimilés* (integrated) to Western culture but uprooted from their own. He denounces the notion of a 'universal man' which he sees as a European imperialistic invention aiming at undermining and eventually annihilating African and Asian cultures.[24] He relentlessly, emphatically states that the *raushanfikr* should aim at reforming his own society, in accordance with its needs and conditions, and that he cannot import his ideas from abroad.[25] The message, Shari'ati implies, must be national in character. For the author does not speak of the Muslim community but of Shi'i Iran. He goes one step further away from the universal concept of Islam by revealing a keen sense for expediency. The *raushanfikr*, he writes, in selecting the means to achieve his ends, unlike the scientist who follows definite precise rules and methods, has to estimate which means fit most the time and place.

> ... sometimes a word of truth [uttered] in the wrong place and at the wrong time, can become a destructive factor. Whereas a wrong word, which might even be scientifically unfounded, [if uttered] in a particular social milieu, could play a positive role.[26]

To illustrate his point, the author explains how some African superstitious belief, when put into use by the natives for the right cause (their fight against imperialism), proved to be effective.[27] But, in a society that possesses a 'proper culture and religion', the *raushanfikr* can rely on its traditions and spiritual possibilities to reach his aim, 'just as F. Fanon's anti-religious pronouncements achieved his own ends.'[28] Hence, 'The *Raushanfikr* must know that the dominant spirit of our culture is Islamic. Islam underlies all our cultural foundation and social structure. It is Islam, and Islamic traditions and values that should guide him in his search for the path to progress and reform.'[29]

And he warns:

> In an Islamic society, an anti-religious *Raushanfikr*, in his fight against religion, would only succeed in repelling the masses who, in their flight, would seek refuge among the reactionary and imperialistic elements that appear to be the protectors of Islam.[30]

The *raushanfikr* thus has to learn to distinguish the 'real' Islam from the corrupt form it is presently assuming.

Shari'ati explains that the Islam he wishes to bring to light is Islam, 'the ideology which inspires *Mujahids* (men fighting a holy war) and *Raushanfikran* (intellectuals), and which creates a sense of self-awareness and responsible leadership', as opposed to Islam, the theology of *mujtahids* and *ulama*.[31] He defines *ummat* (the Muslim community) as a 'human society where all individuals have gathered together to be guided by one common leader, and to move forward to a common goal.'[32] Dismissing other terms for group, such as nation (in transliterated French in the text), *quam* (people) or *qabilah* (tribe) as too static, he shows that the Arabic root word of *ummat* has a progressive and dynamic meaning attached to it, and that, of necessity, it also implies the term *imamate*, guidance to the goal. '*Ummat*', he writes, 'cannot exist without *imamate*.'[33]

The individual member who has freely and deliberately surrendered, has committed himself to the society. And society is committed to motion; motion in turn is committed to leadership, leadership to ideology or faith, and ideology to the realization of the ideal.[34] The ideal is, of course, God. But God is eternity. The motion is therefore never ending. Hence, 'the *ummat* is a society in eternal motion; and the *imamate* is the regime (in transliterated French in the text) which leads it.'[35] The Muslim's life within the *ummat* is not easy, or free, but committed and responsible. His aim is not to be, but to become; not to live well, but to lead a good life. Freedom is not an ideal, but a necessary means to attain the ideal.[36]

Islam, Shari'ati explains, is an ideology for a social revolution. Its aim is to establish a free 'classless society', for individuals who are free and responsible.[37] It was brought about, and put into practice, by the Prophet. But it was the task of the *imams* to continue and complete the historical mission of this movement.[38] The *imam* is thus defined as the political leader, the guardian of society, the *qahriman* (hero), the human being whose existence provides a model for men to follow. But he is also seen as the 'embodiment', the 'reality of an ideology', '... that is, within him, the values and ideas ... have become flesh and blood, and are alive.'[39]

The realization of such a revolutionary ideology is not possible within one generation only. Hence the need for a succession of *imami* guidance until the time when the members of the *ummat* are socially, politically and morally mature enough to assume leadership.[40]

Shari'ati attempts to accommodate the sunni concepts of *bi'at* (oath of allegiance), *ijma* (consensus) and *shura* (consultation), with the Shi'i principle of *vasayat* (the Prophet's will). They are not contradictory, he claims. Both are valid Islamic terms, representing two different phases in the historical evolution of the *ummat*: one, the democratic principle of Islam, the other the will of the Prophet. The latter corresponds to the first stage of social development, the *imamate*, when ideally within twelve generations, the ideological revolution is realized under the direct guidance of the living *imams*. The former is its logical conclusion, when the society stands firmly on its own feet, and democracy takes over. Had the *imams*, Shari'ati argues, been allowed to assume leadership of the *ummat*, undoubtedly the occultation of the twelfth *imam* would not have taken place. He would have lived like the others and, with his death, the *imami* phase would have come to an end. Then the *ummat*, thus rightly staged, would have deserved to choose on its own, according to the principle of *shura*, the worthiest leader.[41] But instead, 'they have relied on democracy and the principle of *shura* when it was the time of *vasayat*, revolutionary leadership.'[42] The *imamate*, following two and a half centuries of holy war and martyrdom, ended up with occultation. 'And the Islamic philosophy of history changed into the philosophy of *ghaybat* (occultation) and *intizar* (expectation)'.[43]

The period we are living in now, the Great Occultation, is the period of *ilm*. There are two kinds of *intizar*. The negative one believes that salvation and the reign of justice will occur only with the manifestation of the Hidden Imam, that in the meantime the prevailing corruption and injustice are natural historical necessities. To oppose them is fruitless.[44] Shari'ati condemns this attitude, and advocates a more positive, more activist belief in the Messianic expectation of the *imam*. It is in the nature of Messianic Faith to believe in 'the comeback of the Golden Age', in the revolution that will bring it about, and in the future reign of peace and justice. It is a progressive, future-oriented ideology, opposed to conservatism, to classicism, to traditionalism.[45]

Intizar means Futurism! The move towards the Future, which must

> of necessity come. A man in expectation, is in expectation of the future. One cannot expect the past! *Intizar* means hope, and hope means life.[46]

Adopting a dialectical terminology, he goes further to assert that *intizar* is the synthesis of two antitheses: Truth and Reality.

> Our faith is true, is just, is redeeming. Our Book, our Prophet, our Way, the best. ... But Reality shows the opposite: the people of Truth are defeated. ... *Intizar* solves this discrepancy. By expecting the final triumph of Truth over Reality.[47]

One therefore has to say no to what is, to revolt against the existing conditions.[48] 'The expecting man is a ready man', ready to fight the final *jihad* which will definitely take place.[49] For *intizar* is historical determinism. There will be a Revolution. This movement will triumph.[50]

* * * * *

Shari'ati's call for reform within Islam is reminiscent of the late nineteenth and early twentieth century Muslim Reformers' movement. Like them, he sees the past as an undeserved decline, and the future as a promise which will be fulfilled sooner or later. Like them, he sees the necessity to 'purify' religion, and to go back to the 'original' Islam. Like them, he refers to the positive results of Luther's revolt in sixteenth century Europe, and to the revitalizing effect it had upon its society. His belief that a cultural and socio-political Renaissance can only occur if religious reforms first take place, reflects, perhaps more so than theirs, a naive faith in the Western case model of development. It indicates his own failure to realize, or to accept the fact, that Iran, and the non-Western world in general, in their race to reach the modern age, have to jump over the centuries of evolutionary change which Europe enjoyed; and that their development does not conform to the Western pattern in any respect.

Whereas earlier reformers were largely influenced by eighteenth century European liberalism in their perception of Islam, and have tried to reveal the democratic root of the Islamic law as practiced in earlier times, his conception of Shi'ism reflects the more radically revolutionary concepts of the socialist schools. In the 1900's, for instance, Muhammad Husayn Na'ini, a then leading liberal *mujtahid*, had tried to accommodate the notions of constitutionalism, popular sovereignty and representative government into Shi'i political theory by claiming that freedom is a God-given right of the people whose duty it is to rise against unlawful despotism; and that the consultative role of the nation in political affairs is a religious imperative. Writing in the 1960's, Shari'ati shows a profound distaste for democracy and individual freedom as practiced in the West.

> Democracy in a society that is in need of rapid revolutionary change cannot be fruitful. The principle of democracy is opposite to the principle of revolutionary change and progress ... Political leadership based on a new ideology that runs opposite to the thought and tradition of that society, cannot be elected and supported by that society. Revolutionary leadership is not compatible with democracy.[51]

He views the Prophet of Islam as an 'engagé' leader committed not to gain votes, but to realize a revolution.[52] Instead of the representative constitutional government which Na'ini and his fellow liberal *mujtahids* accepted as the only legal alternative to the legitimate *imami* rule in this period of Occultation, Shari'ati asserts that the best form of government is an 'engagé democracy', to be led by a qualified group of revolutionary progressive people whose aim is to realize an ideology. 'In a backward nation', he writes, 'the people are not in a position to know what is best for them.'[53]

The élitist disposition he often reveals in his writings is accompanied by an obsessively repetitive need to discuss and define the role of 'the leader'. He quotes, approvingly, Western thinkers 'who believe that history is made by great personalities whose actions civilize ordinary people.'[54] If it were not for these historical figures, he claims, the 'ordinary people' would have continued to lead an 'animal life.' Men are in need of heroes to get out of their base condition and follow the human ideal. The Prophet was such a hero. So was Imam Ali.[55] Shari'ati stresses the need for such a hero to guide men in the present time.

Opposing his own view of Shi'ism as a religion of revolt to the established Shi'i attitude of passive acquiescence, he sees a renovated faith as part of the complete regeneration of society; whereas present conformism he scornfully rejects as only the symbol of general stagnation. Faith must be heroic, hence he calls for an 'Islamic Protestantism.' But he overlooks the essential fact that Luther, a clergyman concerned with the spiritual aspects of religion and the afterlife, directed his fight against the established Roman Church, and succeeded primarily because he gained the support of the German states. Whereas, in his own case, the prime target is, undisguisedly, the state and, in his struggle, he is appealing to some (the revolutionary-inclined) *ulama*. Perhaps Shari'ati, the lay sociologist well-versed in Weberian thought, by radicalizing Shi'ism is aiming at deliberately accomplishing what Luther unintentionally achieved, namely, the secularization of society. He is certainly anti-clerical and anti-traditionalist, and he rhetorically adopts and alters some basic aspects of Shi'i messianism. The conventional Shi'i view of the tragic *imam* figure as a martyr, *shahid*, is transformed into a conquering hero, a *qahriman*, and thus the element of pathos, so essential in the Twelver sect, is undermined by the author's drive for militant action. Similarly, the *intizar* of the *imam zaman*, the Shi'i millenarian ideal, becomes inseparable from historical determinism, from a vision of earthly perfection to be realized through revolutionary action. In fact, Shi'ism, as seen by Shari'ati, is almost totally stripped bare of its spiritual and metaphysical meaning. The emphasis is put on its worldly usefulness. 'Our religion is a religion that makes the ideal possible to realize itself on this earth, and not in our imagination or in heaven only. This *madinah-yi fazilah* can happen on earth.'[56] Shari'ati professes scorn for the various European types of utopia, but his own worldly understanding of the Shi'i *umat*, of the final triumph of good over evil, and the reign of the just is no less utopian. He has almost nothing to say about the practical problem of establishing a Shi'i state. What primarily interests him is the function of intellectuals like himself in the society. The society he is envisioning for the future is a totalitarian society, a 'dictatorship of the intellectuals', at least 'for as long as the social and political revolution has not accomplished its task: the political, social (and) moral maturity of each individual member of the *ummat*.'[57] For he firmly believes that it is in the consciousness of intellectuals alone (and he conceives the Prophet and the *imams* as such intellectual leaders) that great social movements have their origin. But here he is only representing a generally common view held by most modern Iranian intellectuals. For three quarters of a century, they have been prophetically sounding the alarm to warn of the impending cultural doom that is threatening their society. With a feverish intensity, they have questioned, doubted, rejected old and formulated new definitions of themselves. They have discovered their glorious pre-Islamic past, opposed or juxtaposed it to their equally glorious Islamic legacy, and searched for an 'authentic' identity. Painfully aware of their 'decadent present', they have turned their attention to the future, their refuge and last hope for self-realization. Each had a vision of a transformed society. Each aspired to be its chief architect. The turn of the century intellectuals chose the Western model to follow, the contemporary ones prefer to turn against it. The former predominantly wished to secularize, the latter tend to assert the importance of their religion. The present religious revivalism among lay writers, however, which expresses a profound disillusion and disenchantment with the West, is championed by men who have gone to Western-type, if not Western schools. Their whole mental formation is consequently much more secularized than their predecessors. It is therefore inevitable that their understanding and interpretation of their native culture would bear the mark of the West.

Shari'ati is no exception. In fact, in spite of the more violent tone of his attack against the West, the West has permeated his thought even more than that of the earlier reformers, lay or religious. They were all, spiritually and mentally, still deep-rootedly traditional Muslims. He no longer is. He lives in a time when the social system of the *embourgeoisé* class he belongs to through his education, has integrated some of the Western cultural values. He is therefore, whether he wishes to admit it or not, a product of that 'Western-made factory of intellectuals', an *assimilé* himself. One can only attest the fact that most of his references are Western writers. He cites European historians, European philosophers, European Orientalists.He often uses French terms. Even the word *assimilé* he uses instead of the common Persian equivalent: *gharb-zadah*; and in his passionate condemnation of it, he quotes Sartre rather than Al-i Ahmad. More significantly, when he tries to define and explain the Islamic concept of the *dajal*,* he compares it to Picasso's Portrait of a

* The Anti-Christ figure who, on the Day of Judgment, would be destroyed by the *iman*.

Hero, 'with one eye in the middle of the forehead', and calls it 'Herbert Marcuse's one dimensional man.'

> The present world system is a one dimensional system, ruling over a subjugated people rendered also one dimensional. This *dajal* is the symbol of that anti-human system that rules mankind.[58]

Ideologically, Shari'ati seems to reject traditionalism, Westernism and Marxism. And yet he makes use of all three of them. In tradition, he finds an ideal, Shi'ism, which he seeks to reinterpret in order to make it more 'relevant' to contemporary times, and more viable to produce an indigenous, thus acceptable, ideology. Western thought provides him with a frame of reference to update Shi'i concepts and values, and hence, prove them equal, if not superior, to Western ones. Marxism equips him with necessary revolutionary terminology, and a dialectical explanation of some historical developments. His ideologization of Shi'ism helps him to reject traditionalism without seemingly turning to the West for an alternative; and, at the same time, to reject Westernism without necessarily turning to an 'archaic' tradition. And he can thus appeal to two different kinds of follower: those whose impulse is primarily religious and who believe that they should react against the irreligious materialistic tendencies that are overcoming society; and those who are politically minded and want to undertake a revolution.

Shari'ati's personal struggle is two dimensional. On the one hand, he is speaking for a world that is conscious of its difference, proud of its cultural tradition, confronting another world, the West, which he can neither totally reject nor totally accept. On the other hand, within the nation itself, he is opposing two cultures, the old and the new, two systems of values which are reflecting the antagonism existing between social groups. He thus turns against capitalism, democracy and individual freedom which he conceives as distinguishing symbols of the West; and he champions the religious cause since it is symbolic of the masses, the 'oppressed classes'. Inspired by Frantz Fanon, whose works he has translated into Persian, he wishes to assert his native culture against its enemies from within and from outside. His Shi'ism proves to be: 1) a religion for the sake of revolution, and not a revolution for the sake of religion as he claims it to be; 2) in reaction to the West, a militant self-assertive cultural identity which is, ironically enough, reflecting Western concepts.

NOTES

1. My analysis of Shari'ati's ideas is that of a cultural historian who is primarily interested in current trends of social thought: their origin, their development and their impact upon society. I am not discussing the value of his message, but rather diagnosing a present religio-political phenomenon of which he is so much a part. My information regarding his personal life is very little. He is the son of a Khorasani lay preacher. He holds a doctorate in sociology from the Sorbonne (he was a student of the late Massignon, the French Orientalist). Back in Iran, he lectured at Mashhad University, then at Tehran's Husayniyah-yi arshad until the latter was closed down by the authorities. He spent some time in prison for his alleged political activities. News of his death, which occurred in England in the summer of 1977, reached me after this paper was completed.

   This is not an exhaustive study of Shari'ati. I have used only the following works.

   Az Kuja Aghaz Kunim, Tehran, n.d.
   Intizar, Mazhab-i i'tiraz, Tehran, 1971
   Mas'uliyat-i shi'ah budan, Tehran, 1971
   Pidar, madar ... ma muttahimim, Tehran, 1971
   Ummat va imamat, Tehran, 1968
2. *Intizar* ..., p. 19
3. *Ibid.*
4. *Ummat* ..., pp. 5–6
5. *Ibid.*, p. 3
6. Introduction to *Pidar, madar* ...
7. *Ummat*, p. 2.
8. *Ibid.*, p. 9.
9. *Ibid.*, p. 138.
10. *Az Kuja*, p. 56.
11. *Mas'uliyat.*
12. *Intizar*, pp. 23–24.
13. *Mas'uliyat.*
14. *Intizar*, pp. 28–29.
15. *Ibid.*, pp. 20–21.
16. *Ummat*, pp. 11–12; 25–26.
17. *Intizar*, p. 24.
18. *Az Kuja*, pp. 10–11.
19. *Ibid.*
20. *Ibid.*, p. 38.
21. *Ibid.*, p. 11.
22. *Ibid.*
23. *Ibid.*, p. 38.

24. *Ummat*, pp. 52–53.
25. *Az Kuja*, p. 24.
26. *Ibid.*, p. 32.
27. *Ibid.*
28. *Ibid.*, p. 43.
29. *Ibid.*
30. *Ibid.*, p. 45.
31. *Intizar*, pp. 20–21.
32. *Ummat*, p. 37.
33. *Ibid.*, p. 38.
34. *Ibid.*
35. *Ibid.*, p. 43–45.
36. *Ibid.*, p. 43.
37. *Ibid.*, p. 194.
38. *Ibid.*, p. 146.
39. *Ibid.*, p. 97.
40. *Ibid.*, p. 194.
41. *Ibid.*, pp. 195–197.
42. *Ibid.*, p. 197.
43. *Ibid.*, p. 198.
44. *Intizar*, pp. 25–27.
45. *Ibid.*, pp. 32–34.
46. *Ibid.*, p. 35.
47. *Ibid.*, pp. 36–38.
48. *Ibid.*, p. 39.
49. *Ibid.*, p. 45.
50. *Ibid.*, p. 41.
51. *Ummat*, p. 162.
52. *Ibid.*, p. 181.
53. *Ibid.*, p. 182.
54. *Ibid.*, p. 184.
55. *Ibid.*, p. 185.
56. *Ibid.*, p. 68.
57. *Ibid.*, p. 195.
58. *Intizar*, p. 58.

8

Preachers as Substitues for Mass Media: The Case of Iran 1905–1909*

Asghar Fathi

Pye describes the mass media communications process in modern societies as characterized by a distinct and highly organized system operated by professional communicators, while the communications process in traditional societies is not a distinct system, is unorganized, is not operated by a class of professional communicators, and is totally reliant on face-to-face communication. The transitional communication process is described as bifurcated – while part of it operates like a modern system the rest remains traditional.[1]

The object of this paper is to show that in certain traditional societies there is a distinct, organized system of communication operated by a class of professional communicators. Although the communication is face-to-face due to the lack of modern techniques, it is not of a personal nature. In other words, this paper attempts to show the institutional nature of certain 'mass communication' activities in some pre-industrial societies. More specifically, between 1905 and 1909 in Iran there was a series of protests against internal corruption, misgovernment, and foreign influence. In this period of unrest, which led to the constitutional government, the role of the preacher as communicator appears to have been very significant. Informing, agitating, and guiding the illiterate public was an integral part of the movement. The

* I am grateful to the Canada Council whose support enabled me to collect some necessary data in Iran in the summer of 1975.

Royalists, who opposed the movement, also made a significant use of the pulpit and the mosque in promoting their own cause. However, before a discussion of the preachers' role in these uprisings, it is necessary to become more familiar with the setting.

The Constitutional Movement

Toward the end of the nineteenth century in Iran, secret societies and newspapers, which were published abroad and smuggled into the country, advocated social reforms, control of foreign influence, and the end of despotism. Naser-ud-Din Shah of the *Qajar* dynasty, after nearly fifty years of absolute rule, was assassinated on May 1, 1896, by a disciple of the well-known reformist Seyyed Jamal-ud-Din Assad-Abadi, who had been previously banished from the country.

The new monarch, Muzaffar-ud-Din Shah, finally, after a major uprising by the people in Tehran led by prominent religious leaders, granted a constitutional form of government on August 5, 1906, a few months before his death. On January 19, 1907, his son was crowned Mohammad Ali Shah. He began his reign by ignoring Parliament, whereupon mutual suspicion and dissension became the rule. The struggle finally culminated on June 23, 1908 in an attack on Parliament by the Shah's troops in Tehran, and the destruction of the first National Assembly.

After the coup d'état of June 1908, it was only in Tabriz, in the Northwest, that people resisted and kept the Constitutional movement alive. For ten months Tabriz was under siege by the Royalist troops whose persistent attempts to capture the city were rebuffed by the Constitutionalists. This courageous resistance at Tabriz encouraged the Constitutionalists in other parts of Iran to rally, and on July 13, 1909, one group from the city of Rasht in the North, and another from the Southern region in a coordinated effort captured Tehran, thus forcing Mohammad Ali Shah to abdicate.[2]

The Limited Role of the Press

It is true that contact with the West played an important role in the awakening of the Constitutional leaders. The ideas of democracy and equality before the law had come from the West.

Travellers to Europe and the Persian newspapers published abroad were significant in creating a desire for change.[3] But a handful of intellectuals and modernists were ineffectual without the support of the illiterate masses, who were ignorant about their miserable situation.

After recognizing the need to arouse as many people as possible, a few writers and authors tried to change the then fashionable bombastic and high literary style of writing into simple prose very close to the vocabulary of the ordinary people.[4] But this was hardly sufficient. Ordinary people were not accustomed to print, and strict censorship by the despotic government did not allow free circulation of the press. But above all, most people could not read.

To remedy the situation, the liberal intellectuals sought the assistance of the preachers, who, in some cases, were themselves liberal and pro-Western. These preachers were literate and sometimes even learned men.[5] They were also professionally trained to deliver the sermon in the mosque every Friday (the Moslem holiday) after the prayer of the assembly, and on other religious occasions. It would probably be beneficial to turn our attention to the significance of the mosque, the Friday worship and sermon in Islam, in order to clarify and emphasize the role of the preacher in the Moslem community.

The Role of the Mosque and Sermon in Islam

In Arabic there are two words for mosque: *masjid*, or the place of worship; and *jami*, which comes from the verb *jama-a* meaning to gather together. The mosque is not only a place for worship, but also a place where the members of the Moslem community congregate. Because Islam is a religion as well as a state, during the early period of the Islamic empires, and in many Moslem countries afterward, official proclamations were read in the mosque and the new rulers and high officials delivered their inaugural addresses or explained important decisions to the community in that place. Actually in early Islam the mosque was built next to *dar-ul-emara*, or the building which housed the ruler. Thus, for any matter that concerned the community from preparation for an imminent disaster to making an important announcement, the community members would gather in or be called to the mosque. Also, when the community members were dissatisfied with something, they flocked to the mosque to discuss their problem or express their complaints.

The *minbar* or pulpit, which is an elevated seat used by the preacher in the mosque, is said to have been a judge's seat or the seat for the ruler in the pre-Islamic period. Mohammad and his successors used it on many official occasions. It was a kind of throne which could be occupied only by the leader. After Mohammad, the caliph or the governor representing the caliph, sat on the *minbar* during his inauguration ceremony. There he took the oath of office and delivered his first speech in the form of a sermon. Since the ruler was a temporal as well as religious leader, many proclamations from the *minbar* had these dual aspects.

During his sermons, Mohammad often commanded the Moslem community to participate in some mission or expedition from the *minbar*. Gradually as the worship service in the mosque developed, the *minbar* became the pulpit. However, it also retained its earlier significance as a platform from which important decisions, issues, and policies were announced, discussed and defended before a public audience.

In the pre-Islamic era on the Arabian Peninsula, the *Khatib*, which today is the word used for preacher in Arabic, was the man whose role was to extol the virtues and glories of his tribe and to deprecate its enemies in flawless prose. The *Sha-er* or poet did the same in verse. They were propagandists who could arouse enthusiasm for the battle in their own tribe. With the appearance of Islam, the responsibility of the *Khatib* was enlarged. He also became a teacher of religious doctrine and a preacher of the word of God. Originally the caliphs and governors were the official *Khatibs* or preachers. However, later the responsibilities were transferred to men who were learned in religious matters. The office of the preacher should not be confused with that of the *Imam* who leads the prayer of assembly on Fridays in the mosque, although in small communities both roles are often performed by the same person.

Friday in Islam is not a sabbath, or a day of rest. Trading is not forbidden on that day. The phrase, *yawm al-jum'ah*, designates Friday as a 'day of congregation.' Attendance at the prayer of assembly, which takes place in the mosque at noon on Friday, is required of every Moslem male. However, the nature of worship is not different from the prayer required five times daily from every adult Moslem, except that in the mosque during the prayer, the congregation stands behind the *Imam*, or the religious leader in charge of the particular mosque. After the prayer, the preacher delivers a sermon from the *minbar*, reminding the assembly of their religious and moral duties, and often discusses events and issues from a religious point of view. The purpose of the Friday worship in the mosque, therefore, seems to be to gather the Moslems together in order to allow the individual believer to identify himself with the Moslem community, to promote a sense of solidarity among the Moslems, and to announce major decisions or discuss public issues. Thus, from the beginning, the Friday worship service has had more than religious significance.[6]

The Conflict Between the Clergy and the State in Iran

As indicated above, Islam is both a religion and a state. Many Moslem countries have followed this system. A very notable example of this was the Ottoman Empire (1453–1919) where the *Sultan* was considered both the *Khalifa* (successor to the prophet) and the head of the State.[7] In Iran, however, a split developed between the clergy and the State. Whereas the *Sultan* in the Ottoman Empire could legitimize his rule by claiming succession to Mohammad and to some extent keep the clergy under his control, such a legitimacy and control were denied the Iranian monarchs.

Space does not allow a discussion of the developments that led to the split between the State and the clergy in Iran. However, with the increase in the influence of the religious leaders during the *Qajar* rule (1785–1925)[8] the *minbar* also increasingly became the platform utilized to promote the political interest of the clergy and to criticize the ruler and his representatives. Sometimes the interest of the public was also championed by the clergy. For instance, in 1898 a preacher, Seyyed Mohammad Yazdi, in Tabriz, aired the problem of rising prices and hoarding of wheat by the landlords on the *minbar*. In spite of the government's efforts to prevent a riot, the preacher was successful in arousing the people. A large crowd gathered in the mosque and subsequently attacked the houses of the alleged hoarders causing damage and bloodshed.[9]

The Qajar Kings were cognizant of the shaky position of the state with respect to religious legitimacy, and very often tried to placate the influential religious leaders, or even bribe some of them into supporting the State.[10] Both pro- and anti-government religious leaders used the *minbar* for their purposes. The climax of such use was reached during the Constitutional Movement (1905–1909). However, the *minbar* was used most effectively by the Constitutionalists in those years in Tehran and Tabriz as a means of informing the public about foreign influence and misgovernment, as well as arousing and encouraging them to action during the open clashes between the Constitutionalists and Royalists.

The Preachers and the Constitutional Movement in Tehran

The conflict between the clergy and the State was an important factor in the development of the Iranian Constitutional Movement. Two prominent religious leaders in Tehran began this movement. It is not yet clear how the intellectual reformists established an alliance with the clergy in this movement, but a series of incidents which were seized upon by the clergy to attack the despotic court was instrumental in the unfolding of the events which led to the granting of the Constitution by Muzaffar-ud-Din Shah.

In all these incidents the pro-Constitutional religious leaders made effective use of the *minbar*. For instance, the Belgians in the employ of the Iranian Customs Department were strongly resented because of their discrimination against the Moslem Iranian merchants and their pro-Russian activities and sentiments. When a picture of these Belgians at a costume ball, which revealed the chief of the customs, Mr. Naus, a Belgian, dressed as a Moslem clergyman, was 'discovered' in March, 1905, 'this mockery of Islam and insult to the clergy by the infidels' was reproached on the *minbar*. This incident provided an excellent opportunity for the anti-government clergy to criticize publicly foreign influence and thus roused popular sentiments against the court which was 'indifferent to the interests of Islam and the country.'[11]

Further, the Russians in competition with the British had developed a great deal of influence in Iran during the nineteenth century. Most of the clergy and the intellectuals were strongly opposed to this influence. When the Russian bank began constructing an impressive edifice in Tehran, some of the clergy objected because the designated site had previously been a cemetery, and construction there by non-Moslems was considered disrespect to the dead. When both the Russian ambassador and the Iranian court ignored these objections, late in November, 1905, a preacher in the nearby mosque, in accordance with a previous agreement with the prominent pro-Constitutionalist religious leaders, stirred the angered people in the audience from the *minbar* and led them to the construction site where they quickly demolished the half-built edifice.[12]

Another incident exploited by the clergy in their struggle against the Grand *Vazir* Ain-ud-Dawleh was the bastinado applied to two merchants in mid-December, 1905, by the Governor of Tehran because he held them responsible for the rise in the price of sugar. This arbitrary behaviour of the governor angered the merchants who closed the shops and gathered in the nearby mosque. The next day the crowd grew to include prominent religious leaders, and the state officials were strongly criticized from the *minbar* by a preacher. However, because of a clash which ensued between a pro-government religious leader and other clergy, the crowd disbanded. But the anti-government religious leaders did not give up. They established themselves in a shrine south of the capital and, day after day, the preachers persisted in criticizing both the Grand *Vazir* and the court from the *minbar*. Since they had attracted a large crowd, the government became apprehensive. The Shah intervened and in a letter promised to grant their requests.[13]

According to the historians of the Constitutional Movement, the exploitation of these and similar incidents by the Constitutional leaders and the exhortation of such issues from the *minbar* was intended to influence public opinion and arouse the people, thus paving the way for a popular uprising. Actually once such a sentiment was created and had gained momentum, in May, 1906, the two prominent religious leaders who led the Constitutionalist camp decided not to let the friction subside. To sustain their impact, they decided to have someone from their camp preach from the *minbar* regularly. Also, one of them personally preached from one mosque on Thursday evenings and another from a different mosque on Sunday evenings.[14] This arrangement clearly shows that the Constitutionalists knew the significance of the *minbar* as a medium for agitating the people.

The Royalists were also aware of the effectiveness of the *minbar* in arousing the public as well as a propaganda mechanism against the court. For example, Ain-ud-Dawleh, the Grand *Vazir*, humiliated by the success of the Constitutionalists in the shrine incident, insisted and succeeded in sending Seyyed Jamal Isfahani, a very popular and eloquent pro-Constitutional preacher, out of Tehran during the *Moharram* religious holidays (February and March, 1906), so that the latter would not cause any trouble during the days when religious sentiments ran high and many flocked to the mosques.[15]

Thus both the Royalists and the Constitutionalists knew that on certain occasions preaching from the *minbar* would be more effective. That is, preaching as a medium of communication had its 'prime times.' Preachers could command a larger and more attentive audience during the months of *Moharram* (when the martyrdom of Imam Hosein was very elaborately celebrated), and *Ramadhan* (the fasting month). Fridays and religious holidays throughout the year were also 'prime times' for such communication. Accordingly, both the Constitutionalists and the Royalists developed their strategies by taking this fact into consideration. For example, the outcry of insult to the clergy by the Belgians was blazoned from the *minbar* in the month of *Moharram*, and the attack on the Russian bank building took place on the last Friday in the month of *Ramadhan*.

Before examining the role of the preachers in Tabriz, the stronghold of the Constitutional Movement after the destruction of Parliament by Mohammad Ali Shah, it is necessary to discuss the use of the *minbar* by the Royalists in the capital and the Shah's awareness of the significant role of the preachers.

The use of the mosque and the *minbar* was not as readily available to the Royalists at the beginning as it was to the Constitutionalists, who represented the alliance between the clergy and the intellectual reformists. The Royalists had to placate and bribe the clergy in hopes of gaining some support from the *minbar*. As the Constitutional Movement unfolded, some of the clergy found it against their interests and joined the court.[16] Thus, during the months of *Moharram*, *Ramadhan*, or on religious holidays, the anti-Constitutional preachers also climbed the *minbar* and harangued the assembly by attacking the Constitutionalists and calling them *Babies*, or heretics.[17] Using the *minbar* for his purpose, Mohammad Ali Shah once mounted an all-out effort to stir the mob to attack the Parliament.[18] But in the subsequent clashes between the Royalists and Constitutional gangs, the latter somehow succeeded and the court was forced to withdraw.

Mohammad Ali Shah was very much aware of the preacher influence among the public. For example, in one of his many negotiations with the Parliament to settle their differences, he asked for the exile of eight Constitutionalists, three of whom were preachers and two newspaper editors.[19] After the destruction of the Parliament, he arrested and had strangled a well-known Constitutional preacher as well as two newspaper editors. Another popular preacher who had fled from Tehran was caught by the Shah's agent and put to death.[20] Both of these preachers had developed a reputation for their criticism of the court from the *minbar* which had continued until the destruction of Parliament. Again, when a secret agent of the Shah was arrested in Tabriz during the uprising there, he confessed that he had had instructions to shoot four prominent Tabrizi Constitutional leaders, two of them popular preachers.[21]

The Preachers and the Constitutional Movement in Tabriz

It has already been stated that the city of Tabriz in the Northwest was the stronghold of the Constitutionalists and the defenders helped restore the Constitution after Mohammad Ali Shah had bombarded the Parliament. Turning to the role of the preachers in Tabriz, the movement was started by a handful of intellectuals (some of whom were preachers), and by others with anti-government sympathies who took refuge in the British Consulate as an act of protest in mid-September, 1906. Naturally, they were aware of the development in the capital, Tehran, but were unhappy because of signs that the court was resisting implementation of the Shah's decree regarding the Constitution. It had been arranged that these dissenters in Tabriz would attract the attention of the public to their protest. They had also seen to it that once the crowd gathered around the consulate someone would explain the situation to them. The pro-Constitutional preachers took it upon themselves to do so. The next day the British Consulate, the nearby mosque, and even the streets were full of people who attentively listened to the preachers discussing corruption, injustice, and a desire for the rule of law.[22]

In general the preachers in Tabriz were more effective in informing and arousing the public than were the preachers in Tehran. One major reason for their success was probably the fact that the movement in Tabriz was run by twelve dedicated, knowledgeable Constitutionalists called 'the Secret Center', who took the matter into their own hands and in effect erected an alternative government in Tabriz which rivalled the despotic court in the capital.[23]

Space does not permit us to report the course of events and the accomplishments of the Secret Center. With respect to the subject of interest in this paper, it should be reported that the pro-Constitutional preachers were working very closely with the Secret Center. For example, the Secret Center had arranged that on Fridays in three mosques in Tabriz well-known preachers would regularly conduct sermons and discuss issues related to the Constitutional Movement.[24] Some of these services were so popular that the crowd even occupied the roof, the hallways, and the nearby streets of the mosques.[25]

The Constitutionalists in Tabriz had their own newspaper.[26] However, it was obvious to the Secret Center that in reaching the masses the newspaper had a very limited capacity.

The influence of the pro-Constitutional preachers in Tabriz is evident from the following incident. A very influential anti-Constitutional religious leader had sent a large sum of money to a well-known pro-Constitutional preacher, thus trying to attract him to the Royalist camp. But the preacher in question gave the money to the Constitutionalists' treasury and revealed the matter on the *minbar*. Public opinion pressured the anti-Constitutional religious leader to leave the city.[27]

One of the major accomplishments of the Secret Center in Tabriz was the formation of a civilian army. It is not necessary to report the details of success of this army in rebuffing the 30,000 Royalist troops that held the city under siege for ten months. Of interest here is the influence of the preachers in encouraging the people to take up arms and in justifying the importance of this unusual endeavour.[28] Of course, one should remember that in this as well as in other communications the preachers directed toward the public, they were acting in collaboration with the Secret Center.

The preachers in Tabriz not only informed the public about the current events in the capital as well as in other parts of the country and abroad, interpreted the events, and agitated the masses, but also, working under the direction of the Secret Center, they restrained the people and controlled the situation when the crowd was restless or when the occasion required calmness and patience.

Perhaps the best testimony to the significance of the *minbar* and the mosque during the Tabriz resistance comes from the diary of a retired merchant written during the four months of intense fighting between the Royalists and the defenders of the city.[29] He writes about those preachers who preached almost daily in very simple but persuasive language explaining the constitutional form of government, and criticizing both the court[30] and the clergy who supported it.[31] He talks about people going to the mosque to become informed about the events by listening to their preacher.[32] He speaks of the sufferings and complaints that the besieged people of Tabriz expressed to the assembly and the responses the preachers gave to soothe them and ask them for patience.[33]

Reading this diary one realizes that during the Tabriz resistance the mosque and the *minbar* were primarily used as a place and a channel for communication, with the religious ceremonies cut to the bare minimum.[34] For example, the author speaks of people being told to gather in a certain mosque to hear the results of the negotiation with the Royalists, or the announcement of a decision by the constitutional leaders.[35] Even the words *orator* and *speaking* are used synonymously with *preacher* and *preaching* in the diary.[36]

It is not an exaggerated statement to say that without the active role of the preachers in informing, agitating, and guiding the people the Tabriz resistance would have been impossible.

Discussion

There have been a few serious attempts made to study the

development of mass media in the pre-industrial societies. In the observations which exist it is assumed that a society simply shifts from a communication system based primarily on personal contacts and characterized by lack of independent professional communicators to another system characterized by a heterogeneous anonymous audience exposed to similar messages from limited bureaucratic organizations.[37] In such a discussion of comparative statics, the process of transition and development is left out.[38] The purpose of this paper is to investigate the interlinking points between 'traditional' and 'modern' processes of communication. That is, the paper attempts to discover if there are parts in the communication structure of certain pre-modern societies which in some way can assume (at least partially) some of the functions of the mass communication process in modern industrial societies, and the role that such parts play in the process of modernization.

It is the hypothesis of this paper that in the case of Iran (and probably in most Moslem countries), preaching the sermon from the *minbar* in the mosque provides an interlinking point between the 'pre-modern' and 'modern' processes of communication. That is, preaching from the *minbar* has the potentiality of developing into a medium of mass communication at the earlier stage of modernization.

It is important to remember that our investigation in this paper is concerned only with preachers as substitutes for mass media and not with preachers as part of a larger group called the clergy who are the intellectual guardians of certain social values.

In this paper we have seen that newspapers published abroad had an awakening impact on both the Iranian religious and non-religious intellectuals. After the granting of the Constitution and up to the destruction of the Parliament by Mohammad Ali Shah, many emerging newspapers enjoyed freedom in Tehran and other cities of Iran.[39] After that event, pro-Constitution newspapers continued only in Tabriz. But with the bulk of the population illiterate, a national movement could not depend on the newspaper alone.

However, illiteracy does not seem to be the only barrier to the use of print as a mass medium during the Constitutional Movement in Iran. One interesting observation made by Kasravi, the well-known historian of the Constitutional Movement, is that many newspapers during the Constitutional Revolution did not and probably could not relate to the needs and feelings of the populace. Instead of dealing with the issues of the day, many papers published poetry and dealt with philosophical and religious matters. Their language and style also were hardly intelligible to the ordinary people.[40] One explanation of this situation appears to be that prior to the Constitutional Movement print had been a medium used only by the religious leaders and the literate men of the upper class for subjects of interest to them alone. Further, the language was geared to the literary vocabulary and to a lifestyle far removed from the experience of the common man.[41] Transforming print to a medium suitable to the interest of the layman with all the changes that this action would entail was something that many of the newspaper editors (who themselves often belonged to the elite class) could not easily perform. Of course, there were notable exceptions,[42] but this was hardly adequate to sustain a movement of the magnitude of the Constitutional Revolution.

In fact, the term newspaper is a misnomer for most of the materials which appeared in print under this name prior to the Constitutional Movement and during that period. Many of these published materials had little resemblance to the European newspapers of that time. Firstly, as we have seen already, they were directed towards a very small portion of the population, the literate élite. Thus the average newspaper in Tehran enjoyed a circulation of only two to three thousand copies.[43] Secondly, they did not often appear on a regular and daily basis.[44] Some of them were issued once a week. Later, a few became more frequent. Those which were published abroad, naturally, could not and did not reach their readers until weeks after their publication. Thirdly, the topics published in many cases were not timely. That is, even many of those which were directly involved in the movement did not deal with the current daily issues.[45] They were in reality political tracts and pamphlets discussing democracy, scientific achievements of the Europeans, while deploring the condition of Iran.

Thus the newspaper came to Iran as an innovation from Europe, but many of its adopters could not use it the way it had been used in its original cultural milieu. On the other hand, the need which could have been satisfied by the newspaper in France or England during a national uprising such as the Constitutional Movement could be very easily fulfilled by preaching from the *minbar* in the mosque which had existed in Iran as a distinct, organized system of communication for centuries. Of course, the long-standing conflict between the clergy and the court, where the clergy was often the only refuge for helpless people against the despotic régime, greatly facilitated this adaptation.

NOTES

1. L. W. Pye (ed.), *Communications and Political Development* (1963), pp. 24–29.
2. See A. Kasravi, *The History of the Constitutional Movement in Iran* (in Persian, 1965); Nazem-ul-Islam-e Kermani, *The History of the Iranian Awakening* (in Persian; Introduction and Volumes I, II and III, 1967 and Volumes IV and V, 1970–71); and E. G. Browne, *Persian Revolution of 1905–1909* (1910), among others.
3. Kasravi, *op. cit.*, p. 44.
4. Mirza Malkum Khan, the editor of *Qanun* was the trail-blazer in this respect. See H. Kamshad, *Modern Persian Prose Literature* (1966), pp. 14–15. For more on this unusual man see H. Algar, *Mirza Malkum Khan* (1973).
5. For reports on two of the learned and well known constitutional preachers see M. Malek Zadeh, *The History of the Iranian Constitutional Revolution* (in Persian, no date), Vol. 1, pp. 196–212; and I. Safaii, *The Leaders of the Constitutional Movement* (in Persian, 1969–70). Vol. 1, pp. 317–358.
6. See *The Shorter Encyclopedia of Islam* (1961), pp. 330–353; B. M. Borthwick, *The Islamic Sermon as a Channel of Political Communication*, Ph.D. dissertation, University of Michigan, 1965; and O. Grabar, 'The Architecture of the Middle Eastern City from Past to Present: The Case of the Mosque,' in I. M. Lapidus (ed.), *Middle Eastern Cities* (1969), pp. 26–46.
7. B. Lewis, *The Emergence of Modern Turkey*, (1968), p. 403.
8. H. Algar, *Religion and State in Iran 1785–1906* (1969), pp. 257–260.
9. Kasravi, *op. cit.*, pp. 140–142. For a similar use of the mosque and the pulpit in Mashhad, a city in the Northeast in 1906, also see the same source, p. 84.
10. For instance, see Algar, *op. cit.*, pp. 45–52.
11. Kasravi, *op. cit.*, pp. 35–38. See also M. Mokhber-us-Saltana, *Memoirs and Perils* (in Persian 1965–66), p. 141.
12. Kasravi, *op. cit.*, pp. 54–57; and Nazem-ul-Islam-e Kermani, *op. cit.* Vol. 1, pp. 84–87.
13. Kasravi, *op. cit.*, pp. 58–72; and Mokhber-us-Saltana, *op. cit.*, p. 140–141.
14. Kasravi, *op. cit.*, p. 84.
15. *Ibid*, p. 77; and Nazem-ul-Islam-e Kermani, *op. cit.*, Vol. IV, p. 93.
16. Kasravi, *op. cit.*, p. 511.

17. *Ibid.*, pp. 481–482, 505, 512. Also Nazem-ul-Islam-e Kermani, Vol. IV., p. 93.
18. Kasravi, *op. cit.*, pp. 505, 512; and Mokhber-us-Saltana, *op. cit.*, p. 161.
19. Kasravi, *op. cit.*, p. 593. Mokhber-us-Saltana reports that only two preachers were involved, p. 162.
20. Kasravi, *op. cit.*, pp. 659–666; and Nazem-ul-Islam-e Kermani, Vol. IV, *op. cit.*, pp. 160, 170 and 231.
21. Kasravi, *op. cit.*, p. 334.
22. *Ibid.*, pp. 153–158.
23. K. Taher Zadeh Behzad, *The Uprising of Azarbaiyjan During the Constitutional Movement* (in Persian, no date), pp. 44–49, 63–66, and 452–456. Also Kasvari, *op. cit.*, pp. 167 and 467–469.
24. Kasravi, *op. cit.*, pp. 183 and 234.
25. *Ibid.*, p. 235.
26. *Ibid.*, p. 268.
27. *Ibid.*, p. 173.
28. *Ibid.*, p. 183.
29. M. B. Vijaviyaii, *The History of the Azarbaiyjan's Revolution and The Uprising of Tabriz* (in Persian, 1969).
30. *Ibid.*, p. 12, p. 116, pp. 118–121 and p. 148.
31. *Ibid.*, p. 12 and pp. 57–59.
32. *Ibid.*, p. 135 and p. 251.
33. *Ibid.*, p. 121 and p. 212.
34. *Ibid.*, p. 135 and p. 148.
35. *Ibid.*, p. 135 and pp. 181–182.
36. *Ibid.*, p. 45, p. 118, p. 148 and p. 181.
37. Pye, *op. cit.*, and W. Schramm, *Men, Messages, and Media* (1973), p. 35.
38. Lerner might appear an exception. But on closer inspection we find that he only examines the various media such as the press, radio, and motion picture both as agents and indices of modernization. Prior to the introduction of these innovations and in those segments where they have not penetrated, it is the oral system which operates in the traditional society. According to Lerner, in the oral system the channel is personal, the audience is primary group, the content is prescriptive, and the source is hierarchical. See D. Lerner, *The Passing of Traditional Society* (1958), pp. 55–56.

    E. M. Rogers, in his book *Modernization Among Peasants: The Impact of Communication* (1969), like Lerner disregards the indigenous institutions and their history. He deals with social-psychological variables such as empathy and innovativeness.

    Historian Bernard Lewis appears to have identified this problem in cross-cultural research in the following statement:

    'Most techniques of field research in the social sciences relate to one of the two situations: either the researcher is dealing with a sector of his own civilization, whose historical and cultural pattern is known to him as a part of his own education and upbringing, or else he is dealing with a primitive society, where historical and literary evidence can be disregarded because it does not exist. *What has not yet been adequately faced is the problem of field research in a literate, historical society other than that of the field-researcher himself.'* (Emphasis added).

See Bernard Lewis, *Islam in History* (1973), p. 32.

39. Kasravi, *op. cit.*, p. 571.
40. *Ibid.*, pp. 274–275 and 571.
41. According to Browne, the few newspapers which were published in Iran prior to the Constitutional Movement were only valuable from a literary point of view. See E. G. Browne, *The Press and Poetry of Modern Persia* (1914), p. xii. A selection of the poems which appeared during the Constitutional Movement and later in the Iranian press also appears in the same source. See also Kamshad, *op. cit.*, pp. 29–30 and pp. 36–37.
42. A. Deh-Khoda of the Sur-e Esrafil newspaper was one exception. See Kamshad, *op. cit.*, pp. 37–40 and Kasravi, *op. cit.*, pp. 277–278. See also note 4.
43. Browne, *The Press and Poetry of Modern Persia*, *op. cit.*, p. 25.
44. Kasravi, *op. cit.*, p. 275.
45. *Ibid.*, pp. 277–278.

9

The Genesis of the Anglo-Persian Agreement of 1919

William J. Olson

On August 9, 1919 Lord Curzon, in one of his inveterate memoranda, presented to his cabinet colleagues an exposition on negotiations with Persia. He outlined Anglo-Iranian relations during the World War and discussed, at his customary length, the background of British involvement in Iran, mentioning: a longstanding interest in Persia; Persia's strategic importance to India; the chaos in Iran's internal politics; and the machinations of the Germans and Turks to exploit this situation by arousing Muslim sentiments for a holy war against British interests throughout the Middle East. Fortunately, Curzon noted, this last potential had not come to pass and with Britain's victory a new era in Anglo-Iranian relations was possible.[1]

Curzon had taken advantage of Britain's unique post-war situation in Persia to conclude an agreement with the Persians that he believed would consolidate Britain's position in Persia, make Persia a positive asset in India's defences and provide the Persians with the resources and guidance to put their house in order. In making the agreement Curzon fulfilled a long held personal aspiration and became another in a long list of British Foreign Secretaries who tried to resolve the Persian muddle. Curzon was then interim Secretary of State for Foreign Affairs while Balfour was at the Peace Conference in Paris.

The need to protect the Indian Empire and imperial lines of communication was the essential feature of Britain's interest in

Persia throughout most of the nineteenth century and policy-makers in India and London had developed a succession of policies to try to fit Iran into a satisfactory scheme for the defence of India. Initially, when Persia was a strong, independent state, Britain sought treaty relations with Persia to secure India's frontier from foreign machinations and indigenous tribal depredations on India. But as Persia's power declined during the nineteenth century, largely as the result of Russian pressure and internal political turmoil, a policy developed to bolster Persian weaknesses. British statesmen, such as Salisbury, tried to promote economic development and administrative reform as a means to rehabilitate the country and give it the strength to resist Russian influence. But as this policy did not have the desired effect, Salisbury and subsequent Foreign Secretaries abandoned it. Instead they tried to solve the problem of Indian security by reaching an understanding with Russia, the chief threat to Britain's Indian Empire. This too eluded British policy-makers until Russia's defeat by Japan in 1905 and the growing threat of Germany to both Russia and Britain made a mutual settlement of differences more attractive to the Russians.

This settlement was ultimately achieved by Sir Edward Grey in the Anglo-Russian Convention of 1907 which, theoretically, composed the differences of the two powers in the East. Unfortunately for Britain this arrangement failed to give concrete protection to British interests. First, the Convention embittered Persian nationalist sentiment, much of which had regarded Britain as the liberal protection of Persia's integrity against the demands of Russia; the Convention linked Britain with Russia's aggression in Persian minds, and when war came to the Middle East many Persians actively assisted the Turks and Germans against British interests. Second, the Convention did not put an end to security worries, for it merely placated one rival – Russia – while trying to deal with another – Germany. Furthermore, the Convention did not really succeed in reducing Russia's pressure on Persia and therefore on the frontiers of India. Thus, by the beginning of World War I, attempts to fit Iran into a scheme for imperial defence had not been reassuringly successful. The outbreak of the War and its spread to the Middle East made a definitive solution for this problem imperative.

The Germans and Turks were determined to exploit Muslim

sentiments and to capitalize on anti-British, anti-Russian sympathies to engender a revolt and war in the Middle East that would force Britain to divert its attentions from Europe. The Germans and Turks realized that the cooperation of Persia and Afghanistan, as the only other major independent Muslim nations besides the Ottoman Empire, could aid these war efforts and so they actively campaigned – with agents, money and limited military effort – to win them over.

British strategic planners in London and Delhi recognized this threat, and worked to frustrate it. A clear line of policy did not, however, develop from the awareness of the need. The main goal in relation to Iran was to keep the country neutral and minimize its advantage to the enemy. This was ultimately achieved but more as the result of happy accident than deliberate policy deliberately arrived at. The fragmented nature of decision-making – divided as it was between India, the India Office, the Foreign Office, the War Office, the Cabinet, various committees, and local experts – inhibited the development of a clear policy.

Among various alternatives that were employed, alternatives ranging from limited commitment of troops and agreements with locals to the raising of levy corps such as the South Persia Rifles, one of the main efforts was directed at reaching some kind of working arrangement with the Persian Government. These efforts, however, were not especially rewarding. Russian aggression and the apparent support Britain gave to this in the years before the war undermined popular support for the Allied cause in Persia and made it difficult for any Persian Government to reach an agreement with the Allies. Elements within the government supported the Germans and the uncertainties over the course of the war inhibited the chances for an agreement. Furthermore, both Britain and Russia were eager to protect their respective interests and did not want to make commitments to Iran that might have embarrassed their positions after the war. Thus negotiations with the Persian Government did not enjoy notable success and British officials were forced to endure continuing anxiety over the threat to India and imperial communications.

The end of the alarms of war did not bring with it a ready solution for these problems. The immediate threat to British security passed but the necessity of protecting imperial communications remained a cogent issue. Although Germany and Russia had disappeared as the main threats to British interests, victory had not eased the problems of security, for the success of war freighted that concern with a new set of problems. The acquisition of Mesopotamia, the rising tide of regional nationalism, the new importance of oil and newly acquired oil potential, and a new array of international interests all contributed to make the issue of securing post-war interests in Iran as vital as it had been before and during the war. Furthermore, Persia was racked by internal disorder and the Bolsheviks menaced British security by threatening to capitalize on this and spread the germ of communism and revolution.

But victory had left Britain with a unique opportunity in Iran and there were men in London who were willing to seize the opportunity to capture the security that had eluded all war-time efforts. The Anglo-Persian Agreement which Curzon presented to his cabinet colleagues in August, 1919 was to be the instrument for British security. In one stroke it tried to settle all the outstanding issues in Anglo-Persian relations, ministering to Britain's security worries and providing Iran with a renewed sense of integrity.

The chief architect of this agreement was George N. Curzon, the First Marquis Curzon of Kedlestone, former Viceroy of India. He was a recognized authority on Iran, by virtue of his two-volume work *Persia and the Persian Question*, and it had long been his ambition to settle the problems of Indian security.[2] In some aspects Anglo-Iranian relations in 1919 were Curzon–Iranian relations. And in 1919, as *interim* Secretary of State for Foreign Affairs, Curzon, the Persian expert, had an opportunity to finally put Britain's position on a firm basis. He could argue from a position of relative strength – British money supported the Persian Government, British troops or levies provided internal security and the main rivals, Germany and Russia, had disappeared as a menace. With these advantages Curzon's arguments, at least to himself, sounded convincing.

Guided by this personal vision, Curzon set out to settle the issues that had troubled Anglo-Iranian relations during the war and before. He wanted a secure, stable, pro-British Iran that would recognize and protect British interests in the Gulf and provide a buffer to foreign interests and advances on Iran. Curzon came from that group of 'Persophiles' which favoured Persian regeneration.

Curzon's conviction was supported by the fact that Sir Percy Cox, the long-time resident on the Persian Gulf and noted Middle East expert, was Britain's acting minister in Iran; and that the Persian Government of Vusuq ad-Daulah was pro-British. Vusuq ad-Daulah had come to power in 1918 with Britain's active support and the money for meeting his government's expenses was largely provided by a British subsidy. In addition the internal Persian opposition to Britain, led by the so-called Democratic Party, which had offered considerable resistance during the war, was in disarray. Thus the whole weight of circumstance seemed to indicate that the time was ripe for a final settlement.

Two main problems faced the British in their attempt to arrange matters in Iran; first was the perennial problem of how best to secure British interests in Iran, second was the issue of Persia's representation at the Peace Conference and the attendant worry that this would attract unwelcome foreign interests. The British wanted the Persians to appreciate that only Britain could aid them and until the Persian Delegation to the Peace Conference came to realize this Britain avoided contact with and support of Persia's mission.

The British had determined in 1918 to exclude Persia from the Peace Conference if possible and, if not, to secure a mandate for Britain or some pliant second power. Britain wanted to settle her interests in Iran without foreign meddling, a factor that had interfered in Anglo-Iranian relations for a hundred years. If Iran made a successful bid for attention at the Conference then the whole problem would re-emerge. Consequently Britain decided to oppose Persia's representation at the Conference on the grounds that Persia had not been a belligerent.[3] Curzon hoped that by isolating the Persian Delegation and holding out promises to Persia of British assistance the whole issue could be avoided and the Delegation would settle for frank discussions with Britain. Curzon believed, and Sir Charles Marling (the former Minister to Persia, then in London as an adviser) concurred, that Persia needed British support and that only a few radical elements really opposed Britain's sincere interest in rehabilitating Iran. As Marling put it,

> In his heart the Persian, even the rabid 'Democrats' – where Democracy is about as genuine as that of the Committee of Union and Progress in Turkey – know perfectly well that we are really Persia's friend.[4]

It only required waiting until the Persians came to their senses. The Persian Delegation to the Conference were not to Britain's liking, especially since they appeared determined to pursue an independent course outside Vusuq ad-Daulah's control. In this light Curzon decided to have no intercourse with the Persian Delegation to the Peace Conference until they had no choice but to turn to Britain.[5]

The only voice that suggested caution, that urged careful consideration before applying the solutions in Iran that new circumstances seemed to allow, was India. The Government of India realized that a genuine nationalistic spirit was alive in Iran, despite its seeming confusion, and they felt that this force should be recognized and conciliated.

India did not argue that Britain should abandon the position won in Iran, but objected that British policy failed to consider legitimate Persian sympathies. Sir Hamilton Grant, the Secretary of the Foreign Department of the Government of India during the war, who was in London as an adviser for the peace, put forward at a mid-December meeting of the Eastern Committee what he thought were the essential views of India. Grant took exception to Curzon's view that Britain had done everything to reassure Persia of Britain's concern for its integrity. He felt that public opinion in Iran could be influenced in Britain's favour and although he had no illusions as to the 'general meanness or futility of the Persian character,' he felt that there was still a 'curious kind of patriotism and nationalism which is neither to be bought or overawed.' In Grant's opinion Britain might have done everything to reassure Persia, but he felt that the manner in which 'our various announcements and guarantees have been made has not been of a very convincing or ingratiating kind.' He continued:

> There has been a want, if I may say so, of real frankness and kindliness about the tone of our communications to the Persian Government: in the words of the old song, 'It's not exactly what we say but the nasty way we say it.'

In this light he outlined what India expected. India opposed a mandate for Britain as too expensive, politically and economically. They also opposed a mandate for other powers because it would mean footing the bill to secure the interference of another power. But they did not favour abandoning Iran to chaos, proposing instead to assist Persia on a limited scale. They felt it essential to regain the confidence of the Persian people by abolishing the South Persia Rifles, withdrawing British troops from Fars, the Bushire-Shiraz road and other areas as soon as conditions allowed, abolishing the 1907 Convention, and agreeing to revise customs laws. In return they only asked that Persia accept British financial advisers in the regulation of Persia's finances, coupled with a subvention and lenient terms on repayment of debts. Grant believed that a declaration along these lines (a draft of which he had prepared) would reassure Persian opinion and go a long way towards achieving the amiable agreement both Britain and Persia needed.[6]

Officials in London, however, did not share India's concern for Persian nationalistic feelings and regarded this spirit as a German inspiration at worst and a self-seeking political gambit at best. Even Cox, on the scene, with his eyes focused on securing British interest, believed that only a few demagogues thought that Persia could forego foreign assistance, which should rightly come only from Britain.[7] Curzon agreed with Cox and he determined to ignore or discount Persian nationalism and India's opinion and to proceed with a settlement that satisfied his goals.

On January 11 he telegraphed his views to Cox, informing him of the Eastern Committee's decision to avoid the subject of Persia at the Peace Conference. At the same time he expressed a willingness, once it was obvious that Persia would not receive a hearing, to meet with the Persian Delegation to the Peace Conference to discuss questions of future relations. Curzon outlined for Cox the general features of what he had in mind: 1) unqualified renewal of assurances of Britain's respect of Persia's independence and integrity; 2) abrogation of the 1907 Convention, which Britain already considered in abeyance; 3) creation of a uniform force with South Persia Rifles as the nucleus in the south and the Persian Cossack Brigade as the northern focus; 4) appointment of a British financial adviser; 5) withdrawal of British troops at the earliest possible moment justified by the situation.

Curzon regarded these proposals as extremely generous and he made them to assuage Persian doubts as to Britain's good faith. He hoped that Persia would respond in the same spirit and if they did not and if they insisted on unacceptable proposals then Britain might have to consider withdrawing help altogether. Curzon did not want Cox to communicate his proposed terms immediately but first wanted him to 'try to induce atmosphere' suggested above, namely that Persia needed Britain's help.[8]

Cox was able to communicate encouraging news. He reported that Persian public opinion was less hostile than it had been for some time and more inclined to realize that Persia had to depend on Britain. He also had several conversations with Prime Minister Vusuq ad-Daulah, Akhbar Mirza, and Firuz Mirza, the Minister of Justice, concerning advisers and support and they had expressed confidence in Britain. The latter two individuals had been helpful in the past, as had their fathers, the Zill as-Sultan and Farman-Farma, respectively. The British came to call these men 'the Triumvirate' and to put great faith in their judgment. Cox said they broached the subject of British financial aid timidly for fear that if their proposals were rejected they would suffer odium for nothing. On the other hand, if they could receive assurance of Britain's readiness to give effective help to Persia and if a preliminary understanding could be reached then they could undertake the necessary propaganda to carry agreement through. The Triumvirate were anxious for negotiations to begin lest the Persian Delegation at the Conference, the Shah's appointees, should 'queer the pitch' by talking with others in Europe[9]*

The Triumvirate also accepted the idea, opposed late in the war, that any financial adviser employed by Persia should come from Britain.[10] Thus Persia was acknowledging the need for British assistance and removing one of the stumbling blocks that had aggravated British officials, who had felt Britain's

* This hint of rivalry between the Cabinet, or at least the Triumvirate, and the Peace Delegation grew into full-fledged competition before the negotiations were concluded. The reasons are not exactly clear from presently available sources but Vusug ad-Daulah obviously resented the rival source of influence. The Shah encouraged the delegation idea and forbade Vusuq ad-Daulah to join it. Mere personal jealousies may have motivated the animosity. But more likely the Prime Minister seriously believed that Persia had no choice but Britain, and he hoped to get the best terms possible and feared that the Peace Delegation would undermine the chances.

considerable financial support of Persia entitled them to name a financial adviser, in late 1918. On this basis Cox urged that Britain adopt some moderate scheme that would capitalize on Persia's willingness to negotiate.[11]

The Foreign Office appreciated the information and the fact that the three most influential members of the Persian cabinet were aware of 'realities' and ready to adopt a position similar to Britain's; but there was a problem. They felt that the fact that the Persian Government had sent to Paris representatives who seemed to have different opinions from the Government made it difficult to enter into negotiations until it was clear that Persia intended to follow only one policy. The most the Foreign Office, i.e. Curzon, was prepared to permit was to continue to explore the possibilities of an agreement while Curzon consulted with Balfour about convincing the Persian Delegation to give up at Paris and come to London.[12] Presenting this opinion was an attempt to squelch the Persian Delegation from the Persian end while the British endeavored to bury the issue at the Conference.

In the meantime, during early 1919, India had an opportunity to respond to Cox's idea of a moderate scheme for Persia. They agreed that financial reform under British officers was important but they were taken aback by the extent of control suggested. Cox had suggested not only a financial adviser for the Treasury and the Ministries of the Interior, Public Works, Agriculture, Law and Education, but also advisers for each major province. He had also suggested that the British Commander of the uniform force be given virtual administrative independence. In short, he was proposing tight control.

India felt that this full programme of reform might prove too strong meat even for the ultra pro-British Triumvirate. There was another worry:

> ... as we know from experience pro-British optimism of men so bound up with us as Vossuk and the sons of Zill and Farman-Farma are a very uncertain barometer of public opinion. In a matter of such moment we cannot afford a repetition on a large scale of our experience over the South Persia Rifles where recognition of the South Persia Rifles by Vossuk was closely followed by his downfall, and the repudiation of his recognition by successive cabinets contributed directly to our troubles in South Persia.

In India's opinion it was not enough that the cabinet accepted the idea. In their view the proposed reforms had to run so little counter to public opinion that any cabinet could carry them into effect as a matter of course. India doubted that Cox's scheme, which smacked of the Egyptian model, could meet this criterion and so they argued for a minimal agreement. They favoured financial control through an adviser introduced into departments where his presence would produce the best results, rather than an elaborate network of advisers. They also favoured the idea of letting a neutral organize Persia's uniform force. Only in this way, India believed, could Britain help Persia and guarantee the chances of successful reform.[13]

Curzon, however, was not sympathetic to India's view. He wanted an agreement with Persia and had confidence in Cox; his objection to proceeding being the problem presented by the Persian Delegation. Two factors made this problem less pressing. First, the Peace Conference decided against non-belligerents' representation, thereby reducing the threat that Persia could claim a hearing. Second, the Shah, who had supported the Delegation at Paris, became more tractable.

Although Ahmad Shah was receiving a British subsidy, negotiated during the war, threats to curtail the subsidy had not appreciably altered his stand over the Delegation and he was a source of trouble. But in February, 1919 the Shah conceived a desire to go to Europe, which required money, and that meant British support. Cox tried to discourage him but the Shah was determined to go and he was not opposed to British help to arrange the trip. He suddenly became willing to support British-sponsored reform, though he did feel that there would be little public support for the idea while the Peace Conference was still in session. He suggested that the cabinet begin with propaganda to win support for the idea while he went to Europe; then in five or six weeks he could wire his approval of the idea and with the proper groundwork laid the scheme would have every chance of success. The Triumvirate felt that the Shah was being sincere and so Cox sought Curzon's view.[14]

Curzon opposed the Shah's visit. He felt that the Shah's presence in Europe would give him the opportunity to link up with the Peace Delegation and add considerably to Britain's difficulties at Paris. Curzon suggested that Cox delay the issue and have Vusuq ad-Daulah say that his cabinet could not function without the Shah's presence.[15] But the Shah would not be put off. He developed the opinion that Britain was being unfriendly, which opened the possibility that he would revert to his former intrigues and troublemaking that had caused difficulties for Britain during the war. Therefore, it became worth considering whether it might not be better to get the Shah out of the country in exchange for his approval of an agreement.

Meanwhile the Persian cabinet continued to express interest in an agreement. In late February, 1919, they asked Britain to give them some grounds on which to build up popular support. They suggested permission: (1) to employ or encourage Persian capital for necessary railway construction; (2) to create a transportation company; (3) to establish a public works company; (4) to announce the British readiness to discuss specifically and sympathetically the possibility of meeting the Persian Government half-way on some of the desiderata which they had proposed to seek at the Peace Conference. In this connection they asked that the Allies (a) guarantee Persia's independence; (b) support efforts to secure war damages from Turkey and Russia; (c) agree in principle to a revision of the tariff; and (d) assist in the possible recovery of some lost territories.[16]

The Foreign Office, in a reply drafted largely by Lancelot Oliphant, still felt unable to pursue the matter officially so long as the Persian Delegation was in Paris. But this did not prohibit comment. The Foreign Office felt that Persian capital would naturally be encouraged to invest in railways but Britain could give no guarantees. They also thought a purely Persian transport company would fail and that it was premature to discuss public works projects. As to point four, the Foreign Office had the gravest objections to inviting others to guarantee Persia's independence but no objections to items 'b' or 'c'. The Foreign Office were unwilling to comment on item 'd' lest this be used as a lever by Persia to force their way into the Conference.[17]* Discussions over an agreement and the Shah's trip all hinged on the fate of the Delegation in Paris. The Shah continued to press for permission to leave and Curzon continued to stall.[18] But in

* In fact, the British hesitated to comment specifically to the cabinet for they had indications that information passed to the Persian Cabinet found its way to Mushavir al-Mamalik, the head of the Persian Delegation in Paris.

mid-March Cox began to urge that Britain find some way of circumventing the stalemate.

On March 20 Cox informed Curzon that the Shah's attitude was more than satisfactory. He was keeping his promises, avoiding intrigues and discouraging the practice in others. He was friendly, amiable and supportive of the cabinet. Consequently, Cox felt that if something were not done to reassure him he would have reason to believe that his change of attitude had been for nothing. Cox reported that the atmosphere in Tehran and elsewhere was less hostile than it had been in years, but he felt nonetheless that the Shah's acquiescence and goodwill were essential to Britain's expectations of a settlement. Cox urged a reply that would not discourage the Shah, even if it did not promise immediate compliance with his wishes.[19] Curzon decided to waive his objections to the Shah's journey but on the condition that the monarch promised to abstain from all intrigues or associations with 'undesirable persons' and not to visit Paris during the Peace Conference. He also had to give the Prime Minister full authority before he left to conclude an agreement and he had to promise not to leave until the agreement was reached (Curzon was afraid that Vusuq ad-Daulah would use the Shah's absence to renege on negotiations).[20]

In any event the situation in Paris no longer looked so threatening and by winning over the Shah it became easier to box in the Delegation.

The improvement in conditions in Tehran and the growing likelihood that the Persian Delegation in Paris was hopelessly isolated meant that negotiations could move ahead. Britain could put an end to the anomalous position of exerting every effort on Persia to seek only British assistance while delaying negotiations until the Paris Delegation was no longer a threat. Reaching this resolution quickly became more important because of growing post-war pressure in Britain to cut back on obligations in the East, particularly military ones.

In late December, 1918 J. M. Keynes, acting for the Treasury and as the vanguard of a trend to cut expenditures, informed the Eastern Committee that the Vote of Credit, passed by Parliament at the beginning of the war, would expire in March 1919, and all new demands on the Treasury would require a Parliamentary vote. Keynes pointed out that the level of expenditures in Iran, about £2,550,000 per month, not counting the military stores brought in, were out of proportion to the results obtained and that every economy would have to be employed to cut future expenditures.[21] Since most of these funds went to the various military missions, the Treasury was, in effect, serving notice on the British military presence in Iran. To Curzon and Cox this meant withdrawing the only reliable forces in Iran capable of defending the country from internal chaos and worse, the Bolsheviks. The most that these architects of the Persian settlement could hope for was a delay in withdrawal and thus there was an urgent timetable for securing the agreement.

Curzon opposed this post-war policy of cut and run. In the Eastern Committee meeting of December 30, 1918 he characterized this policy and the India Office's tendency to support it as 'immoral, feeble and disastrous.'[22] It threatened to undo all the gains of the war, to abandon Britain's traditional position in Persia and to desert Iran in the face of the Bolshevik menace. But the most that Curzon could win – or assume, since no definite decisions but Curzon's were reached – was a delay in the proposed evacuations. In the meantime Curzon outlined to Cox his proposals for negotiating with Persia (outlined on page 191 above). Curzon intended to push ahead.

But Curzon's policy was challenged by Edwin Montagu, the Secretary of State for India. Montagu had not been present at the meeting in December, and in early January, 1919 he wrote to Curzon protesting at the manner in which the affair was being handled.

> I notice in the draft minutes [of the Eastern Committee's meeting] a statement that the Committee agreed with the Chairman. Surely you will not allow this to stand? For the situation was this: Mr. Balfour was away: I was away: I do not see it recorded that C.I.G.S. was present: Lord Robert Cecil (I don't know whether he is a member of the Committee or not now) had left before he had heard either Sir Hamilton Grant or Sir Arthur Hirtzel. And therefore the Committee consisted of the Chairman: and the Chairman, of course, not unnaturally, agreed with the Chairman.[23]

Montagu did not favour Curzon's plans and refused to commit India to paying half the expenses. Under attack from the Treasury and 'betrayed' by the India Office, it seemed Curzon's policy was doomed. But Curzon was able to convince Montagu of the need for resolution of the Persian situation and he had reason to believe that his plan, an eventual economy, could be got past the Treasury.

The problem of evacuation remained, however. Curzon disliked it and Cox argued that a too rapid withdrawal would deprive the Persian Government of the means to maintain order and leave the country open to renewed disorder. He urged a slowdown.[24] With the improving conditions in Tehran, the successful isolation of the Persian Delegation at Paris, and the winning over, ignoring or silencing of opposition, all obstacles to a settlement were disappearing. It only remained to conclude the negotiations.

In early April, 1919 Cox reported that the Persian Government was still interested in an agreement and was fully prepared to rely solely on Britain. Even the Shah was urging that something definite be done. The Triumvirate favoured an agreement but they felt that quick action was necessary while all the factors were favourable.[25] They urged that negotiations begin on the general terms of an agreement and, since they had already given thought to this, passed along a draft for an agreement plus a confidential subsidiary agreement. They further proposed that, when these instruments were concluded, the Persian Government would then inform Mushavir al-Mamalik, head of the Persian Delegation, that his mission to Paris was finished, thus presenting him with a *fait accompli*. Cox passed the Persian proposals to Curzon and in the ensuing weeks a preliminary agreement emerged.

The text of the Persian proposal runs as follows:

> In virtue of the close ties of friendship which have existed between the two Governments in the past and in the conviction that it is in essential and mutual interests of both in future and that these ties should be cemented and progress and prosperity of Persia should be promoted to utmost, it is hereby agreed between the Persian Government on the one hand and His Britannic Majesty's Minister, acting on behalf of his Government, on the other as follows:
>
> 1. British Government reiterates in the most categorical manner the understanding which they have repeatedly given in the past to respect the independence and integrity of Persia.
> 2. British Government will supply at the cost of Persian Government

the services of such expert advisers as may be necessary for the several Departments of the Persian administration.

These advisers shall be engaged on contracts and endowed with adequate powers, the nature of which should be a matter of agreement more or less between the Persian Government and advisers.

3. British Government will [group omitted] provide at the cost of Persian Government such officers and munitions and equipment of modern type as may be adjudged necessary by a Joint Commission of military experts, British and Persian, which shall assemble forthwith for the purpose of estimating the needs of Persia in the direction of a uniform force which the Persian Government proposes to create for the establishment and preservation of order in the country and on its frontiers.
4. British Government in consultation with Persian Government shall seek in customs revenue or other sources of income at the disposal of the Persian Government adequate security for a substantial loan to be provided or arranged by British Government for Government of Persia for the purpose of financing the reforms indicated in clauses 2 and 3 of this agreement, and pending the completion of negotiations for such a loan, British Government shall advance such funds as may be necessary to provide personnel and equipment for initiating the said reforms.
5. British Government, fully recognising the urgent need which exists for the improvement of communications in Persia, both with a view to the extension of trade and prevention of famine, are prepared to co-operate with Persian Government for encouragement of Anglo-Persian enterprise in this direction both by means of railway construction and other forms of transport, subject always to examination of the problems by experts, and to agreement between the two Governments as to particular projects which may be most necessary, practicable, and profitable.
6. British Government agree in principle, in so far as they are concerned, to the examination of existing treaties with a view to their revision in conformity with the present-day requirements, and will be prepared to enter into special negotiations for the purpose as soon as, in the opinion of the two Governments, a suitable moment has arrived.
7. The two Governments agree to appointment forthwith of a joint committee of experts for examination and revision of the existing customs tariff with a view to its reconstruction on a basis calculated to accord with the legitimate interests of the country and to promote its prosperity.

8. British Government will lend their full support to Persian Government for the establishment of her position as a member of the League of Nations.[26]

In addition to this draft the Persian Government also included the outlines of a subsidiary agreement. It included the following:

> In continuation of the agreement come to and executed this day between the two Governments on the subject of the provisional advisers, &c., a confidential agreement is hereby entered into by parties on following two further subjects. It shall, for the present, remain secret:
>
> (a) It being hereby mutually agreed and decided between the parties that British and Persian Governments will make no claims against one another for losses incurred by one Government from the other resulting from recent World War, the British Government undertakes to support the claims of Persia to obtain compensation for material damage suffered by Persia from action of other belligerents.
>
> (b) It being understood that Persian Government is anxious to obtain a rectification of the frontier of Persia in certain localities, the British Government accordingly agree to receive confidentially the detailed explanations of the desires of the Persian Government and to examine them with an open mind; furthermore, in case of any particular item the justice or expediency of which in the interest of the people concerned they may become convinced the British Government will endeavour to the best of their power to assist the Persian Government to attain their object in such manner and by such means as may be decided between the parties to be possible and expedient.[27]

These terms were remarkably similar to proposals put forward by a variety of Persian Governments, some of which the British regarded as distinctly unfriendly, in the course of negotiations during the war to resolve British security worries. There had been sixteen cabinet changes between 1914 and 1919, reflecting the strains and fluctuations of war and internal politics; but, despite the supposed differences in sympathies of these cabinets for various of the belligerents, they had all sought similar concessions. They tried to limit the degree of foreign interference in internal Persian affairs, to cancel the 1907 Convention, to end extra-territoriality, to secure financial independence, to recover lost territory, to develop a national army and to win foreign guarantees for Iran's independence. The British baulked at these terms when presented by a supposedly unfriendly cabinet but were prepared to consider them favourably when presented by one that appeared cooperative and that owed its life to British support. Thus, when the Triumvirate outlined their desiderata they received sympathetic consideration.

Cox received the Persian proposals favourably. He had no comment to make on articles 1, 3, 4, and 5. He felt article 6 was worded innocuously and vaguely enough but that Britain might want to make some changes. Article 7 was mainly interested in securing more revenue and the Persian Government included article 8 in order to captivate public sentiment. The article that most concerned Cox was article 2 of the main draft and articles 'a' and 'b' of the subsidiary agreement.

Cox said in regard to article 3 that the power of the adviser should be a matter for agreement between the two Governments but the Triumvirate felt that this might cause difficulties if stated explicitly. They argued that, since Britain would not allow advisers to accept terms Britain did not approve, the result would be the same. Cox also wanted to include a clause that would prohibit Persia from looking elsewhere for advisers and loans. Again the Triumvirate objected that this would cause trouble because it sounded very similar to an ultimatum. Instead the Triumvirate argued that this did not need explication since Britain would be supplying advisers and controlling the finances.[28]

The Triumvirate made the inclusion of the proposals of the subsidiary draft an essential point of their position. Cox was aware that these subjects were sensitive to officials in London but he felt obligated to pass them along. He also expressed the hope that Britain could accommodate some of these proposals, especially since some concessions would make the acceptance of the agreement more palatable to public opinion. He suggested something in the Caucasus, Central Asia or along the Turco-Persian border that would not violate self-determination and at the same time compensate Persia for the damage caused by Turkey and Russia.[29]

In addition to the formal terms the Triumvirate and the Shah had additional requirements. The Shah expected something in return for his support – personal assurances of support, support for the dynasty, and 20,000 tomans a month for life.[30] The Triumvirate, on the other hand, wanted guarantees of personal support and considerable sums of money to help overcome potential opposition.

The Triumvirate, according to Cox, were convinced that the policy under consideration was the best one but they were also aware that a good many persons or elements, acting for selfish reasons they mistook for patriotism, would oppose the agreement. This opposition had to be overcome either by coercion or persuasion. The Triumvirate were prepared, with British support, to do both, but a policy of persuasion would require a great deal of secret service funds in order to 'square' the rest of the cabinet, the newspapers, and the Majlis. They asked for 500,000 tomans paid down with no questions asked. The Triumvirate also asked for guarantees of asylum and assurances of an income in the event that things went wrong and they had to leave the country. With these preliminaries out of the way, it was possible to get down to serious haggling over conditions and wording.[31]

Curzon approved Cox's efforts and he found the draft proposals generally acceptable. The only immediate change he suggested was the insertion of '*all* such expert advisers' in article 2 and the inclusion of a stipulation that would put the financial adviser in the service of Britain and not the Persian Government. Although it was too soon to comment in detail on the main proposals, he had some observations concerning the subsidiary agreement and the desiderata of the Shah and the Triumvirate. In fact the majority of the correspondence between Curzon and Cox dealt with these private arrangements. But Curzon basically approved Cox's efforts; he did, however, object to secret agreements because of the prevailing feelings against them, and he did not want to bind Britain to maintain the Qajar dynasty or to subsidize the Shah in perpetuity. He also felt that payment of 500,000 tomans, if approved, would have to be part of the general advance.

> I desire to express my appreciation of the manner in which you have conducted the negotiations. ...
>
> In view of strong feeling against secret agreements, it would appear desirable, if anything is to be done on these points [subsidiary agreements], to embody it in subsequent letter to Minister. His Majesty's Government would like further time to consider (a) and (b). It would need addition of such words as 'if and when opportunity offers.'

Colonel Wilson is being consulted about the frontier.

His Majesty's Government could not commit themselves to maintenance in perpetuity of Kajar dynasty, or to subsidy to Shah, which would amount at present rate to 120,000 l. a year.

If Persian finances are properly administered rise in revenue would beneficially affect civil list of Sovereign.

Further payment of 500,000 tomans would, if ever approved, have to be merely an advance out of any prospective loan.[32]

Cox proceeded to deal with these comments. He pointed out that it was not the Persian Government who desired secret arrangements, for they were willing to see their inclusion in the principal agreement. Cox added, however, that if the

> ... compact between ourselves and Persian Government in first clause of (a) would be considered 'unholy' if published, perhaps the understanding could be arranged by exchange of letters and only last clause, beginning with 'British Government' come unto agreement.

After dealing with these problems Cox turned to the remarks on the expectations of the Shah and the Triumvirate. Cox was aware that these subjects were uncomfortable but he believed in their necessity and he had some rather cynical suggestions to match the Persian requests. He pointed out that the life of the present Shah was not likely to be a long one because of his increasing obesity. In regard to the dynasty he wondered if it would not be possible to say ' "Shah and his successors will have our friendly support [?as long as]." etc., or that "we will not support any change of dynasty as long as"?' Cox also felt that some settlement was necessary over the 500,000 tomans.

> If advanced out of a loan it would be less palatable, because item would have to appear in Government accounts, which would be inconvenient to parties whose palms were greased.

Cox urged at least a diluted form rather than a complete rejection and suggested that the Anglo-Persian Oil Company might be persuaded to share the cost.[33]

Curzon and the Foreign Office appreciated the ins-and-outs of negotiating in Persia and had some cynical observations of their own. Oliphant minuted:

> I am very doubtful whether we s[houl]d be justified in gambling on the Shah's life. It is true that he is so stout as to be almost deformed; but

even if his life be precarious one must not forget 'creaking hinges.'

He also objected to 'oiling the wheels,' especially since the Treasury would cause trouble and the Foreign Office did not want to involve the A.P.O.C.[34]* Cox was informed that the most that Britain was prepared to do was to continue the subsidy already paid to the Shah so long as he supported Vusuq ad-Daulah and to agree to offer the Qajar dynasty Britain's friendly support. In view of the difficulties in finding a source of funds for the 500,000 tomans the Foreign Office wondered, that if the funds were forthcoming in the near future 'might it not be possible for the Persian Government to accept it, even though only as an advance before their Ministry of Finance is reorganized.' They did not suggest how to explain the missing funds to a reorganized Ministry of Finance.[35]

Cox asked for clarification. He had not held further talks with the Triumvirate since he presented their proposals and he wanted a clear understanding of Britain's position before he resumed the negotiations and he was still unsure of Britain's position on the subsidiary agreement – whether it was to be treated separately. His main interest, however, was in settling the private arrangements.

He agreed on the suggestion of 'support' for the dynasty but he tried once again to see if something could not be done about the Shah's subsidy. Vusuq ad-Daulah's incumbency was uncertain and presumably the Shah's support would still be necessary if Vusuq ad-Daulah left. Cox wanted to know if it would not be possible to continue the subsidy for ten years with the following reservation: 'until such time as improved administration has increased total revenue by double amount of subsidy.'**

The payment of the 500,000 toman gratuity also remained in doubt. Cox felt that as a last resort the 500,000 toman payment could be made as an advance – presuming that the item was not queried in the future (Cox saw the flaw in the Foreign Office's

* The A.P.O.C. was making far-reaching demands for oil and railway concessions in the Middle East and the Foreign Office had not made up its mind to approve these claims. In fact they eventually rejected them, but at this point they did not want to compromise themselves by asking the A.P.O.C. for financial support.

** which was running about £70,000 a year.

suggestion). In any event, Cox believed some arrangement was necessary and if the above scheme proved difficult he wanted to know if he could offer half the amount; or if a system could be devised whereby Britain would pay an extra month of the monthly subsidy of 350,000 tomans being paid to the Persian Government. Cox could suggest no method, or at least none that would not come under scrutiny, and he still had nothing definite to say to the Persians on the personal assurances asked for by the Triumvirate.[36]

On April 30, while Cox waited for answers to his inquiries, the Government of India entered into the debate. India appreciated Cox's success with the Shah and Triumvirate; because of this and their earlier opinion against relying on such a small base they regretted even more that their views had been ignored. The very fact that the Shah and the Triumvirate were asking for guarantees and money corroborated India's misgivings about placing faith in them. They remained chary of Cox's financial, military and political commitments. Particularly India worried that the scope of Cox's plan would 'insensibly decrease to zero' Britain's chances of ever being able to withdraw from Persia. There were other serious worries:

> On the other hand, chances of our having sooner or later to use force based on India to maintain our position in Persia against wave of nationalism would arise sooner rather than later. Existence of anti-British feeling among Moslems in Egypt and India and threat of it in Kurdistan, coupled with unsettled condition of Afghanistan, renders the present a highly dangerous moment for initiation of so hazardous an experiment.[37]

Cox was prepared to defend his position. He regretted that India had misgivings about the negotiations but he believed that the position they felt obligated to take up inclined them to see phantoms. Cox tried to minimize the differences of opinion, or to point out that the differences were more apparent than real. India too wanted to offer financial assistance and to provide an instruction mission for the uniform force if Persia desired it. In Cox's view this was not appreciably at variance with his own suggestions except that he wanted to avoid a hodge-podge of foreign advisers and neutral officers who would be a source of friction and delay.

Cox could not help but feel that the time was ripe for an agreement, especially since Britain could still provide protection in the north with its own forces, and he took exception to the tenor of India's comments on his negotiations. It was not, as India would have it, 'Cox's latest scheme,' but the policy of the British Government and in Britain's imperial interests; and contrary to India's military worries the situation was opportune for a settlement that would strengthen Persia, whereas if the opportunity were lost, Persia would relapse into anarchy, necessitating large-scale intervention.[38]

Cox was not prepared to see much value in India's opinion. Cox, the former servant of the Government of India, shared the views of another old India hand – Curzon. Together they were ready to override all opposition that interfered with their vision for a Persian settlement. Cox and Curzon had long been critics of the bungling of relations with Iran and now they were determined to prove the worth of their convictions.

On May 9, 1919 Curzon informed Cox that the Eastern Committee* had been able to review carefully the text of the proposed agreement, which they were anxious to conclude. The Interdepartmental Conference, held on May 7, discussed the situation in Iran and the best means of securing the stability of Britain's future position there.

Curzon termed the negotiations, if successful, a notable act of State policy. The question that worried him was whether or not the negotiations would be successful. He realized that an agreement would require further financial commitments, and given the climate for economy in Britain it was not obvious that such a step would be sanctioned. The Treasury was urging thrift and India's objections to paying half the expenses of a new cabinet jeopardized the chances. The most the Treasury was willing to do was briefly continue the subsidies currently paid.[39] Curzon hoped to reverse this, since he had succeeded in convincing Montagu of the importance of the agreement, and now he turned to winning over the Treasury.

* In January, 1919 the Eastern Committee had recommended its own demise to the Cabinet, who approved it. An Interdepartmental Conference, to be called from time to time as Curzon felt necessary, was to replace it. The term, however, survived and Curzon refers to it in this telegram to Cox. For demise of Eastern Committee, see PRO-CAB 23/6/512/2, 1/10/19.

In the Conference Curzon carefully detailed his reasoning and the need for haste. He wanted to avoid the issue of Persia at the Paris Conference and the longer it remained unsettled the greater were the chances of Persia attracting foreign attention. Curzon had no faith in the Paris Conference's ability to settle matters in the Middle East. He had asked himself what the duty of a British politician should be and had replied that it was to build up the bastions of India, 'which had always been and must be the pivot and focus of British interests in the East.' In his opinion the war had changed the position of Persia from the point of view of British interests.

> She [Persia] now lay between India and Mesopotamia, and a tranquil Persia was of vital importance to the prosperity of both countries. He [Curzon] looked on the present opportunity of establishing Persian stability as one which ought not to be lost. ... He wished to make it clear that these negotiations, which involved large questions of statesmanship, ought not, in his opinion, to be handled in any narrow or small-minded spirit.

Montagu agreed with Curzon. The Treasury still had to decide whether or not to sanction any further payments, but Curzon was marshalling his forces. Only India remained recalcitrant, and Curzon had already isolated their position by winning over Montagu. It remained to settle the outlines of the agreement and the conference turned to considering the Persian proposals.[40]

They had only minor changes to suggest in the wording of the principal agreement and preferred to dispense with references to renegotiation of treaties (clause 6) and territorial compensation, which might involve the attentions of other nations, unless differently worded and included in a separate letter. They wanted specifics on the security Persia was prepared to offer for the proposed loan and they expressed a desire that its payment would be in sterling, which was easier to remit. In regard to the private arrangements, they were unprepared to go beyond general assurances of friendly support for the Qajar dynasty and doubted that Parliament would consent to paying the Shah a subsidy. They were also unimpressed by the Triumvirate's request for additional money, remarking: 'If Ministers are so frightened of proposed agreement as to fear expulsion, agreement itself would not rest on very secure foundation.'[47]

Cox discussed these suggestions with the Triumvirate, who agreed to the various changes and to the idea of transferring clause 6 to a separate letter. They were willing to have a separate letter dealing with tariff revision, compensation for war-damages, and rectification of frontiers but they stressed that these points were indispensable in helping to check public opinion and to ensure the success of the agreement. They too did not want the issues raised at the Peace Conference and Cox suggested the separate letter contain vague promises along these lines that would have the matter wait on the conclusion and dispersal of the Conference. The Delegation in Paris still haunted negotiations.

In regard to the Shah, Cox felt he would be disappointed but that he could be controlled. The Triumvirate were also willing to forgo personal assurances and made it clear that they had no apprehensions about the success of the policy. They were willing to extend the security of the proposed loan to include the customs of Sistan, Kermanshah and Azerbaijan. They were also willing to have the loan paid in sterling, but they still needed the secret service money which could be paid as an advance on account of the loan.[42]

The agreement was moving towards a conclusion but certain perplexities still remained. Curzon wanted to avoid delays but he also did not want to rush into accepting terms that would later cause trouble. Specifically he wanted clarification of the terms to be covered in the proposed separate letter. He did not want to commit Britain to embarrassing tariff revisions, compensation schemes or territorial readjustments that would involve other countries. He was also concerned about the 500,000 tomans requested by the Triumvirate. Curzon had never been pleased with what he considered a bribe and he worried that if it ever became public it would effectively damn the career of the Triumvirate and excite severe criticism in Britain. Curzon was ready to conclude the agreement at once if he could receive reassurance on these points.[43] Cox was prepared to give it.

Cox argued that something along the lines of the separate letter was necessary to give the Cabinet the ability to show that they had obtained by other means what had been expected from the Peace Conference. The Cabinet, however, did not expect Britain to commit itself to modifications of treaties or abandonment of privileges. As far as the money was concerned, it was possible to reduce the amount but some substantial secret service payments were necessary to give the Cabinet the ability to stay in power at least long enough to ensure that the new policy was firmly established. Cox suggested a more euphonious definition of the 'bribe' such as '"education of public opinion"' or '"costly initiation of reforms"' in order to avoid the contingency Curzon feared.[44]

It is difficult to believe that Curzon could have found too much solace in this reply but the momentum for settling was mounting. On May 30 Curzon informed Cox that the Chancellor of the Exchequer had agreed to a loan of £2,000,000 to Persia secured on the customs of the south and of Sistan, Kermanshah and Azerbaijan, provided that India paid half. Curzon could already count on India Office support and so the last hurdle had been passed.[45] India admitted its defeat, but not without a parthian shot: 'In view of our misgivings with regard to present scheme we trust liability now accepted by you will not be further extended.'[45] It only remained to settle the fine points.

The negotiations in June settled the issue of interest rates and payment schedules. The Persian Government wanted to repay the loan at 7 per cent per annum over a twenty year period with the right to pay off the loan at any time from any future advances from Great Britain. The British wanted an interest rate of 8 per cent over a fifteen year period but they accepted the Persian terms.[47] In early July the negotiations entered the final phases.

On July 7 Cox informed the Foreign Office that the French text of the principal agreement was ready. He wanted to know if he needed special authorization to sign, since he was a minister *ad interim*, and what assurances were to be given the Shah.[48] Curzon authorized him to sign the agreement and told him to assure the Shah, who was still receiving a subsidy, of Britain's friendly support as long as he acted in accordance with the policy and advice of the British Government. He also informed him that Britain was prepared to extend asylum to the Triumvirate if the occasion developed.[49]

With these personal matters out of the way, Curzon tried to scale down the Triumvirate's request for 500,000 tomans (about £200,000 or 10 per cent of the total loan). He suggested £20,000. However, the Triumvirate felt that such a sum would do more harm than good, as it would only stimulate the appetites of numerous people who could cause difficulties if not satisfied. They saw two alternatives: 1) pay nothing and fight out the agreement on its merits; or 2) pay liberally and establish the policy without a fight. Cox believed that the Triumvirate would have to pay freely to get things moving and he urged accommodating them so things would go smoothly. Cox did not want to fight out the agreement on its merits.

Curzon did not want to pay – not £200,000 at any rate.

> We have offered £20,000. They ask for £200,000. *This is not merely exorbitant it is corrupt.* [my emphasis]
>
> I thought I had said this to Cox a dozen times over but I cannot get it into his head.[50]

And Curzon did not want £200,000 worth of corruption. He tried to get the message across:

> Advance of 10 per cent of entire loan for suggested purposes cannot possibly be considered small advance. You know my intense dislike of this phase of the transaction and with this expression of my opinion I must leave you to make the most suitable terms you can.[51]

This sounded vaguely like Pilate washing his hands; and the Triumvirate would not respect Curzon's scruples. The most suitable terms remained £200,000.*

On July 27 Cox began sending to the Foreign Office the final drafts of the principal agreement, the loan agreement, the letter of assurance to the Shah, and the separate letters on tariff revision, etc. for the Triumvirate. These required only minor changes. On August 4 the India Office approved the texts and the Treasury followed suit. The last obstacle disappeared.

On August 9, 1919 the long delayed agreement settling Anglo-Iranian relations was signed. Curzon had succeeded in putting Anglo-Iranian relations on a firm basis. He had assured the glacis of empire. In one stroke he had concluded an issue that had evaded resolution throughout the war and throughout the nineteenth century and had given form to his dreams. In the euphoria of success he could hardly be expected to realize that he had built his foundation, his policy, his dreams on Persian sand.

There were inherent flaws in Curzon's policy that undermined its chances of success from the beginning. First, according to the

* The sum actually paid was £131,000.

Persian Constitution, the Agreement needed the approval of the Majlis. Elections were a lengthy business in Iran and as the elections dragged on, aided by the procrastination of the Cabinet, the opponents of the Agreement had time to marshal their forces. They began using the Agreement, which they characterized as a sell-out of Persia, to arouse Persian nationalism and to shake the Government's position. The momentum of this movement eventually stalled the Agreement beyond hope. Second, Curzon had not counted on the vehemence of the foreign reaction. Both America and France reacted as if Britain were trying to establish an Egypt in Iran. Curzon could deny this but no one believed him. America would soon have the example of oil and Britain's attempt to lock up all sources of it outside America, to excite the imagination.* The French, on the other hand, had a long memory, still remembering Egypt. Third, the hostility expressed by these powers gave sympathy to Iranian nationalists, who could point to outraged foreign opinion as a sign of what the Agreement really meant. Once again a comprehensive agreement had run foul of nascent Persian nationalism and after another half-century of development, a revolution and a war, that nationalism had a new cause. In the atmosphere created by the nationalists it became increasingly difficult for the Persian Government to uphold the Agreement. Before the end of 1919 they were seeking modifications and by the end of 1920 the issue was dead.

It also became increasingly difficult for Curzon to withstand pressures at home that wanted to cut commitments in Iran. Curzon had intended the 1919 Agreement to do exactly that, but before it could have an effect Persia needed stability, and without adequate armed force the central government was virtually powerless. Only the various British missions and troops gave the Government any real armed force, a fact that undermined the Government even further with the nationalists. The country remained sharply divided, with separatist movements in Kurdistan, Azerbaijan and in the Caspian provinces. In addition,

* For American fears, see 'Multinational Oil Corporations and U.S. Foreign Policy,' Report by the Senate Subcommittee on Multinational Corporations of the Committee on Foreign Relations, 1/2/75. U.S.G.P.O., Washington, D.C., 1975. For the development of British oil policy in the Middle East in this period, see Marian Kent, *Oil and Empire: British Policy and Mesopotamian Oil, 1900–1920*, Macmillan, 1976.

British involvement in Russia had aggravated the Soviets, who were sending agents and troops to Iran to challenge the British. In the face of these mounting pressures Persia needed British troops – a fact that India had predicted. Unfortunately for Curzon's policy, officials in London were determined to reduce those very forces.

As Britain lost the conviction to pursue the anti-Bolshevik campaign in Russia, the military presence in Iran lost much of its rationale to an economy-minded Government. Curzon could not halt this process at home and he could not force the pace in Iran, despite biting telegrams to the new Minister, Herman Norman, to see that the Agreement did not fade away. Even Montagu would not support Curzon, who resorted to the spectre of Persian anarchy and rampant Bolshevism to save his masterstroke. It was of no avail. British troops continued to evacuate their position in the north assumed almost before they left by Soviet forces. Ironically India came to Curzon's defence and argued that withdrawal would open Britain up to the charge of breach of faith, having agreed to aid Persia and then abandoning it; India worried that this would further difficulties with Afghanistan.[52] Even this support, however, could not halt the pace of withdrawal. This was the final flaw in Curzon's policy, for as India had feared, it needed British troops in large numbers 'sooner rather than later.'

In the meantime the Persian Government came under increasing criticism from the nationalist press. In addition the Jangali movement in the Caspian provinces, thought to have withered away, re-emerged with Soviet support and began exercising control over much of the area. There were also separatist movements in Azerbaijan and Khorasan and social unrest throughout the country. These factors, plus the British withdrawal in the face of Soviet advances, influenced the Persian Government to seek an agreement with Russia. Curzon objected to this course, worrying that it might firmly establish the Bolsheviks between Mesopotamia and India, but Curzon's wishes and imperious orders to Norman, Cox's replacement, could not halt the collapse.[53] Vusuq ad-Daulah's Government fell in July, 1920 under intense pressure and the Persian Government continued its efforts to negotiate with the Russians in the hopes that an agreement would halt the menace.[54] Although the British had, in the late days of 1918 and in 1919, come to believe they could do without Vusuq ad-Daulah, he had been in power well over a year and his presence had given a certain sense of continuity to relations. His departure under fire only weakened the Agreement more, and the succeeding Cabinet of Mushir ad-Daulah had to worry about the menacing internal crisis created in part by the 1919 Agreement.

Norman, who had replaced Cox so that he could return to Mesopotamia, tried all the old methods for overcoming Persian resistance. He threatened the Shah with the loss of the subsidy paid by Britain, and he urged the Foreign Office to give him more money to help him defray certain expenses.[55] Curzon also instructed Norman to impress on the Persian Government that Britain's continued support depended on the loyalty of the Government to the Agreement.[56] Money was of no avail, for the Shah was not impressed and Britain's support only contributed to Persia's worries. The pressure did not have its old effect. By late 1920 Curzon was admitting the obvious – the 1919 Agreement was in abeyance, if not dead. It went to its grave on February 21, 1921 when a *coup d'état*, led by a newspaper editor and politician, Sayyid Zia ad-Din Tabataba'i, and an Iranian military officer in the Cossack Brigade, Riza Khan, replaced the wobbling central government and the ratification of the Agreement ceased to be a possibility. Within the week this new régime concluded a treaty of friendship with Russia and began to reorganize the country's armed forces to restore internal order. The 'noble act of state policy' was a shambles and Curzon was bitter:

> Personally I will never propose another Agreement with the Persians. Nor unless they came on their knees would I even consider any application from them, and possibly not then. In future we will look after our own interests in Persia not hers.[57]

Even Curzon, the Persian expert, had been unable to secure the position in Iran. He had succeeded in making an agreement but he was no more successful in making it stick than other Foreign Secretaries who had tried to settle the Persian situation under less advantageous conditions.

In his determination to secure the Agreement, Curzon had over-powered all opposition. He knew the answers and he turned a deaf ear to voices that raised inconvenient objections. India had urged a new policy, one of reconciliation based on the realization that Persian nationalism was not just the occupation of a few extremists. But Curzon had not been interested in dealing with Iran, seeing Iran as a means to an end, not as a legitimate end in itself. He saw the opportunity to secure India's frontiers and was determined to do this in a manner he saw fit. He convinced himself that he spoke for Persia and then found the men who would listen.

This tendency, to rely on the right men in office, on winning influence, had characterized British practice through the war. In part this was a rationalization of political practice in Persia; nevertheless it blinded the British to change, and it tended to base Anglo-Iranian relations on personalities not on policies.

Both Cox and Curzon were aware of political opposition to their efforts but they believed that most of this was trumped-up, inconsequential, and easily won over or subdued. It might have been better if they had checked more closely into numbers when the Triumvirate told them that a good many persons and elements might oppose the Agreement. Instead Curzon relied on his brand of personal diplomacy, and rather than working out a policy in resonance with Persian realities, he thrust his ideas upon a Government he had created for the purpose. In forcing the Agreement he excited the elements he despised and put a weapon in their hands to bring down the whole structure.

India had been right. The new nationalism of such re-emerging nations as Turkey, Iran, Egypt and the lands of Arabia and Mesopotamia and even India could not be ignored. In the post-war era they came into direct conflict with European imperialism; but on new terms, for the emerging nationalistic sentiments were much less willing to deal with the Europeans than of old.

The British emerged victorious from the First World War but it was not a happy triumph. Britain, as all the countries of Europe, had spilled much blood and treasure to make a peace that settled none of the problems that had made the war. In addition the war let the genie of nationalism and revolution out of the bottle. To win a European war the British had to turn to outsiders. They had to make promises to peoples that their power had held in thrall; they had also to mortgage their policy to the ideas of yet another outsider, Woodrow Wilson. In doing so they made more promises than they could keep. British policy in the interwar years was much concerned with dealing with the problems raised by these conflicting promises. It had been a wearying war; it would be a trying peace.

NOTES

1. Curzon's Memorandum on Anglo-Persian Agreement circulated to the Cabinet, *British Documents on Foreign Policy* (BDFP), Series I, IV, p. 1120.
2. Harold Nicolson, *Curzon: The Last Phase, 1919–1925* (New York: Houghton Mifflin Co., 1934), pp. 120–121.
3. Curzon–Cox, 1/14/19, FO 371/3858.
4. Memorandum by Charles Marling, 12/20/18, FO 371/3263.
5. Curzon–Balfour, 3/1/19, FO 371/3859.
6. Memorandum by Sir Hamilton Grant, 12/10/18, FO 371/3858.
7. Cox–Balfour, 11/27/18, FO 371/3263.
8. Curzon–Cox, 1/11/19, FO 371/3858.
9. Cox–Curzon, 1/13/19, FO 371/3858.
10. Cox–Curzon, 1/14/19, FO 371/3858.
11. Cox–Curzon, 1/22/19, FO 371/3858.
12. Curzon–Cox, 1/23/19, FO 371/3858.
13. Viceroy–SSI, 1/28/19, FO 371/3858.
14. Cox–Curzon, 2/6/19, FO 371/3858.
15. Curzon–Cox, 2/13/19, FO 371/3858.
16. Cox–Curzon, 2/25/19, FO 371/3858.
17. Curzon–Cox, 3/5/19, FO 371/3859.
18. Curzon–Cox, 3/17/19, FO 371/3859.
19. Cox–Curzon, 3/20/19, FO 371/3859.
20. Curzon–Cox, 3/28/19, FO 371/3859.
21. Memorandum by J. M. Keynes, 12/31/18, FO 371/3863.
22. Quoted in Nicolson, *Curzon*, p. 132 and Busch, *Mudros*, p. 135.
23. Quoted in Nicolson, *ibid.*, p. 133.
24. Cox–Curzon, 1/19/19, FO 371/3858; Cox–Curzon, 3/14/19, FO 371/3859.
25. Cox–Curzon, 4/9/19, FO 371/3860.
26. Cox–Curzon, 4/10/19, FO 371/3860.
27. Cox–Curzon, 4/10/19, FO 371/3860.
28. Cox–Curzon, 4/10/19, FO 371/3860.
29. *Ibid.*
30. Cox–Curzon, 4/11/19, FO 371/3860.
31. *Ibid.*
32. Cox–Curzon, 4/17/19, FO 371/3860.
33. Cox–Curzon, 4/19/19, FO 371/3860.
34. Minute by Oliphant, *ibid.*
35. Curzon–Cox, 4/23/19, FO 371/3860.
36. Cox–Curzon, 4/25/19, FO 371/3860.

37. Viceroy–SSI, 4/20/19, FO 371/3860.
38. Cox–Curzon, 4/30/19, FO 371/3860.
39. Treasury–FO, 4/21/19, FO 371/3860.
40. Minutes of Inter-Departmental Conference on Middle Eastern Affairs, 5/7/19, FO 371/3860.
41. Curzon–Cox, 5/9/19, FO 371/3860.
42. Cox–Curzon, 5/13/19, FO 371/3860.
43. Curzon–Cox, 5/17/19, FO 371/3860.
44. Curzon–Cox, 5/21/19, FO 371/3861.
45. Curzon–Cox, 5/30/19, FO 371/3861.
46. Viceroy–SSI, 6/13/19, FO 371/3861.
47. Cox–Curzon, 6/5/19; Curzon–Cox, 6/10/19, FO 371/3861.
48. Cox–Curzon, 7/7/19, FO 371/3861.
49. Curzon–Cox, 7/11/19, FO 371/3861.
50. Cox–Curzon, 7/17/19, with a minute by Curzon, FO 371/3861.
51. Curzon–Cox, 7/30/19, FO 371/3861.
52. Richard Ullman, *The Anglo-Soviet Accord* (Princeton: Princeton University Press, 1972), fn. p. 367.
53. Curzon–Norman, *BDFP*, Series I, XIII, Nos. 406 and 407.
54. Norman–Curzon, *BDFP*, *ibid.*, nos. 500, 503, 521.
55. Norman–Curzon, *BDFP*, *ibid.*, no. 463.
56. Curzon–Norman, *BDFP*, *ibid.*, no. 487.
57. Minute by Curzon to a note from Montagu, 2/23/21, FO 371/6409, quoted in Busch, *Mudros*, p. 286.

10

The Military and Politics in Iran: The Uneasy Symbiosis*

Farhad Kazemi

The phenomenal build-up of military power in Iran, and the annual expenditure of several billion dollars for military hardware, have been the subject of much discussion in the past few years. The implications of such a build-up are numerous and touch directly on international politics, regional politics in the Middle East, and domestic politics in Iran. The international and regional ramifications have received considerable attention in recent months among academic, governmental, and other interested circles. The domestic aspect of military and politics in Iran, however, has rarely been discussed or analysed. This is due at least partially to the sensitivity of the subject matter from the viewpoint of the Iranian government and the paucity of reliable information on the military's relationship to political authority. Even Professor Zonis' scholarly analysis of the Iranian political elite had to exclude the military leadership from his study because he was unable to secure permission to interview key military officers.[1]

Given these apparent difficulties, this paper will attempt to present a sketchy picture of the military in Iranian politics emphasizing the following aspects. In the first place, a brief

* This research was supported with a Faculty of Arts and Science Research Grant at New York University. The author is also grateful to I. William Zartman for comments on an earlier draft of this paper. The paper was written before the 1978–79 events in Iran.

background will be presented on the establishment of the Iranian national army by the founder of the Pahlavi dynasty and the father of the present monarch, Reza Shah. Secondly, the place of the military in Mohammad Reza Shah's reign will be discussed with a special emphasis on the activities of the Tudeh (Communist) Military Network in the 1950s. And finally the Shah's policies for control of the military and security forces will be analysed in the context of politics in Iran.

Historical Antecedents: Reza Shah and the Establishment of the National Army

Although Iran has had a long history of military might and has seen a succession of powerful empires within its borders, it has never had a standing national army.[2] The emperors and monarchs of Iran had traditionally relied on separate units of armed groups and tribal support to fight wars or to dispel invaders. In the nineteenth century the Qajar dynasty (1779–1925), which like most Persian dynasties was of tribal origin, attempted to exercise a tighter control over the tribes by nominating or appointing their leaders. These tribal chiefs were entrusted with duties of tax collection and of providing military forces for the government.[3] As the Qajars grew weaker due to a combination of internal problems, unrest, and pressures from Russia and England, the tribes were able to demonstrate a greater degree of autonomy and independence from the government. By the turn of the century, a system of *Muluk al-Tavayif* (autonomous tribal lordship) was well established throughout the country. These tribes were often able to challenge successfully the central government's exercise of authority. Hence the expected military contingents from the tribes were not always forthcoming.

Faced with this situation, the Qajar rulers developed other methods for enlistment of fighting men. This consisted either of new arrangements or a more vigorous application of some older practices. One of the least effective of these developments was a greater reliance on provincial levies. The provincial levies were a disparate group drawn from artisans, tradesmen, and peasants who were paid small salaries for their services.[4] These were supplemented by an essentially ceremonial unit known as the palace guards which had lost its previous position of prestige. But these efforts were to no avail as the military weakness of the Qajars was becoming apparent to all. According to Hurewitz, by 1919 the combined number of the provincial levies and tribal contingents had fallen to below 10,000 and the morale of the armed forces had slackened.[5]

The most effective fighting forces were the remaining three units, which oddly enough were organized and controlled by foreign governments and advisers. The Swedes established the gendarmerie in 1911 for the protection of the rural areas and placed its regiments under the direct command of Swedish officers. The British in 1916 created the South Persian Rifles in the southern part of the country as essentially an arm of the British government. This unit was used primarily to combat rebellious tribes and Swedish and German agents opposed to British interests in the region. And finally there was the Persian Cossack Brigade which was originally created in 1879 by Russian officers at the behest of the Qajar king Nasir al-Din Shah (1848–1896). The Brigade remained under direct Russian control and was used as a tool of Russian policy in Iran.[6] With the onset of the Bolshevik Revolution, the Brigade fell under Iranian officers and continued to function as a relatively efficient force in the country. Reza Shah rose to power as an officer of the Persian Cossack Brigade.

It is clear that what passed for Iranian armed forces was no more than a collection of fragmented and conflicting groups often controlled by foreign governments. This in many respects was an accurate reflection of a social order torn apart by centrifugal forces with no real leadership. Reza Shah stepped into this vacuum using regiments from the Cossack Brigade and joining hands with important political figures in Tehran.[7] A coup was staged on February 21, 1921 which resulted in the naming of Ziya al-Din Tabataba'i, a Tehran journalist of stature with connections to the British Legation, as prime minister and Reza as his war minister.[8] This new alliance lasted for no more than three months. The independent Ziya was soon ousted and a new prime minister was named in his place. Although Reza did not become prime minister until 1923, this cabinet as well as its successors were generally subservient to his will. The last barrier to Reza's ambition, the figurehead Qajar king Ahmad Shah, left for Europe in 1923 never to return.

From the day of the coup until December 1925 when he was named the King of Iran by the Constituent Assembly, Reza applied his relentless energy to bring order to the country under central government authority. He succeeded in these efforts mainly because of his establishment of a standing national army and his control over the military forces. He dissolved some military units and integrated the rest into a unified national army. Upon Reza's behest, the Iranian parliament in 1925 enacted the law of compulsory military service for all men at the age of twenty-one. The conscripts were to serve for two years of active service and twenty-three years of reserve duty. In addition, many officers were sent abroad for training and military staff colleges were established in Tehran. A naval unit and a small air force were also created in due time.

Thus in less than two decades the Iranian military was transformed from a potpourri of inefficient and divergent forces into an organized and effective military establishment. By 1941, Reza Shah was able to mobilize 400,000 men for the war effort.[9] Although this army proved incapable of resisting the Allied invasion of Iran and Reza Shah's forced abdication in favour of his son, it had nevertheless succeeded in establishing the authority of the central government and Reza Shah's absolute power in every corner of Iran.[10] Even the rebellious tribes were no longer a match for Reza Shah's forces and had to comply with his wishes.

From a historical perspective, the rise of Reza Shah and the establishment of the Pahlavi dynasty signals two interesting developments in modern Iran. Firstly, the Pahlavi dynasty was not of tribal origin and came to power without reliance on tribal support. This clearly pointed to the demise of tribes as an essential force in Iranian politics. Secondly, from the very beginning the Pahlavis were closely identified with the military. Not only did Reza Shah come to power by using regiments of the Cossack Brigade, but he was also able to wield absolute power through the newly created and loyal national army. The military therefore became the chief political instrument of Reza Shah's reign. It is not so surprising to note that his heir has also come around to use the military and security forces as the essential base for the enforcement of his will and policies.

The Years of Turmoil: 1941–1953

Mohammad Reza Shah's ascension to the Peacock Throne in 1941 was accompanied by several years of instability and turmoil. The young and inexperienced monarch was confronted with a number of major economic, political, and military problems in his first few years on the throne. The termination of the war did not diminish these problems as Soviet sponsored autonomous régimes were established in Azarbaijan and Kurdistan. The insurrection in Azarbaijan began officially in December 1945 with the establishment of an autonomous Communist and pro-Soviet régime. Then in late January 1946 another pro-Soviet autonomous régime was organized by the Kurdish leaders in Kurdistan. The formation of these two régimes was due to both domestic and international factors. The international factors were related to the Allied occupation of Iran in 1941 to ensure the quick passage of war supplies and material to the Soviet Union. The Allies divided Iran into three zones with the British in the southern and central parts, the Russians in the northern provinces, and a neutral zone which included Tehran and Mashhad.[11]

This and other arrangements were confirmed in the Tripartite Treaty of Alliance between Iran, Great Britain, and the Soviet Union on January 29, 1942. The major provisions of the Treaty included the defence of Iran against 'aggression on the part of Germany or any other power,' respect for 'territorial integrity, sovereignty and political independence of Iran,' and the pledge to withdraw 'from Iranian territory not later than six months after all hostilities between Allied Powers and Germany and her associates have been suspended.'[12] These provisions were further confirmed in the Anglo-American-Soviet Declaration of December 1, 1943 in Tehran where the three governments pledged to maintain Iran's 'independence, sovereignty, and territorial integrity.'[13]

At the conclusion of the war, the Soviets refused to adhere to the terms of these two agreements and encouraged separatist activities in the provinces of Azarbaijan and Kurdistan. By March 2, 1946 (the deadline set by the Tripartite Treaty of Alliance for the evacuation of the Allied troops from Iran), the American and British forces were removed but the Russians remained in occupation of most of the north including Azarbaijan.

The refusal of the Soviet Union to evacuate the occupied areas brought about a crisis in the Iranian government. The Iranian officials protested to the United Nations and the support of the United States was actively sought. President Truman, who was sympathetic to the Iranian cause, sent a note to Stalin urging immediate withdrawal of the Soviet forces from Iran.[14] In response to a combination of pressures from the United States, the United Nations, and clever manoeuvring by the Iranian prime minister, Ahmad Qavam, the Soviets agreed to withdraw the Red Army from Azarbaijan in return for an oil concession in the northern provinces.

The withdrawal of the Soviet troops in May 1946 left the autonomous régimes of Ja'far Pishihvari in Azarbaijan and Qazi Mohammad in Kurdistan without a major supporter. In December the Iranian government decided to send troops to the two provinces. Not much resistance was offered to the Iranian army by the insurrectionists and the two provinces were recovered. The oil concession agreement reached between Qavam and the Soviet government was rejected overwhelmingly by the Iranian parliament in the fall of 1947.

As a result of this confrontation, the Iranian army once again emerged as an important force in maintaining order and peace. The lost prestige of the army for its poor showing against the Allies in 1941 was partially restored by this action. The day of this victory has ever since been celebrated as the national military day in Iran. Perhaps another important side effect of this episode was to make the Shah aware of the crucial significance of the military for the preservation of the Pahlavi throne.

Aside from the rebellion in the two provinces, the Shah found himself faced with many other major domestic problems. The most important of these was the drive for oil nationalization and the concerted effort by a coalition of political groups known as the National Front to wrest control of the oil industry from the British. The National Front formed in 1949 and led by Dr. Mohammad Musaddiq was the active spokesman for oil nationalization. The oil nationalization law was finally passed by the parliament in March 1951, and soon after that Musaddiq was named prime minister.

Musaddiq's government brought a noticeable decline to the Shah's power and authority. One of the central issues in the conflict between the Shah and his prime minister was control over the military forces. When in July 1952 the Shah refused to allow the prime minister control over the armed forces and Musaddiq resigned in protest, massive demonstrations and riots immediately forced the monarch to bring back the popular prime minister. Musaddiq purged the military through forced and early retirement of a large number of pro-Shah officers. Some of these officers along with other disgruntled politicians led a coup in August 1953 to overthrow the prime minister. The unsuccessful coup prompted the Shah to hastily leave the country. This pattern was reversed three days later when a second coup aided by the Central Intelligence Agency toppled Musaddiq's régime and reinstated the Shah on the Peacock Throne.[15]

Consolidation of Power: The Post-1953 Period

The period since 1953 has been one of consolidation of power by the Shah. Ever since his return to Iran, the Shah has attempted to re-establish his position as the commander-in-chief in absolute control of the armed forces. As part of this process the Shah has rapidly increased the size and quality of the armed forces relying heavily on assistance from the United States. The State Security and Intelligence Organization (SAVAK) was also created in 1957 to combat domestic opposition to the Pahalvi régime.

The Shah's efforts to consolidate his power were severely challenged on two occasions in the post-1953 period – one within the military in the 1950s, and the other by a coalition of opponents of the régime in the early 1960s. The military opposition organized by the Tudeh Party will be discussed in full shortly. The opposition from the non-military opponents of the Shah came about as a result of a combination of widespread economic and political discontent. What precipitated these political clashes was the elections to the parliament in 1960, contested by the loyal and government-sponsored parties. Contrary to the promises, the elections turned out to be anything but free. The prime minister's party had rigged the results so blatantly that even the loyal opposition protested. The prime minister, Manuchihr Iqbal, was forced out of office and the Shah asked all deputies to resign their newly won seats to allow for new elections. The elections took place in midwinter, but did not satisfy the people and the opposition who felt that this was no more free than the first election. The National Front was vocal in its opposition and openly challenged the elections. The situation became very acute with a massive general strike of teachers in Tehran and most other cities in May 1961. The Shah soon acquiesced to the teachers' demands. The parliament was dissolved, the prime minister was replaced by the well known and independent Dr. Ali Amini, and the teachers' chief spokesman was named the minister of education.

Elections were not held until the latter part of 1963. In the meantime, Amini undertook a number of actions including a land reform programme. Political activity was again curtailed and a few prominent political figures including some leaders of the National Front were arrested. Amini was replaced in July 1962 by Asad Allah Alam, the Shah's trusted friend and companion. Then in January 1963, a referendum was held to ratify the Shah's Six-Point Programme of Reform. The referendum was boycotted by the National Front and many religious groups.

Throughout this period the religious leaders were showing their opposition to some of the Shah's reforms, especially the distribution of religious lands. The combination of economic problems, political discontent, and religious opposition resulted in the massive anti-government riots of June 1963 in Kashan, Mashhad, Qum, Shiraz, Tabriz, and Tehran. Many were killed during these riots. Estimates run as high as 10,000. The military, however, supported the regime and the Shah was able to silence the opposition, though at a very high cost.[16]

The Tudeh Military Network

The opposition within the military was the work of the Tudeh Party, officially outlawed since 1949 but openly active in the early 1950s. The Tudeh Military Network is significant not only for its Communist orientation, but also because it so successfully recruited among the lower ranking and younger military men of middle class background. This is precisely the group which the Shah has courted in the more recent years as part of his efforts to create a loyal military force. There may be, however, a basic problem in attempting to coopt middle and lower-middle classes to support monarchical régimes. As Huntington points out, the middle classes tend 'to describe even the most benevolent despotism as feudal anarchism. Monarchy is simply out of style in middle-class circles.'[17] Whatever the case may be, these middle and lower-middle class officers were susceptible to anti-régime activities and readily embraced the radical ideology of the Communist Party.

The Tudeh Military Network was a vast organization within the military with members in practically all branches of the armed forces. This military arm of the Communist Party was engaged initially in 'organizational expansion and doctrinal consolidation,' but after the return of the Shah in August 1953, it 'began preparing for an armed insurrection.'[18] The Network was discovered by the military governorship of Tehran in 1954 and about 600 officers (none above the rank of colonel) were arrested. Of these, 458 (including 7 civilian employees of the armed forces) were tried and given sentences ranging from execution (27) to 18 months' imprisonment. In addition, two other officers had died (one in an apparent suicide, the other in an air crash) before the arrest and trial of others. It was also discovered during the trials that more than three-fourths of these officers were recruited in late 1952 and early 1953.[19]

The background analysis of the Tudeh military officers that follows is based on a document published by the military governorship of Tehran known as *Kitab-i Siyah* (The Black Book) which provides partial and at times detailed information about the accused and the trials.[20] *Kitab-i Siyah* is divided into nine chapters and two appendices. The first eight chapters give reasonably extensive information about various aspects and operation of the Tudeh Military Network. These include information about the Network's history, organizational system, hierarchy, intelligence and propaganda division, clandestine activities, and the auxiliary organization of the wives of the Tudeh officers. Chapter nine is an account of the Network's discovery by the military governorship and the confessions and trials of the accused. The two appendices give the Network's organizational chart and list name, rank, division, and final verdict of the military court for all the accused. The book is illustrated throughout with pictures of the officers at various levels of the trials and some of the documents discovered by the government. There are also frequent photocopies of the Tudeh officers' confessions in their own writing.

FIGURE 1

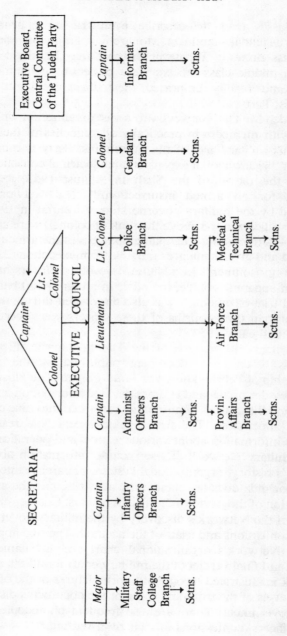

ORGANIZATIONAL CHART OF THE TUDEH MILITARY NETWORK

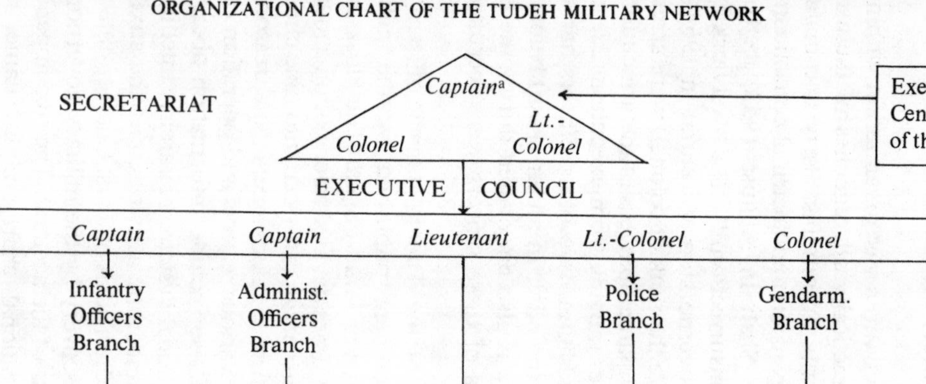

[a] These were the military ranks of the specific individuals who held key positions in the Network. A top figure in the organization was Khosro Ruzbeh who had been expelled from the army while holding the rank of captain.

Source: Adapted from Iran, The Military Governorship of Tehran, *Kitab-i Siyah* (Tehran, 1334/1956).

Structure and Administration Although the Network was founded probably as early as 1944, it had no governing regulations or constitution until March 1953. Up until 1953, the Network essentially followed the general guidelines and directives of the Tudeh Party. In 1953 the central committee of the Tudeh Party ratified the proposed 31-article constitution of the Tudeh officers. The constitution spelled out the conditions for membership and the general organization of the Network.[21] Accordingly, a candidate for membership had to be nominated by a member with at least one year's experience in the Network. The candidate had to spend six months of apprenticeship before he could qualify for full membership. During this period he received training and 'party education.' The secretariat of the Network would then either approve or deny the candidate's membership or require additional training. Utmost care was taken to admit only those who were loyal and dedicated to the Network and its goals.

The top position in the hierarchy belonged to the three-member secretariat (six-member before 1953) who were appointed to their posts by the central committee of the Tudeh Party. The secretariat had considerable power in the Network and could freely appoint, reassign, or dismiss others in the organization provided that it was not contrary to the wishes of the central committee of the Party.

The members of the secretariat were in turn part of the seven-member executive council, which was entrusted with specific responsibilities and duties for the operation of the several branches of the Network (Figure 1). The head of each branch was charged with organizing the needed local sections. Each section was made up of at least three members and was led by an officer with no less than two years' experience in the Network. The sections routinely carried out the actual operations of the Network and worked to expand the organization's role among the rank and file in the military.

The Network also had an auxiliary organization for the wives of the Tudeh military officers. The conditions for the wives' membership were similar to the requirements of the main organization. The wives were also subject to a period of apprenticeship and final approval by the secretariat before admission to full membership. The Network apparently made every effort to bring a large number of the wives into the organization. The husbands were urged to submit reports on the background and characteristics of their wives and their 'attitude and sincerity' about the Tudeh Party. The auxiliary organization of the wives cooperated closely with the Network and facilitated its activities. It did not, however, develop into a large-scale operation. As late as 1954, a substantial number of the Tudeh officers' wives were still not members of this organization.

Ideology and Goal The goal of the Network was to eventually bring about a socialist republic. In the words of one of the accused, the Tudeh members believed in 'Marxism and dialectical materialism and it was the Party's programme to establish socialism as the first step toward creation of a Communist régime.'[22] The Tudeh Party's various publications and other communication channels were often used as vehicles to strengthen these beliefs among the members.

The officers also generally thought that religious beliefs and practices had no place in their ideology. As one officer stated to the prosecutor,

> The first principle of Islam is belief in God's existence and oneness. In the Tudeh Party's philosophy of materialism, there is no such belief ... From another point of view, Islam believes in private ownership ... while the Tudeh Party speaks of social and governmental ownership.[23]

Some of the officers' harshest criticisms were levelled at the Iranian monarchical system and the person of Mohammad Reza Shah Pahlavi. They believed that the foundations of the monarchical system had to be destroyed and the Shah toppled. It was clear to all the officers that a socialist republic could only be created after the Iranian monarchy was eliminated. Thus to the Tudeh officers, the régime's downfall was the first step toward their final goal.

Division and Rank The largest single group in the Network was based in the army numbering 277 or about 61 per cent of the total. This is expected since the army has been the most important and the most numerous division of the Iranian military. It is surprising to note that the next largest concentration of the Tudeh officers was in the small air force. There were 103 Tudeh members in the air force accounting for 23 per cent of the total. The other divisions included the police with 53 (about 12 per

TABLE 1

NUMBER AND PERCENTAGE OF OFFICERS IN THE TUDEH MILITARY NETWORK BY DIVISION AND RANK

Rank	*Army*	*Air Force*	*Police*	*Gendar-merie*	*Other*	*Total*	*% by Rank*
Colonel	6	—	1	2	—	9	
Lieutenant-Colonel	13	—	—	1	—	14	
						23	5.0
Major	49	6	—	9	—	64	14.1
Captain	79	11	11	—	—	101	22.3
Lieutenant (Level I)	100	12	24	3	—	139	
(Level II)	30	15	11	—	—	56	
(Level III)	—	1	—	—	—	1	
						196	43.3
Sergeant (Level II)[a]	—	15	—	—	—	15	3.3
Non-commissioned (Students in Military College)	—	43	6	—	4[b]	53	12.0
Total	277	103	53	15	4	452	100.0[c]
% by Division	61	23	12	3.3	0.7	100.0[c]	

[a] This group includes 14 *Ustuvar-s* and 1 *Gruhban*, both Level II.

[b] Division was not specified.

[c] Some percentages were rounded to equal 100.0.

Source: Adapted from Iran, The Military Governorship of Tehran, *Kitab-i Siyah* (Tehran, 1334/1956).

cent) and the gendarmerie with 15 (about 3 per cent) members. There were apparently no Tudeh officers in the very small naval division.

The Network was made up almost exclusively of younger and lower ranking officers (Table 1). The highest ranking officers in the group consisted of 9 colonels and 14 lieutenant colonels. The combined number of these two groups (23) was only 5 per cent of the total. Lieutenants made up the largest single group amounting to slightly over 43 per cent of the total. The next two largest groups were captains and majors with 22 and 14 per cent respectively.

At least two relevant observations may be made regarding the composition of the Tudeh Military Network: (a) the presence of so many lower ranking officers in the organization, and (b) the relatively large concentration of the Tudeh officers in the air force. The first situation may be explained by pointing out that scholars of military affairs in the developing societies have frequently noted that most coups or attempted coups are undertaken by lower and middle ranking officers especially colonels. There are very few coups where the leadership consists of generals. This has been especially the case in the Middle East in the past two decades.[24] Deutsch probably offers the best explanation of this phenomenon. While discussing the strategic importance of the 'middle level' command, he makes the following observation:

> [The 'middle level'] command is that level of communication and command that is 'vertically' close enough to the large mass of consumers, citizens, or common soldiers to forestall any continuing and effective direct communication between them and the 'highest echelons:' and it must be far enough above the level of the large numbers of the rank and file to permit effective 'horizontal' communication and organization among a sufficiently large portion of the men or units on its own level. From this point of view, there are usually too few generals to receive direct information from, or give direct orders to, the large mass of private soldiers; and there are too many sergeants and lieutenants in most armies to permit effective organization for political purposes. On both these counts, colonels seem to be most favourably placed for political intrigue.[25]

The colonels, of course, were not the largest group in the Tudeh Military Network. But they were in important leadership positions. The central committee of the Network was composed of three individuals two of whom were colonels; the third was an expelled captain and a well known figure in the Tudeh Party. Judging by the sentences they received, the colonels were clearly thought to be of great importance in the Network. Of 23 colonels and lieutenant colonels, 6 were executed, 10 received life sentences with labour, 4 were given 15-year sentences with labour and the other three received sentences ranging from 3 to 10 years of solitary confinement. Moreover, if we combine the number of colonels with the next two ranks immediately below them (majors and captains), then they account for 41 per cent of the Network's membership.

Another explanation for the predominance of the colonels and lower ranking officers in the Network may be related to the question of social mobility. It is well known that the military in highly stratified societies such as Iran provides an important vehicle for social mobility. Many individuals from the lower socio-economic strata who may not be able to climb the social ladder rapidly in civilian occupations, will opt for the military career. It is possible that a good number of these officers will find their career progress and ambitions thwarted beyond a certain rank in the military.[26] In other words, socio-economic background and family connections may not be as important in the military establishment up, say, to the rank of colonel, but beyond this rank family connections and other such factors again become significant. An examination of the family names of the 452 Tudeh military officers seems to at least partially substantiate the impression that many of these Tudeh officers were not from the upper class families of Iran. The end result of all this is that social class may be a significant factor in military intervention in politics of certain societies and may explain the attraction of a radical party that aims at a fundamental reorganization of the social order to officers from the lower socio-economic strata.

A similar line of reasoning may also be offered for the relatively large concentration of the Tudeh officers in the air force. The air force had traditionally been the smallest and the least important of the Iranian military divisions. It had also been relatively easier to move up the ranks of the air force than other divisions.[27] Therefore it is likely that at the time of Tudeh Party recruitment, the relative number of officers from lower socio-economic groups was larger in the air force than in other divisions of the armed forces.

An examination of the educational profile of the Tudeh Military Network seems to indicate that these officers had more education and technical specialization than average officers with similar ranks. Of 263 officers whose area of specialization was stated, 111 or 42 per cent were assigned to units within the armed forces where specialized training was needed (Table 2). Included

TABLE 2

FIELD OF SPECIALIZATION OF OFFICERS IN THE TUDEH MILITARY NETWORK

Field of Specialization	*Number*
Medicine (physician)	49
Medical Assistant	3
Engineering (engineer)	15
Engineering Division	29
Communications Division	8
Financial Division	6
Administrative Division	1
Other Divisions	152
Total	263

among these were specializations in medicine and engineering where a high level of education and training is required. This may reveal that the expectations of these officers and their hope for achievement were probably greater than those of their brethren. They may well have been impatient with what they had so far been able to achieve in the military.

The Tudeh Military Network is a thing of the past. The Tudeh Party probably does not enjoy much support within the military any longer. Effective scrutiny of all activities within the armed forces and control of the outlawed Tudeh Party by the SAVAK has prevented any systematic recruitment of the officers. However, the occurrence of two incidents subsequent to the events of 1954 may indicate that perhaps as late as 1957 there were still remnants of the Tudeh Party in the military. One was the discovery of a spying operation on the borders of the northern provinces where an officer was among those apprehended.[28] The other was the arrest of several officers for theft of arms from the military in 1957.[29] These may well have been minor incidents, especially since nothing of major significance has been reported in the 1960s and 1970s.

Nevertheless, the extensive Tudeh military organization of the earlier years indicates that potentially some segments of the military may be responsive, if not to the Tudeh propaganda, at least to anti-régime sentiments. The Shah has been aware of this possibility and his actions in the past decade have attempted to rout any actual or potential military threat to his régime. This has been achieved, on the one hand, by expanding the size and capability of the armed forces and staffing them with loyal officers, and on the other, by tightly controlling the affairs of the military.

Expansion of the Armed Forces

The size of the Iranian armed forces has increased rapidly over the years. In the early 1970s the armed forces in active duty numbered over a quarter of a million. Moreover, the quality of the military in terms of equipment and manpower has been raised very sharply. The air force in particular enjoys substantial improvement in personnel and material. This growth of the armed forces has been supported by increases in the defence budget (Table 3). The military budget has increased over 34 times from 2,544 million rials in 1954 to 92,100 million rials in 1972. For the same period, the national budget increased 24 times. From 1946 through 1972 on the average approximately 24 per cent of the national budget had been earmarked for military use.

Further analysis of the budget indicates that the military has enjoyed a higher share of the budget in the period since the Shah's proclamation of his reform programme (1963 on) than in the preceding period of 1954 to 1963. While 23.5 per cent of the budget was used exclusively for the military in the earlier period, 25.7 per cent of the budget was set aside for the armed forces in the later period.[30] This may indicate that there is relatively greater reliance on the military and security forces in the more recent years.

The allocation for defence and security expenditure as

TABLE 3

DEFENCE BUDGET (EXPENDITURE IN MILLION RIALS[a]): 1939–1972

Year	*National Budget*	*Defence Budget*	*% Defence*
1939	1,375	357	25.9
1940	2,411	380	15.7
1941	2,732	485	17.7
1942	3,760	593	15.7
1943	2,663	700	26.2
1944	3,993	1,000	25.0
1945	4,419	1,117	25.2
1946	4,312	1,096	25.4
1947	5,995	1,545	25.7
1948	8,021	1,479	18.4
1949	6,904	1,651	23.9
1950	10,687	2,478	23.1
1951	10,060	—	—
1952	9,550	—	—
1953	—	—	—
1954	12,456	2,544	20.4
1955	22,154	3,725	16.8
1956	23,445	5,298	22.5
1957	30,829	6,457	20.9
1958	39,660	8,378	21.1
1959	47,920	13,992	29.1
1960	52,594	16,174	30.7
1961	54,761	13,084	23.8
1962	54,667	14,448	26.5
1963	55,743	14,064	25.2
1964	64,151	14,604	22.7
1965	74,725	17,163	22.9
1966	106,900	24,400	22.8
1967	134,000	33,300	24.8
1968	162,800	41,900	25.7
1969	174,100	46,800	26.8
1970	204,200	58,200	28.5
1971	231,000	65,000	28.1
1972	302,000	92,100	30.4

[a] 67 rials equalled approximately one dollar in 1974.

Source: United Nations, *Statistical Yearbook*, 1951, 1952, 1957, 1958, 1961, 1962, 1963, 1964, 1965, 1966, 1967, 1968, 1970, 1971, 1973.

percentage of the Gross National Product has also increased from 3.3 per cent in 1961 to the relatively high figure of 8 per cent in 1970.[31] The great increase in oil revenues since 1973 and the massive purchase of arms by the Iranian government has substantially changed these figures and ratios. According to Anne Cahn, the defence expenditure as percentage of the GNP amounted to 14.2 in 1974–75. For the year 1975–76, she estimates that this percentage may well reach the staggering figure of 27.8.[32] The decision to construct nuclear reactor power plants, and to continue to purchase several billion dollars of arms annually from the United States, will most likely result in even a larger allocation of the Gross National Product to the military.

Control of the Military: Cooptation and Divide and Rule

It is clear that the Shah's policies for control of the military and security forces have been successful. The armed forces have consistently supported the Shah in the post-Musaddiq era. And since the armed forces have a monopoly over the means of physical violence, this support has been immensely valuable to the régime. However, the few instances of covert anti-régime activities by segments of the military (such as the Tudeh Military Network) have made the Shah cautious in his dealings with the armed forces. This caution is warranted especially since the officers of the armed forces generally possess some degree of social and political consciousness. All officers of the Iranian military are graduates of military staff colleges while some also have degrees in medicine, law, or engineering. They are a mobile group mostly residing in major urban centres and are exposed widely to mass media. And if we accept the analysis of scholars such as Morris Janowitz who attribute a high degree of esprit de corps, 'ethos of public service,' and other such factors to the military in the developing societies, then the armed forces must also have a high level of organizational cohesiveness.[33]

The armed forces' loyalty to the régime is secured through material benefits and the Shah's clever control of factions or groups within the military establishment. The military and the secret police enjoy prestige and high salaries. The officers' salaries have been rising consistently. Even the economic crisis of 1964 did not prevent the king from raising the officers' salaries in the army and the gendarmerie.[34] In addition, the officers enjoy a large number of fringe benefits not available to the civilian bureaucracy.

The Shah has been very careful not to allow any officer to become too powerful within the military. In the past decade, several high-ranking generals have been removed because of the Shah's fear of potential threats to his rule. In most instances, these generals were not accused of harbouring political ambitions, but they were rather labelled corrupt and charged with financial misconduct. There are at least two exceptions to this pattern. One is the case of the first director of the security organization, General Taymur Bakhtiyar, who was accused of both financial misconduct and participation in plots to overthrow the régime.[35] The other is the charge of political insubordination levelled against General Qarani for allegedly leading a plot against the régime in 1958.

The Shah has also exercised control over the military and the security forces through a policy of divide and rule which assigns overlapping duties for gathering of intelligence to separate organizations. There are three different agencies which are responsible for security matters. One is the State Security and Intelligence Organization (SAVAK) which operates an extensive network of intelligence gathering units. The other is the Special Intelligence Bureau of the SAVAK which is 'physically separate and financially independent' of the SAVAK and is headed by the Shah's former classmate and trusted friend. And finally there is the J-2 branch of the armed forces which is charged with the same functions as the other two organizations. There are also other divisions within the military-security network, all headed by trusted senior officers, which are responsible in one way or another for security matters. These include the Town and City Police, Imperial Guard, Gendarmerie, and Military Police. With this overlapping of duties and functions, and acute rivalry among senior officers leading these organizations, there is very little chance of any development within or outside the military not reported to the king.[36]

The policy of divide and rule, the provision of more than adequate financial benefits for military officers, and the generally high prestige of military and security occupations has so far paid off handsomely for the Shah. But the recent attempted coups in

Morocco led by 'loyal' officers who also received high rewards and held prestigious positions, raises some doubts about loyalty secured through such devices. Furthermore, it may be possible that the younger officers in the Iranian armed forces are not as committed to the régime as the conservative Old Guard. Since many of the younger officers are in active command of the army units, their potential impact, if and when they choose not to support the Shah is substantial. Although Westwood's words of caution in the early 1960s about the younger officers have not been borne out, they nevertheless underline a potential area of conflict in the armed forces. Westwood maintains that

> The active officers in many of the higher and almost all of the lower commands are younger men, often university graduates and generally drawn from the middle class. They appear to share the discontent and attitudes of their civilian contemporaries in the middle class. Considerable care has been taken to give these younger officers economic privileges, but they have no opportunities to become wealthy or powerful and they owe their positions not to the Shah alone, but to a variety of persons and factors. In a violent clash with the middle class opposition the conservative Old Guard would probably support the Shah with alacrity, but the younger officers would face very difficult choices.[37]

Both the younger officers and the conservative Old Guard supported the Shah in the bloody riots of June 1963. It remains to be seen whether any faction from within the military would defect to the opposition in the foreseeable future.

NOTES

1. Marvin Zonis, *The Political Elite of Iran* (Princeton: Princeton University Press, 1971).
2. Amin Banani, *The Modernization of Iran: 1921–1941* (Stanford: Stanford University Press, 1961), p. 64.
3. Ann K. S. Lambton, *Islamic Society in Persia* (London: Oxford University Press, 1954), p. 7.
4. Banani, p. 53.
5. J. C. Hurewitz, *Middle East Politics: The Military Dimension* (New York: Frederick A. Praeger, 1969), p. 269.
6. Firuz Kazemzadeh, 'The Origins and Early Development of the Persian Cossack Brigade,' *American Slavic and East European Review*, XV (October, 1956), pp. 351–363.

7. Bahar points out that Reza contacted Modarris and Vusuq al-Dowlah suggesting his readiness to assemble forces to overthrow the government. See Mohammad Taqi Bahar, *Tarikh-i Mukhtasar-i Ahzab-i Siyasy-i Iran: Inqiraz-i Qajariyyah*, Vol. 1, (Tehran: Rangin Press, 1945), p. 61.
8. Yahya Dowlatabadi, *Tarikh-i Asr-i Hazir: Hayat-i Yahya*, Vol. IV, (Tehran: Ibn Sina Press, 1951), p. 177. See also Donald Wilber, *Riza Shah Pahlavi: The Resurrection and Reconstruction of Iran* (Hicksville, N.Y.: Exposition Press, 1975).
9. Banani, p. 57.
10. *Ibid.*, p. 57.
11. George Lenczowski, *Russia and the West in Iran: 1918–1948* (Ithaca: Cornell University Press, 1949), p. 174.
12. For the text of the treaty see Lenczowski, pp. 319–322. See also *ibid.*, pp. 174–175.
13. For the text of the declaration see *ibid.*, pp. 322–323.
14. See Harry S. Truman, *Memoirs*, Vol. 2, *Years of Trial and Hope* (Garden City, N.Y.: Doubleday and Company, 1956), p. 95. In recent years some scholars have questioned the nature of this note and its actual usefulness in this dispute.
15. For a good discussion of this period see Richard Cottam, *Nationalism in Iran* (Pittsburgh: University of Pittsburgh Press, 1964), chapters 13 and 15. See also Donald Wilber, *Contemporary Iran* (New York: Frederick A. Praeger, 1963), chapter 4.
16. For a detailed account of these years see T. Cuyler Young, 'Iran in Continuing Crisis,' *Foreign Affairs*, 40 (January, 1962), pp. 123–135. Hossein Mahdavy, 'The Coming Crisis in Iran,' *Foreign Affairs*, 44 (October, 1965), pp. 134–146. Hafez Farman Farmayan, 'Politics During the Sixties: A Historical Analysis,' *Iran Faces the Seventies*, ed. by Ehsan Yar-Shater (New York: Praeger Publishers, 1971), pp. 88–116.
17. Samuel Huntington, *Political Order in Changing Societies* (New Haven: Yale University Press, 1968), p. 163.
18. Sepehr Zabih, *The Communist Movement in Iran* (Berkeley: University of California Press, 1966), p. 180.
19. *Ibid.*, p. 178.
20. See Iran, The Military Governorship of Tehran, *Kitabi-i Siyah* (Tehran, 1956). Although this important document has been available to Persian speaking scholars for some time, its contents (to my knowledge) have not so far been analysed.
21. For the text see *ibid.*, pp. 75–79.
22. *Ibid.*, p. 45.
23. *Ibid.*, p. 64.
24. There have been a few examples of coups or attempted coups led by the generals in Morocco, Pakistan, and the Sudan. But on the whole, colonels have been the dominant group in the Middle Eastern coups.
25. Karl Deutsch, *The Nerves of Government: Models of Political Communication and Control* (New York: Free Press, 1966), p. 154.
26. Some observers have pointed out that there is no pressing need for the generals to risk their careers on coups since they have already 'arrived.'

They possess prestige, power, and authority and except for the overly ambitious generals, it may be more advantageous to stay out of direct involvement with political intrigue.

27. The Iranian air force has gone through dramatic changes in recent years. It is now a powerful and extremely important division of the armed forces. It is also probably even more difficult to move up within the ranks of the air force than within other divisions.
28. *Ittila'at*, January 24, 1956.
29. *Ittila'at*, March 13, 1957.
30. Because of the absence of data, no military budgets were calculated for 1951–53. For these three years only monthly or bi-monthly authorizations were approved. The authenticity of the military budgets should not be taken for granted. Most likely some of the expenditure set aside for internal security purposes is not reported in the military budget even though the defence budgets reported in the U.N. sources claim to include internal security expenditure.
31. United Nations, General Assembly, 26th Session, Report of the Secretary General, *Economic and Social Consequences of the Armaments Race and its Extremely Harmful Effects on World Peace and Security* (A/8469/ Add. 1, November 12, 1971), p. 57. In his prepared statement in the hearings of the Committee on Foreign Affairs, Marvin Zonis makes the following observation: 'Between 1967 and 1970, the budget of the gendarmerie was increased by 331 per cent. The budget of the national police was raised by 50 per cent, while the budget of the imperial armed forces increased 100 per cent. In 1970–71 the defence allocation was budgeted at a staggering $781.3 million.' See U.S., Congress, House, Committee on Foreign Affairs, *New Perspectives on the Persian Gulf*, Hearings before the Subcommittee on the Near East and South Asia, 93rd Cong., 1st sess., 1973, p. 67. See also Manoucher Parvin, 'Military Expenditure in Iran: A Forgotten Question,' *Iranian Studies*, I (Autumn, 1968), pp. 149–154.
32. Anne Hessing Cahn, 'Determinants of the Nuclear Option: The Case of Iran,' *Nuclear Proliferation and the Near-Nuclear Countries*, ed. by Onkar Marwah and Ann Schulz (Cambridge, Mass.: Ballinger, 1975), p. 197.
33. Janowitz generally explains military intervention in the politics of developing societies through factors related to the internal structure of the military such as the 'ethos of public service,' internal cohesion, etc. This explanation, as Huntington has observed correctly, is misdirected because the reasons for military intervention in politics are essentially political rather than organizational. It should also be kept in mind that the armed forces have a monopoly over the organized means of physical violence which puts them in a favourable position to intervene in politics whenever they deem it necessary. See Morris Janowitz, *The Military in the Political Development of New Nations* (Chicago: University of Chicago Press, 1964), pp. 27–29. Huntington, pp. 193–94. See also James Bill, 'The Military and Modernization in the Middle East,' *Comparative Politics*, 2 (October, 1969), pp. 41–62.
34. Zonis, *Political Elite of Iran*, p. 112.

35. On rumors of a plot masterminded by Bakhtiyar in 1962, see Wilber, *Contemporary Iran*, p. 166.
36. For a good discussion of the policy of divide and rule within the military and intelligence organizations see Zonis, *Political Elite of Iran*, pp. 84–86; and James Bill, *The Politics of Iran: Groups, Classes and Modernization* (Columbus, Ohio: Charles E. Merrill, 1972), pp. 42–44. The above discussion is based on the analyses by Zonis and Bill. Bill also discusses briefly the role of the Minister of War, the Chief of Police, the Commander of the Air Force, and the head of the Special Office in military and intelligence matters.
37. Andrew Westwood, 'Elections and Politics in Iran,' *Middle East Journal*, 15 (Spring, 1961), p. 156.

11

The Impact of Increased Oil Revenue on Iran's Economic Development 1973–76

Hushang Moghtader

The quadruple increase in the oil prices, decided by OPEC countries in the last quarter of 1973, and the subsequent price rises resulting from participation agreements between Arab Gulf producers and oil companies, which benefited Iran through the 'balancing margin principle', effectively increased Iran's revenues from oil from some $2.4 billion in 1972 to $18.5 billion in 1974. This dramatic rise in income was welcome to a government whose outstanding debt at the end of 1974 stood at no less than $5.900 million[1] and whose ambitious development plans had been held back in the past by lack of cash. The Government, therefore, seized the opportunity to embark on an ambitious economic, social and military development Plan with the declared aim of transforming the country into a major economic power by the end of the century. Fifth Development Plan targets were revised and expanded in scope and size; enormous economic cooperation agreements were signed with various foreign concerns; loans, aid and credits were granted to various countries, developed and underdeveloped, as well as international financial agencies, and investments were made in such prestigious Western industries as West Germany's Krupp.

Characteristics of the Iranian Economy

A Decade of Rapid Economic Growth

The Iranian economy has recorded one of the highest growth

rates in the past decade. During the Fourth Plan period (1968–1973) Gross National Product increased by an annual average of 11.8 per cent in real terms, which was in excess of the 9.4 per cent target of the Fourth Plan. With an oil revenue increase of 161.1 per cent in 1973/74 and 171.7 per cent in 1974/75 (the Iranian year starts on March 21st of one Gregorian year and ends on March 20th of the following year), GNP increased by 34 and 42 per cent respectively, while a drop of 11.1 per cent in the oil revenue during 1975/76 led to a GNP increase of only 2.7 per cent,[2] despite an increase of 18 per cent in the non-oil sector (table 1). The amount of GNP has increased from $16.5 billion in 1972/73 to $53.2 billion in 1975/76, resulting in a per capita income of $1.605.[3] With the increase in the oil revenue, the importance of the oil sector in the Iranian economy has increased while the relative importance of some other sectors, such as agriculture, has decreased. Thus, the oil's share of GNP increased

TABLE 1

IRAN'S NATIONAL INCOME IN 1975/76
(BILLION RIALS)

	Amount		*Per cent change*	
	Current	*Constant*[1]	*Current*	*Constant*
Agricultural group	333.9	324.0	10.1	6.8
Oil group	1,311.7	1,233.9	– 5.5	– 11.1
Industrial group	689.7	582.1	45.3	22.6
Services group	1,231.8	1,101.6	34.2	20.0
Gross domestic product	3,567.1	3,241.6	15.7	5.1
Gross domestic product (excluding oil)	2,255.4	2,007.7	33.0	18.4
Net factor income from abroad	10.8	10.8	– 41.0	– 41.0
Net indirect taxes	59.1	51.6	22.4	6.8
Gross national product	3,637.0	3,304.0	15.4	4.9
Terms of adjustment	0	– 47.4	—	—
Gross national income	3,637.0	3,256.6	15.4	3.4
National income	3,415.9	3,060.8	14.6	2.7

[1] Constant 1974 prices
$1 = 68 rls.
Source: Central Bank of Iran: *Annual Report, 1975/76.*

from 27 per cent in 1972 to 45 per cent in 1974/75 at current prices, while agriculture's share dropped from 16.5 to 9.4 and industry's from 20 to 15.4 per cent during the same period (table 2).

TABLE 2

SHARE OF ECONOMIC ACTIVITIES IN GROSS NATIONAL PRODUCT (PER CENT)

	1972/73	*1973/74*	*1974/75*	*1975/76*
Agriculture	16.5	12.4	9.8	9.4
Oil	27.0	40.8	45.0	36.8
Industry	20.1	17.6	15.4	19.3
Services	36.4	29.2	29.8	34.5
	100.0	100.0	100.0	100.0

Source: Bank Markazi: *Annual Report*

The Importance of the Oil Sector

Oil obviously has a prominent place in the Iranian economy. Revenues from oil amounted to $18.5 billion in 1974/75 and $19.05 billion in 1975/76, contributing respectively 45.0 and 36.8 per cent to the country's GNP. In terms of Government's revenues and foreign exchange earnings, oil is also important in that it accounts for nearly 80 per cent of the Government's revenues and 90 per cent of the country's foreign exchange earnings (table 3). Oil finances all the development budgets as well as a good deal of day-to-day administrative running. Iran's oil reserves, estimated at 66,000 million barrels in 1973, are due to run out, at the present rate of extraction, by the end of the century (table 4). Iran, in contrast to some Arab producers, like Kuwait and Algeria, who have adopted conservation policies to preserve their exhaustible assets for a longer period of time, has not so far adopted such a policy. It has, rather, pushed for more oil lift by the major oil companies (the former Consortium group) and for higher sale prices for oil in order to finance its large-scale economic and military plans (table 5). Iran's plan is to transform the country through rapid industrialization into a regional economic and military power by the time the oil exports come to an end. By then, it is hoped that the economy will reach a stage of development where growth will be self-generated and self-sustained.[4]

TABLE 3

RELATIVE IMPORTANCE OF OIL IN THE IRANIAN ECONOMY (PER CENT)

	1971/72	*1972/73*	*1973/74*	*1974/75*	*1975/76*
Contribution of the value added of oil to GDP at current prices	17.8	17.9	30.3	45.0	36.8
Contribution of oil revenue to total Government revenue	56.6	54.7	63.1	84.3	76.7
Contribution of oil sector receipts to total current foreign exchange receipts	77.3	76.0	81.4	89.4	87.3

Source: Central Bank of Iran: *Annual Report*

Industry

Industrialization lies at the heart of the Government's development drive, organized through a series of five-year Development Plans. During the last decade, industrial growth reached 15 per cent on annual average which was far above the 9.4 per cent target set down in the Fourth Plan (1968–1973). During the first three years of the Fifth Development Plan (Fifth Plan runs from March 1973 to March 1978) industrial growth has been in the range of 18 per cent. This phenomenal growth has

TABLE 4

RESERVES OF OPEC'S MIDDLE EAST MEMBERS

	*Proven Reserves** *(000 million barrels)*	*Oil-life* *(years)*
Saudi Arabia	148.6	48
Kuwait	68.0	73
Iran	64.5	29
Iraq	34.3	50
Abu Dhabi	29.5	57
Libya	26.1	47
Nigeria	20.2	25
Venezuela	17.7	16
Indonesia	14.0	28
Algeria	7.4	20

* at end 1975

Source: MEED, 2.4.1976

TABLE 5

CRUDE OIL PRODUCTION IN MAJOR MIDDLE EASTERN COUNTRIES

Main Middle East producers	*Production per day*	*1973*	*1974*	*1975 1 Qtr*
Kuwait	'000 barrels	2,753	2,278	1,937
Saudi Arabia	'000 barrels	7,344	8,210	6,827
Iran	'000 barrels	5,896	6,058	5,677
Iraq	'000 barrels	2,018[a]	1,871[a]	2,044[a]
Libya	'000 barrels	2,175	1,566[a]	919[b]
Neutral Zone	'000 barrels	512	544	466
Abu Dhabi	'000 barrels	1,308	1,418	907
Qatar	'000 barrels	517	519	481
Oman	'000 barrels	293	291	302

[a] Partly estimated. [b] Average for two months.
Source: Petroleum Intelligence Weekly.

come about in a mixed economy brought into being by both private and public sectors. While private sector investment has concentrated mainly on construction, consumer goods and food-processing industries, the Government has assumed responsibility for such key and basic industries as oil and gas, iron and steel and petrochemicals.[5] This industrial drive has been highly import-consuming. Imports of goods and services have risen sharply since 1973 oil price rises, encouraged by the Government in part to help the balance of payments of the oil-consuming countries.[6] Iran's import bill has risen from $3.5 billion in 1972 to $19.0 billion in 1975, an increase of 543 per cent.[7] The 1976 imports of goods are estimated to have risen by a further 55 per cent. Imports have ranged from capital goods and industrial raw materials to consumer goods and foodstuffs. The thrust of Iran's industrial drive is to achieve self-sufficiency in consumer goods and to reach a level of productivity where it can successfully export manufactured goods to replace the export of crude oil and traditional products. In order to do so, Iran has placed emphasis on the development of those industries which best suit its resources and conditions, such as export refineries, gas projects, petrochemicals, iron and steel, and copper industries.[8]

Many of the major agreements concluded with industrial countries in recent years, particularly those with Japan, West Germany, France and Britain, relate to the construction and development of petrochemical, steel and oil-related industries. USSR has also been involved in the construction and development of the Arya Mehr steel mill in Isfahan, the first steel mill ever to be built in Iran, in 1967. Nuclear energy has also received particular emphasis with recent agreements concluded with France, United States and Germany for the supply of a number of nuclear reactors together with the required nuclear fuel.

There is also a gradual shift from assembly plants towards more manufacture of local products, a good example of which is in the motor industry, where Iran is now producing component units for passenger cars, buses and trucks. These are produced mainly for the domestic market but some have been exported to such Middle Eastern countries as Egypt and to Eastern Europe on concessionary terms. Other important industries include textiles (carpets), clothing, food processing and metal products (household appliances). The share held by industrial goods in Iran's exports, although increased recently, still accounts for less than a quarter of all non-oil exports. Two thirds of that total is represented by 'traditional' goods: carpets, cotton, fresh and dried fruits, hides and caviar. In 1975/76, Iran's total non-oil exports amounted to

PRODUCTION OF CERTAIN SELECTED INDUSTRIES

		1971/172	1972/173	1973/174	1974/175	1975/176	% change 1974/75	% change 1975/76
Milk (pasteurized)	Million litres	59	69	77	91	109	18.4	19.7
Pasteurized buttermilk and yoghurt	Million litres	13	11	9	8	12	−9.0	48.9
Pasteurized butter	Tons	3,529	4,022	5,514	6,860	7,954	24.4	15.9
Pasteurized ice-cream	Tons	3,684	3,418	4,264	5,274	6,295	23.7	19.4
Vegetable shortening	Thousand tons	164	183	189	244	265	29.1	8.6
Lump sugar	Thousand tons	157	160	169	216	212	27.8	−1.9
Granulated sugar	Thousand tons	509	509	531	531	558	0	5.1
Non-alcoholic beverages:	Million large bottles	256	307	486	710	939	46.1	32.2
	Million small bottles	78	140	122	90	38	−26.2	−58.1
Cigars and cigarettes	Millions	13,452	12,923	13,449	14,389	15,314	7.0	6.4
Tobacco	Tons	5,384	6,154	6,117	6,044	5,563	−1.2	−8.0
Paints	Thousand tons	19	21	25	33	36	34.3	7.6
Cement	Thousand tons	2,882	3,372	3,401	4,628	5,145	36.1	11.2
Refrigerators	Thousand sets	171	196	257	309	437	20.2	41.4
Water heaters	Thousand sets	60	73	87	114	130	31.0	14.0
Heaters	Thousand sets	139	159	219	307	336	40.2	9.4
Gas stoves	Thousand sets	228	319	313	291	327	−7.0	12.4
Coolers	Thousand sets	94	143	134	144	227	7.5	57.6
Radios	Thousand sets	159	222	281	351	345	24.9	−1.7
Televisions	Thousand sets	158	185	242	326	356	34.7	9.2
Automobiles and jeeps	Thousand sets	40	51	51	73	90	44.6	22.4
Minibuses, station wagons and ambulances	Sets	1,981	2,652	1,551	4,359	5,354	181.0	22.8
Buses	Sets	1,284	1,237	1,627	1,989	2,388	22.2	20.1
Trucks	Sets	2,549	3,442	5,850	8.415	10,592	43.8	25.9
Vans	Sets	8,297	12,035	17,373	21,272	32,216	22.4	51.4

Source: Central Bank of Iran: *Annual Report, 1975/76.*

$592.2 million of which 70 per cent or $413.7 million was 'traditional' and agricultural goods, and 24 per cent such industrial products as: detergents and soaps, pharmaceuticals, chemicals, knitwear, clothes and shoes, which were mainly exported to neighbouring and socialist countries.[9]

TABLE 7

INDUSTRIAL EMPLOYMENT 1972

	Establishments	*Employees*
Food Manufacturing	28,853	181,118
Beverages	89	4,880
Tobacco	3	5,708
Textiles, Carpets, etc.	49,577	715,964
Clothing	47,462	223,542
Wood and Furniture	14,324	92,467
Paper and Cardboard	297	8,707
Printing and Binding	1,239	15,026
Leather and Hides	1,497	20,300
Rubber and Rubber Products	1,244	13,491
Chemicals	1,447	37,012
Non-metallic Minerals	6,655	72,203
Petroleum	15	37,700
Base Metals	944	31,415
Metal Products	29,058	107,595
Non-electrical Machinery	1,653	16,194
Electrical Machinery	3,924	33,704
Transport Equipment	13,788	74,902
Miscellaneous	7,077	23,402
Total	209,146	1,715,330

Source: *Middle East and North Africa Yearbook 1976/77*, Europa Publications Ltd., London, 1976.

Agriculture

Agriculture, which employs about 40 per cent of the total labour force, has remained mainly underdeveloped. Agricultural output increased by 3 per cent during the Fourth Plan period. Although the rate of growth has increased in recent years, nevertheless, the

TABLE 8

ACTIVE AND WORKING POPULATION BY URBAN AND RURAL AREAS (MILLION PERSONS)

	1971/72		*1972/73*	*1973/74*	*1974/75*	*1975/76*		*Per cent change*	
	Number	*Share of total population (p.c.)*	*Number*	*Number*	*Number*	*Number*	*Share of total population (p.c.)*	*1974/75*	*1975/76*
Total population	30	100.0	31	32	33	34	100.0	3.0	3.0
Urban	12	40.0	13	14	14	15	44.1	4.7	4.6
Rural	18	60.0	18	18	19	19	55.9	1.7	1.8
Active population[1]	8.6	28.7	8.0	8.2	8.4	8.8	26.0	2.7	3.9
Working population	8.5	28.4	7.9	7.1	8.4	8.7	25.7	2.7	3.9

[1] Active population includes ages 12 and above after year 1972; whereas before it was 10 years old and above.

Source: Iran Centre of Statistics.

TABLE 9

DISTRIBUTION OF ACTIVE POPULATION BY BRANCH OF ECONOMIC ACTIVITY

	1966		*1971*	
	Thousands	*Percentage of Active Population*	*Thousands*	*Percentage of Active Population*
Agriculture, forestry, hunting and fishing	3,168	41.8	3,410	42.2
Mining and quarrying	26	0.3		
Manufacturing	1,267	16.7	1,392	17.2
Construction	509	6.7	509	6.3
Electricity, gas, water	52	0.7	100	1.2
Commerce	552	7.3	642	8.1
Transport, storage and communication	224	3.0	277	3.4
Services	929	12.2	833	10.3
Other	127	1.7	79	0.9
Unemployed	725	9.6	837	10.4
Total of active population	7,579	100.0	8,079	100.0

Sources: International Labour Organisation, *Yearbook of Labour Statistics*, Geneva, 1971.
Middle East and North Africa Yearbook, Europa Publications Ltd., London, 1974.

impact of the growing population (which increases at about 3 per cent a year) and the rise in the level of incomes has led to an increase in the demand for agriculture and dairy products far beyond the level of domestic supply. The Government has had to rely heavily on foreign markets to meet domestic demands and has poured more than $1 billion a year into food subsidies. During 1975 alone, Iran imported more than $1.5 billion worth of food and live animals. The major agricultural food imports included 1.4 million tons of wheat, 596 thousand tons of sugar, and 282.9 thousand tons of rice.[10]

The advent of increased oil revenue has had some adverse effect on the agricultural sector since it has drained the hitherto cheap labour force from the agricultural rural to the industrial urban areas and has enabled the Government to import foreign agricultural products while maintaining tight control on the prices of domestic agricultural produce.

The Government is, however, aware that the policy of importing and subsidizing food and agricultural products cannot continue into the indefinite future and has, therefore, taken steps to increase the level of domestic supply by setting up various joint ventures for the production of meat and dairy products with foreign participation. It has also drawn up long-term plans to raise the level of productivity and output by modernizing the agricultural sector and bringing greater acreages under cultivation. There is also increasing awareness of the key role that agriculture will have in the future in the Iranian economy. Agriculture has not only to sustain a population of over 60 million by the end of the century, but it has also to provide the

TABLE 10

ESTIMATED MAJOR FARMING CROPS (THOUSAND TONS)

	1971/72	*1972/73*	*1973/74*	*1974/75*	*1975/76**	*Per cent change 1974/75*	*Per cent change 1975/76*
Wheat	3,700	4,546	4,600	4,700	5,500	2.2	17.0
Barley	900	1,009	923	863	1,400	– 6.5	62.2
Rice (paddy)	1,050	1,200	1,334	1,313	1,430	– 1.6	8.9
Corn	00	20	31	50	65	61.3	30.0
Cotton (raw)	459	600	615	715	470	16.3	– 34.3
Sugar beet	3,990	3,918	4,240	4,300	4,670	1.4	8.6
Sugar	594	700	1,050	1,100	1,100	4.8	0
Tea (green)	64	88	93	96	80	3.2	– 16.7
Oil seeds	46	54	57	79	85	38.6	7.6
Tobacco	19	24	15	14	15	– 4.7	4.9
Pulses	196	176	200	210	225	5.0	7.2
Potatoes	400	420	481	533	506[1]	10.8	– 5.0
Onions	250	258	307	305	297[1]	– 0.6	– 2.5
Pistachios	18	28	31	42	26	35.5	– 38.1

[1] Bank Markazi, Iran.
* Provisional.
Source: Ministry of Agriculture and Natural Resources.

feedstock for the country's ambitious industrial schemes. Although capital formation in agriculture has increased rapidly in recent years (54 per cent in 1974, and 18 per cent in 1975), nevertheless the share of agriculture in domestic capital formation remains the lowest, around 6 per cent (table 11).

TABLE 11

GROSS DOMESTIC FIXED CAPITAL FORMATION BY SECTOR (BILLION RIALS)

	At current prices		Growth rate at constant prices (per cent)		Share of total constant prices (per cent)	
	1974/75	*1975/76*	*1974/75*	*1975/76*	*1974/75*	*1975/76*
Agriculture	53.1	72.2	54.4	17.9	9.4	6.5
Manufacture and mining	119.5	235.1	30.3	79.2	21.2	22.1
Oil and gas	48.7	105.2	18.8	83.4	8.7	9.2
Transportation, communications and telecommunications	101.7	234.0	31.9	108.1	18.1	21.8
Residential and nonresidential construction	121.6	210.7	10.1	47.0	21.6	18.5
Other	118.5	243.0	15.9	79.7	21.0	21.9
	563.1	1,100.2	23.3	72.2	100.0	100.0

Source: Bank Markazi: *Annual Report.*

The Impact of 1973 Oil Price Rises

Revision of the Fifth Plan

Following the 1973 oil price rises, the Government decided to revise the Fifth Development Plan in the light of new developments in the oil industry. Estimate of the Government's total revenue during the Plan period was set at $122.8 billion of which $98.2 billion (80.5 per cent) was to come from oil and gas revenues and $18 billion (15 per cent) from taxation. Total expenditure was doubled to $122.8 billion of which $50.2 billion was earmarked for current expenditure (including $29.1 billion for defence, $11.1 billion for social affairs) and $42.2 billion for investment (table 12). Total investment during the Plan period which was originally projected at $35.5 billion was almost doubled to $69 billion of which the public sector was to provide $46.18 billion or 66 per cent and the private sector $23.4 billion.

TABLE 12

REVENUES AND EXPENDITURES/5TH PLAN PROJECTIONS (1973–1978)

	Billion rials	*Billion dollars*
Revenues		
Oil/Gas	6,628.5	98.2
Direct taxes	547.0	8.1
Indirect taxes	668.0	9.9
Other*	253.0	3.7
Foreign loans	150.0	2.2
Bank credits (net)	—	—
Government bonds (net)	50.0	0.7
Total	8,296.5	122.8
Expenditures		
Current expenditure	3,393.3	50.2
Public affairs	(452.8)	(6.7)
Defence	(1,968.7)	(29.1)
Social affairs	(745.0)	(11.1)
Economic affairs	(217.8)	(3.2)
Fixed investment	2,848.1	42.2
Repayment of foreign loans	405.0	6.0
Miscellaneous payments	905.0	13.4
Investment abroad	745.1	11.0
Grand total	8,296.5	122.8

* Including 135 billion rials (2 billion dollars) revenue from foreign investments and loans.

Source: Plan Organization: Fifth Development Plan.

$1 = 67.5 Rls.

Total fixed investment by the public sector was composed of $39.5 billion to be directly invested by the Government, and $6.7 billion to be invested by State-owned public enterprises. A further $2.7 billion was to be transferred to the private sector in the form of bank loans.

Allocations for the oil sector were increased by 156 per cent, for natural gas by 112.5 per cent and for industry by over 95 per cent. Other major increases in allocations included those for

TABLE 13

FIFTH PLAN: FIXED CAPITAL FORMATION (BILLIONS OF DOLLARS)

	Public Sector	*Private Sector*	*Total*
Public affairs	*5.64*	—	*5.64*
Social affairs	*8.76*	*10.30*	*19.06*
Education	1.88	.07	1.95
Culture and arts	.13	.02	.15
Health	.62	.05	.67
Urban development	1.09	—	1.09
Rural development	.89	—	.89
Housing	3.56	10.15	13.71
Environment	.09	—	.09
Regional development	.15	—	.15
Social welfare	.13	—	.13
Physical education	.22	.01	.23
Economic affairs	*31.78*	*13.12*	*44.90*
Agricultural & natural resources	2.62	1.96	4.58
Water resources	2.40	.06	2.46
Electricity	4.60	—	4.60
Manufacturing	4.11	7.45	11.56
Oil	7.93	1.30	9.23
Gas	1.78	.70	2.48
Mining	.92	.07	.99
Transportation	5.95	1.34	7.29
Post & telecommunication	1.35	—	1.35
Tourism	.12	.24	.36
Total	46.18	23.42	69.60

Source: Plan Organization: Fifth Development Plan.

electricity generation, which were more than tripled, for port, railway, road and other infra-structure projects, up by 128 per cent and for agriculture up by nearly 100 per cent. The biggest single allocation in the revised Fifth Plan went to housing, followed by industry. The revised Plan called for a 51.5 per cent growth rate in oil and gas, 18 per cent for industry, 16.4 per cent for services and 7 per cent for agriculture. The overall rate of growth, originally set at 14 per cent, was also uprated to 25.9 per cent annually.

TABLE 14

FIXED INVESTMENT OF PUBLIC SECTOR FUNDS UNDER THE FIFTH PLAN (1973–78)

	Original	*Revised*	*Increase*	*% increase*
		IR '000 million		
Agriculture	121	239.6	118.6	98
Water	106	160	54	51
Industry	180	352.1	172.1	95.6
Mines	46	62	16	34.6
Oil	130	333	203	156.1
Gas	24	51	27	112.5
Electricity	53	240	187	352.8
Communications	177	404	227	128.2
Telecommunications	36	91.4	55.4	153.9
Rural development	36	60	24	66.7
Urban development	32	45	13	42.2
Government buildings	91	320	229	251.6
Housing	90	230	140	155.5
Education	127	130	3	2.4
Culture	5	10	5	100
Tourism	7	11	4	57.1
Health	24	43	19	79.2
Welfare	5	9	4	80
Sport	9	15	6	66.7
Provincial development	—	10	10	—
Public affairs	—	32	32	—
Total	1,299	2,848.1	1,549.1	—

Source: Plan Organization: Fifth Plan.

The Spending Spree

Following the 1973 oil price rises, Iran went on a spending spree such as it had never experienced before. The Government increased its expenditures in practically every field of activity: large sums were made available for social and educational services; education up to university level was made free; social insurance services, especially medical insurance, were expanded to include a greater number of people. Large sums, estimated at $1.5 billion a year, were allocated to food subsidies, and tax exemptions were granted to lower paid employees. Given the availability of money and the Government's readiness to spend, many public and private projects were approved and large contracts were awarded to Iranian and foreign concerns. Credit to the private sector was also increased enormously, through the banking system, supported by the Government.*

The explosion of expenditure which followed these activities increased the volume of money supply in an unprecedented manner (Central Bank figures put the increase at 61 per cent for 1974 alone) which gave rise to a high rate of inflation. As a result of the increase in the aggregate demand, the manufacturers were forced to maximize their productive capacities which in turn intensified inflationary pressures on the factors of production. In order to alleviate internal inflationary pressures, the Government relaxed import regulations and liberalized tariffs which resulted in an unprecedented influx of imports, which led to the congestion

* According to official figures, in 1974/75, Government expenditures (out of the general budget) totalled Rls. 1,076.5 billion, an increase of 125.2 per cent over the previous year, of which Rls. 920.9 billion was paid for current expenditures and Rls. 526.8 billion for fixed investment. During the same year, Government spent Rls. 161.2 billion on grants, loans and investments abroad, Rls. 60.8 billion on the repayment of foreign debts and Rls. 37.2 billion on the repayment of domestic debts (during the same period Government obtained Rls. 9.5 billion new forieign loans and Rls. 30.0 billionnew domestic credits). During 1975/76, Government current expenditures increased by 26.5 per cent and fixed investments by 51.1 per cent. During that year, Government's repayment of its foreign loans amounted to Rls. 13.4 billion and repayment of domestic loans to Rls. 10 billion (these figures represent the balance between new loans acquired and the actual repayments). Loans, aid and investments abroad in 1975/76 showed an increase of 3.9 per cent and reached Rls. 167.5 billion.
($1 = Rls. 0.68.)[11]

of ports, roads, railroads and transit frontiers. These not only revealed the infrastructural weaknesses of the economy but also caused a considerable amount of waste (it is estimated that Government had to pay as much as $1 billion a year for demurrage charges of ships which had to wait for up to six months to find a berth at the southern ports).[12]

In the economic boom which followed the increase in the oil revenue, the propertied classes, the industrialists, the contractors, etc. made quick fortunes while the unpropertied classes and those with fixed incomes were faced with higher rents and a rising cost of living. Although the Government took action to raise the salaries and wages of Government employees and workers, these measures fell short of bridging the gap between rich and poor which was widening, giving rise to social tensions.[13]

Aside from these, there were other unsatisfactory developments which began to unfold in 1975. As a result of world inflation, Iran was forced to pay much higher prices for imported goods and services than it had expected. In June, the Minister of State and Director of the Plan and Budget Organization, Abdol Majid Majidi, complained that Iran was paying 50 per cent more for goods and services than it had expected.[14] The Shah of Iran, in an interview with *Business Week*, gave two examples of how inflation in the West was eating into Iran's oil money: 'We talked to E.I. du Pont de Nemours', said the Shah, 'about building a factory in Isfahan that would have cost $250 million. Now, a year later, they say it will cost $450 million. The Japanese petrochemical complex was to cost $1 billion. Now they say it will cost $1.8 billion. This is what the West is inflicting upon us'.[15]

There was also concern over the decline in the oil revenues brought about by world recession. In early 1975, the Government realized that its oil revenue would amount to $19 billion, instead of $22 billion on which it had counted, which made it difficult for the Government to meet some of its financial commitments. The speed with which the oil money had been spent came as a surprise even to Government itself.[16]

The cumulative effect of these developments – inflation, infrastructural bottlenecks, widening gap between rich and poor, waste and corruption – finally prompted the Government to introduce a number of measures to put things in order.

TABLE 15

IRAN'S CURRENT ACCOUNT

	1974/75	*1975/76* (*$ bn.*)	*1976/77**
Current receipts	20.89	21.89	23.50
(incl. oil)	(18.67)	(19.05)	(21.00)
Current payments	12.39	19.02	20.50
(incl. services**)	(1.75)	(2.97)	—
Net current account	8.5	2.79	3.0
Net capital account	− 3.22	− 3.48	—
Errors and omissions	0.02	0.03	—
Overall	5.07	− 0.99	—

* Financial Times estimate.
** Mostly defence items.
Source: Financial Times.

In the first of these measures, it was declared by the Government, in April 1975, that by 1978 all major private enterprises would have to sell 49 per cent of their shares to either workers or farmers (who would have first options) or to the public. This measure was designed to provide for a more equitable basis of distribution of wealth and to end the dominance of a minority group on the country's big businesses. The said measure was later proclaimed as the 13th principle of the Revolution of the Shah and People which is the new name for the White Revolution.

This was followed in July by a fierce anti-profiteering and anti-corruption campaign which were designed respectively to fight internal inflation and eliminate waste and corruption on the Government level. The anti-profiteering campaign which led to the fining and imprisonment of many businessmen for violating the Government's price regulations was effective in the short run in that it led to an immediate decline in the inflated prices of consumer goods, but in the long run the combined impact of the share participation requirement and the rather crude anti-profiteering campaign, which ignored economic facts, led to further shortages of food and consumer goods and the flight of some $2000 million of capital from Iran.[17] However, both the anti-profiteering campaign and the share participation regulations were later relaxed to allow for a more reasonable and moderate application of these principles which were regarded as indispensable for a just and tolerable economic order.

The extent of the spending spree was revealed towards the end of 1975 when, instead of an anticipated budget surplus, the Government was faced with a budget deficit of about $1.7 billion and the country's balance of payments plunged into a deficit of some $1 billion, a deterioration of nearly $6 billion over the previous year. In view of these developments and the prospect of a slump oil market, the Government was forced to re-assess its development projects and to revise its priorities. Thus, the Fifth Development Plan was once again subject to revision, as the result of which the targets of the Plan were trimmed back again and private and public projects were dropped or postponed.

TABLE 16

IRAN'S GENERAL BUDGET FOR 1355 (1976/77)

	IR *million*	$ *million*	% *of totals*
Revenues	*1,911,800*	*27,600*	
Oil & Gas	1,409,000	20,350	73.7
Taxation	312,900	4,520	16.4
Goods & Services	66,700	965	3.5
Government Monopolies & State-owned Companies	29,700	430	1.6
Interests on Loans & Foreign Investment	13,500	195	0.7
Foreign Borrowing	80,000	1,155	4.2
*Expenditure**	*2,056,800*	*29,700*	
Economic Affairs	579,100	8,360	28.2
Defence	566,800	8,180	27.6
Social Affairs	397,900	5,745	19.3
Public Affairs	251,000	3,625	12.2
Miscellaneous	58,100	840	2.8
Foreign loans, credits & aid	105,000	1,515	5.1

* No figures available on the shortfall of IR 98,900 million (4.8% of the total) in expenditure allocations.
Exchange rate: $ = IR 69.25.
Source: MEED, 13.2.76.

(Government officials later declared that none of the basic development projects had been cancelled and only secondary projects had been temporarily dropped.[18]) Examples of these included the cancellation of a proposed huge airport for Tehran and a health scheme involving the construction of 12 hospitals in Tehran.

When the budget for the fiscal year 1976/77 was disclosed in February 1976 (much later than usual), it contained a budget deficit of $2.4 billion which the Government proposed to fill through saving and foreign loans. Thus in 1976, Iran was once again in the international money market to borrow in order to

TABLE 17

IRAN: BUDGET RECEIPTS AND EXPENDITURE
(IN DOLLARS BN.)

		1975–76	*1976–77*	*1977–78*
1. *General Budget*				
(a) Taxes		3.84	4.39	5.89
(b) Oil/gas		17.68	19.98	19.47
(c) Others		0.91	0.98	1.18
(d) Domestic loans		—	—	2.12
(e) Foreign loans		0.08	1.14	1.41
(f) Special revenue		3.14	0.64	0.95
Total		25.6	27.2	31.04
2. *Total State Receipts* (including State enterprise borrowing)		32.76	42.67	47.43
3. *Total expenditure*				
	32.76			
	44.73			
	49.17			
4. *Gross deficit*				
	—			
	2.05			
	1.74			

Source: Financial Times, London, 27 February 1977.

meet its already committed obligations. However, due to higher oil purchases by the oil companies towards the end of 1976, in anticipation of the OPEC meeting in December to raise oil prices, Iran's income from oil exceeded the initial estimates and reached the $22 billion mark in 1976.

On presenting the 1976/77 budget to the Parliament, the Government indicated the desirability of a slow-down in the economic activities in order to cool off the over-heated economy. On that occasion, the director of the Plan and Budget Organization, Abdol Majid Majidi, stated that 'after a period of rapid economic growth it is necessary to accept a more modest rate that is possible to maintain'. He added that the economic growth rate was expected to be 17 per cent during the following years and the next five year Plan.[19]

The announcement of the 1977/78 budget in February, with a projected record expenditure of over $49 billion (up 9.5 per cent over the previous year), however, indicates the Government's determination to push ahead with its stated plans, despite temporary drops in the oil revenue and infrastructural problems encountered in the previous years.

NOTES

1. 'Iran: Oil Money and the Ambitions of a Nation', *Hudson Letter*, Paris, 1975, p. 13.
2. *Bank Markazi Iran: Annual Report and Balance Sheet*, 1975, p. 2.
3. *Ibid.*
4. For further information see: Firouz Vakil, *Determining Iran's Financial Surplus: 1352–1371*, Tehran Papers No. 2, (The Institute for International, Political and Economic Studies, Tehran, 1975) and: *Iran: Past, Present and Future*, Aspen Papers, 1976.
5. For a brief and useful review of Iran's industrial development see: Jane Perry Clark Carey and Andrew G. Carey, 'Industrial Growth and Development Planning in Iran', *The Middle East Journal*, Summer 1975, pp. 1–15.
6. See the statement by the President of Iran's Chamber of Commerce, Industry and Mines, Taher Zia'i, reported in *Kayhan International*, October 30, 1976.
7. *Bank Markazi*, *op. cit.*, p. 13.
8. See *Iran's Fifth Development Plan*, Revised edition, August 1974.
9. For these figures, see *Foreign Trade Statistics of Iran*, 1976.
10. *Ibid.*

11. *Bank Markazi*, *op. cit.*, p. 51.
12. See the Survey on Iran in *The Economist*, August 28, 1976.
13. *Ibid.*
14. The *Economist*, Dec. 20, 1975, p. 68.
15. *Business Week*, November 17, 1975, p. 69.
16. The *Economist*, 'A Survey on Iran', August 26, 1976.
17. The *Economist*, Dec. 20, 1975, p. 69.
18. *The Middle East Economic Digest*, 20 June, 1975.
19. *Facts on File*, 1976, p. 102.